Bird Dog Guide

Larry Mueller

Stoeger Publishing Company

Bird Dog Guide is a completely revised and updated version of the author's earlier *Bird Dogs*.

Published by the Stoeger Publishing Company,
55 Ruta Court, South Hackensack, N. J. 07606.

ISBN: 0-88317-068-X

Manufactured in the United States of America

Distributed to the book trade by Follett Publishing Company, 1010 West Washington Boulevard, Chicago, Illinois 60607 and to the sporting goods trade by Stoeger Industries, 55 Ruta Court, South Hackensack, New Jersey 07606

In Canada, distributed to the book trade by Nelson, Foster and Scott, Ltd., 299 Yorkland Boulevard, Willowdale, Ontario M2J 1S9 and to the sporting goods trade by Stoeger Trading Company, 900 Ontario Street East, Montreal, Quebec H2L 1P4

Contents

About the Author

To most bird dog enthusiasts Larry Mueller needs little introduction; he's been involved with bird dogs, in one way or another, for most of his forty-six years. He has done a considerable amount of free-lance writing for a large variety of hunting, shooting and dog publications.

Larry's first experience with a scattergun came at about age five, when his dad lined him up on a rabbit with a 12-bore side-by-side. Larry bagged the rabbit but sacrificed his dignity in the process. He's been close to dogs and guns ever since.

Larry figures he's served an apprenticeship of about thirty years in the dog-field. Starting with a local newspaper while still a student, he has served almost the same amount of time learning his trade as a writer.

His qualifications for writing this book are therefore well established.

Foreword

This is a most complete and up-to-date book about sporting dogs. Author Mueller has approached the topic as broadly as anyone I know. He is not especially "high" on any breed or "down" on any breed. All too often by the time a writer is knowledgeable enough to write a book, he is also (probably unwittingly) encumbered by numerous prejudices. Larry Mueller shows no "kennel blindness" in this book.

Another thing which commends this volume to your attention is that the author is not serving "leftovers." Some writers are guilty of reading or talking to other writers and then writing their piece based only on this source. It may not be pure plagiarism, but reading such an article cannot expand the knowledge of the reader if he has done much reading previously.

I can personally vouch that Larry Mueller has done considerable leg work on this book. I know he has sought out leading specialists regarding training, breeding, dog care and other specialized facets of the book. This is added to his knowledge gained from lifelong dog ownership. Totaling up all this makes a book that is a valuable addition to any bird hunter's library.

—John W. Ingram

To my dad, Bill Mueller, who is really to blame for this.

1/Hunting with a Dog

Once you begin to hunt with a dog, your stature grows in the eyes of those of us who understand your motives. But being a notch above and a cut apart from other hunters can sometimes make your purposes misunderstood by the very people you hope will appreciate them.

It's obvious to other dog men that you are committed to sound game management and hunting practices. How you feel about losing cripples is one of the motives behind paying a high price for a good pup and spending either hundreds of hours or hundreds of dollars on his training. But all this coupled with a willingness to spend a hundred dollars a year at a minimum to feed the dog, may lead others to believe that it's highly profitable to own a gun dog. I've seen landowners fearful of letting men with dogs on their property because they regard a canine as a kind of olfactory radar. They believe dogs have an uncanny, infallible sense of smell that will ferret out every last bird on their holdings. In truth, your dog will preserve the game population. Every cripple it finds that you wouldn't is one less kill required to fill a limit. Try to make sure the landowner understands.

You are committed to conservation, and not crippling, but even hunting buddies may not believe it. Unlike the landowner, they don't fear that the dog's nose will be infallible—some of them fully expect and depend upon it. They may openly criticize your dog for what they think are mistakes. I've heard dogs cursed for not finding birds where none existed.

If you have a good dog and a good friend, keep both by letting the friend know how to hunt with a dog and what to expect. Scenting conditions are often less than perfect. When an ordinarily consistent dog isn't performing well, the friend should understand that humidity, temperature, wind direction, barometric pressure and other variables may be factors as well as the dog itself. Dogs have bad days just as we do, and we know that getting yelled at doesn't help matters. If no one handles, commands or yells at your dog but you, then there will be no confusion detrimental to the dog's training.

Be sure friends understand that dog training never ends. Dogs are conditioned by whatever we do. The dog has been carefully trained to hold his points, but this training can be destroyed. At some time or another, the dog is bound to stumble into a bird or covey while running downwind. He can't smell them in time, and they flush. If he stops to flush he's obeying his training and can't be faulted. But if your friends shoot in these instances, it encourages the dog to flush instead of point. Before long, your dog is ruined. Make it clear that good sports do not shoot over dogs' mistakes.

Know your dog's range and pace and try to plan hunts accordingly. If you have a close-working dog that hunts at a leisurely pace, don't join a four- or five-man war party. The dog can't cover ground for that many men, so they become impatient, move on at a fast walk, and do their own hunting. The dog finds himself continually hunting to the rear.

Even merely crowding the dog too much can spoil a hunt. Just about the time the dog smells birds, they flush to the noise of the close-following hunters. The dog gets the blame, of course, for the birds not holding.

It's not always possible to hunt into the wind. Many dogs naturally make a straight run downwind, then return quartering and hunting. Encourage this and caution your friends to slow down and let the dog hunt back to you, instead of rushing through cover to meet the dog.

A difficult thing to teach friends (and sometimes yourself) is to exercise restraint when the dog points. Don't charge in like a wild bull. The excitement can be infectious, and it urges the dog to break point and chase, or at the very least, break to flush or gun. The dog is holding birds by using self-control. Help him by teaching your friends to do the same.

Manners for shooting over dogs evolved through the years, and it was, and still is in some places, the accepted practice for the dog owner to be granted first shot at the birds his dog has pointed. That's a very satisfactory arrangement when each hunter has a dog and birds are plentiful. But I don't consider it practical when I'm the only hunter with a dog, and birds are scarce. I want the others to have an equal opportunity to enjoy the hunt with the few birds we'll see. When hunting with new acquaintances, it's wise to learn their customs before going afield.

I'll put up with customs and traditions wherever I find them, but I'm not "hung up" on any of them. The only thing about dog work that really offends me in the field is the character whose dog is his ego. He hasn't had time—or taken time—to train his dog, so it blunders. His reaction is, "The s.o.b. can't do that to me!" I can understand the untrained dog and forgive all his shortcomings. I can't put up with the man who blames the dog for not knowing the things he should have taught it.

Dogs require little while in the field and frequently get along with less, but there are things we can do to make their job easier and their performance better. Many Springer Spaniel field trialers carry a plastic soap bottle (thoroughly rinsed, of course) filled with water to squirt in the dog's mouth whenever necessary. That's a great idea for anybody hunting dry country. The bottle takes up little room in a hunting coat.

Dog boots are something to consider when hunting in cactus country or on especially rough terrain. And be sure to use a blaze orange collar for safety when hunting in heavy cover.

Many hunters—probably most—still have the notion that sweets are damaging to dogs. Actually, dogs rarely get cavities in their teeth. Sugar gives the dog quick energy, just as it does you. If you carry candy bars for fuel on long hunts, don't hesitate to share some with your dog.

Some hunters also have the notion that a dog must be hungry to hunt. Obviously, a dog would feel groggy and sluggish if stuffed right before a hunt. But he should be given his normal meal. The dog burns up a tremendous amount of energy while hunting. Weakness from hunger can seriously slow the dog's performance.

Is it really worth the time, trouble and expense to hunt with a dog? You bet it is! Many hunters become so enthusiastic that they won't hunt anything that can't be flushed, retrieved or held by point. Why? The dog finds birds we'd pass and retrieves cripples we'd lose, but the practical side of the dog is dwarfed by the fact that men and dogs are held together in the freedom of the field by the bonds of affection. This rapport, friendship and loyalty has no price.

I've noticed that enthusiasm for the hunt sometimes wanes as men grow older. If they're blessed with a son, interest revives and even expands when they teach the boy and enjoy his successes more than their own. The man who hunts with dogs finds a bit of the boy in every one. Some men train pup after pup and enjoy the anticipation of what each will learn day by day. The dog's success or failure, the contest between it and the game (not the bag limit) becomes the hunter's real reason for being afield.

Nothing heightens enthusiasm for the hunt like watching your own dog's success in bringing game before the gun.

2/The Pointing Breeds

Pointers

Pointers or English Pointers? We're told over and over that simply Pointer is the correct name. And that's the name we'll use most often. But there are many pointing breeds around the world. Forgive me if I sometimes say English Pointer to indicate the origin of their development. I may even refer to American Pointers on occasion. They've become different in some ways from their English cousins.

Whatever we call them, Pointers have won the title of number one quail dogs in anyone's book. They've earned it wherever the bobwhite whistles in open country. And they've won it in the tough competition of the National Championship on the Ames Plantation at Grand Junction, Tennessee. Hunters may be critical of the "racehorses" that win derby trials without ever stopping to point, but it's a long way from a local derby event to Grand Junction. It takes a polished bird-finder to get entered in the National. To win, the dog must be adaptable to terrain. A big runner that can't widen or shorten his range to suit the cover doesn't have a chance. Since World War I, Pointers have carried off the honors every year except five. When Johnny Crockett won the National in 1970, he was the first English Setter to win the crown from Pointers in 24 years.

Lest anyone think I'm prejudiced in favor of Pointers, forget it. I have a Pointer that I often can't turn loose because he'd be hunting neighbors' posted ground in minutes. I said the Pointer has earned the number one position as a quail hunter, and I mean in traditional open quail country. I didn't say he's the number-one choice for all bird hunters. The choice of breed depends upon game species, type of country and other factors.

One such other factor is how many fellows normally hunt together. My young Pointer ranges between 75 and 300 yards to the front and either side. He's seldom within gun range and rarely casts behind me. He runs flat out as hard as he can go, and it takes a long while to slow him down. That way of searching takes his nose into more bird cover in ten minutes than my Brittany hunts in an hour. If there are several of us hunting a wide area, that's fine. Someone is always near the dog. For a single hunter, however, that kind of running pattern can create a brisk pace and long walks to points.

I acquired this particular Pointer for big country hunting. And unfortunately, it won't be long before the West and some parts of the South will be the only places left for the king of quail dogs to show his best. He's too efficient for small coverts. The hunt is over almost before it starts.

Not all Pointers range that far, however. A great many Pointers range comfortably for the foot hunter; those that don't can be hacked back by a reasonably good trainer.

No dog can be hacked ahead, however. Desire to hunt and independence to run wide, yet master-oriented enough so as not to bolt or become lost—all have to be a part of the dog's nature. These things can never be put into a dog by training; they can only be *developed* by training. And that's why hard-running, hard-hunting Pointers were bred. A dog was needed to hunt wide country with relatively little cover and do it in a hurry because the hunter might be following on horseback or mule-drawn wagon.

Generations of foot hunters have also followed Pointers. Of course, the majority had more territory to hunt than we do today; today's hunters, probably through lack of experience with dogs, seem sincerely worried that their dog will run away or become lost. Quite often, with more experience and understanding, these hunters would find that some of the closer-ranging individuals of the Pointer breed would suit them to a tee. Some old-timers like my father became so accustomed to the snap, dash and intense style (class is the word that's used to sum it up) of Pointers that they can't look favorably upon any other breed.

I'm without prejudice. One man says he doesn't need a dog if it hunts within gun range because he'd kick up those birds anyway. The man with a close dog says the wide ranger is running past a lot of birds while its master is equally unaware of those *he's* walking past. There is no right or wrong in choice that I can see. It's a matter of terrain, cover, bird habits, manner of hunting, *and the hunter's personality*. Fortunately, there are dogs to fit every preference.

It's hard to imagine that at one time Pointers didn't fit the needs of quail-hunting specialists. Before the turn of the century, Pointers were considered so inferior to English Setters that separate trials were held. When Pointers were allowed to run with Setters, Pointers didn't always win even when they won.

One of the greatest of the early Pointer handlers, Nat B. Nesbitt, told about this prejudice in an article published in the January 9, 1915, issue of *The Ameri-*

Pointer retrieving a woodcock.

Hunting sharptails with an English Pointer.

can Field. Nesbitt recalls the first Pointer he started in field trials:

"The dog was Trinket's Bang by Croxteth-Trinket, and he was drawn with Bryson's English setter, Lillian, by Gladstone-Sue. I knew I had a good dog, but felt beaten before the start from the fact that he was a pointer, just simply a dog of a discredited breed. . . . Looking backward now after a lapse of so many years, I have to smile. The pointer found those bevies of quail, pointed them staunchly, and some singles. The setter found no bevies and pointed a few of the scattered birds, none of which she located. The pointer was ordered up while on point and the heat awarded to Lillian (the Setter)."

Nesbitt said that almost from the initiation of field trials in the United States, he began trying Pointers "confident that the short-haired dogs would soon begin to catch up with the procession."

"We all know that we had to contend against trying to convince the world—and especially the field trial world—that he (the Pointer) had any durable qualities whatever. To Edward Dexter, who furnished the sinews of war, and to Captain MacMurdo, who went abroad and brought back the dogs which furnished the 'lever' in the shape of Mainspring and his sister Hops, our thanks are due mainly to the present high standard of the pointers. From the union of Hops to King of Kent was produced Rip Rap and from the union of Mainspring and Queen III came Jingo. Here the prepotency of the 'Mike-Romp pointer blood' had its

chance to demonstrate itself on this side of the herring pond."

Nat recalled the field-trial judge who advised him, "Nat, you are wasting your time trying to improve the short-haired dogs. They are not and never will be the **English Setters.**"

Nesbitt, Dexter, MacMurdo, S. A. Kaye, who imported Faust at a cost of $1,350 in 1879, U. R. Fishel, and others were only spurred on by the prejudice against the breed. They were willing to make the effort to prove the superiority of their dogs, and their efforts have sustained until today.

From the inception of the National Championship in 1896 until 1909, no Pointer had taken the event. In 1909, Manitoba Rap, less than three years old, trounced the Setters. The Setters held on four more years after that, but in 1914 Commanche Frank won it for the Pointers as did his brother John Proctor in 1916. Commanche Frank sired Mary Montrose, an almost unbeatable bitch that was the first of any breed to win the National three times (1917, 1919 and 1929).

A Setter won in 1918, but Pointers were already dominating the field. Feagin's Mohawk Pal won it three times for the Setters (1926, 1928 and 1930), Sport's Peerless Pride took it in 1939, Mississippi Zev in 1946 and Johnny Crockett in 1970. The trials were declared off three times, so from John Proctor's time until 1972, Pointers won 48 times to the Setters' 6.

The major field trials seem to be tailor-made for

Pointers. In fact, the two have an inseparable history. For a hunter to express fondness for Pointers and dislike for trials is ridiculous. One has made and sustained the other.

Let us illustrate how closely Pointer bloodlines are tied to major field trials. During a visit to Gunsmoke Kennels, head trainer C. L. Owens expressed a liking for the genes passed down from Spunky Creek Boy. In a telephone conversation some time ago, William F. Brown of *The American Field* and Field Dog Stud Book told me that John Proctor has had a strong influence on Pointer pedigrees right up to the present. Since the Field Dog Stud Book registers almost all of the Pointer and Setter hunting stock and all of the dogs that run in major trials, nobody is in a better position to know. To get a better picture of where Spunky Creek Boy and John Proctor fit into Pointer history, I checked copies of *National Field Trial Champions* and *Field Trials,* both written by William Brown.

Without having pedigrees on either dog and simply by checking lists of major wins, I was able to trace both dogs easily. The lists show the winner's sire and dam, one of which usually turned up as an earlier winner themselves.

Spunky Creek Boy was sired by National Pheasant Champion Village Boy, who was sired by Scarview Rap, an excellent stylist that didn't win often but was great as a breeder. Village Boy's dam was Village Girl, sired by Ferris' Manitoba Rap, who was a son of the great Manitoba Rap, first Pointer to win the National.

It's well known that Manitoba Rap carried both Rip Rap and Jingo bloodlines.

Coming back the other way, Rip Rap also sired Fishel's Rip Rap. This dog, owned by U. R. Fishel of Hope, Indiana, wasn't well known or a great winner, but he sired Fishel's Frank, himself the sire of 58 field-trial winners including the famous Commanche Frank and John Proctor. Commanche Frank sired Mary Montrose. John Proctor sired the 1921 National winner, Ferris' Jake, the sire of Air Pilot, who himself sired the 1937 winner, Air Pilot's Sam. The most famous son of Sam was three-time winner Ariel, whose bloodline carried John Proctor genes into such notables as National Champions Palamonium, Wayriel Alleghany Sport, Home Again Mike, and The Arkansas Ranger.

My own young Pointer is related to the Arkansas Ranger and Tyson, a grandson of Spunky Creek Boy. The leading all-time producer of Pointer winners had been Boy until Tyson surpassed him.

This is a terribly narrow look at field-trial Pointer ancestry. We've left out many great dogs by only touching on a few National winners. We didn't even examine Amateur and Shooting Dog winners. But it illustrates how closely Pointer pedigrees are tied to field trials.

My brief search also unearthed the startling fact that the All-America Club's Chicken Championship was won by Highland Boy in 1926, the year I was born in Highland, Illinois. So I'll accept that as a prediction of my going to the dogs. And Highland Boy, being a son of Ferris' Manitoba Rap, takes us once again back to Rip Rap, who sired 19 field winners at a time when prejudice against Pointers was strong.

The black and white Rip Rap did so well that even today someone occasionally passes along the fairy tale that there once was a breed of black and white Pointers called Rip Raps.

Rip Rap's sire was King of Kent, an English import sired by Priam, a son of Price's Champion Bang. Bang also sired Croxteth and Mike, whose son Mainspring gave us the famous Jingo.

Bang's dam was a daughter of Brockton's Bounce, one of the four great names considered to be most influential in molding and holding the fine qualities of Pointers down through history. The other three dogs were Garth's Drake, a dog so fast that he continually skiddled into points until his seventh year; Statter's Major, a large dog of good conformation that traced back to Spanish origin; and Whitehouse's Hamlet, a lemon and white (not admired at the time), and far more racy and lithe than the others. Bounce was liver and white, and a large dog by today's standards.

Pointers were perfected in England.

Price's Champion Bang was the color of his grandsire Bounce, and was not only the most handsome and popular stud of his day, but the fountainhead of Pointers in America.

The Pointer was developed in England, but it did not originate there. It was long thought that the first Pointers were bred in Spain, but short-haired pointing breeds seemed to surface all over Europe about the same time some 400 years ago.

There is evidence, however, that the first dogs that pointed did come from Spain, but it's almost certain they were long haired. (That's discussed in more detail in the sections on Setters and Spaniels.) From the nature and characteristics of short-haired pointing dogs, it's fairly obvious that they arose from crosses of hounds of the period to pointing Spaniels. Short hair and pointing are both dominant genetic characteristics, so such outcrosses could be made fairly easily without entirely destroying bird-hunting ability.

The early short-haired pointing dogs were slow—probably a necessity when men hunted with falcons and nets. With the advent of firearms suitable for hunting, the sport took on a new look in the early 1700's.

The English wanted more speed and used foxhound infusions to get it. In fact, they almost didn't know when to stop, carrying on the practice until the dog shows began in 1859. It may be the one time that ability in a hunting breed was saved by shows.

Pointers in America don't exhibit quite the dished face of their English cousins, but they continue the pace and bird-finding qualities of their predecessors. They learn their trade early in life; this eliminates the years of wondering and waiting that hunters have experienced with some other breeds or strains of breeds. Field trialers especially like this early working trait. Most Pointers have to be force-trained to retrieve, but pro trainer Delmar Smith of Oklahoma tells me dogs of the Baconrind strain in his part of the country are natural retrievers. Pointers catch on to obedience and bird hunting quickly, but require more refresher training than some breeds that never seem to forget what they've learned. There seems to be just a hint of the independent hound nature still showing through and making the Pointer try it his way one more time. And like the hound, most Pointers just want to hunt; they don't care who takes them. Comradeship is enjoyed, but deep attachments seldom occur.

While these wide-running dogs are already excluded from areas of small coverts in America, there's no need to fear that fine stock won't be available for those who love and can use these birdy dogs in the future. Field trials are well entrenched in America, and field trialers are a tough and dedicated bunch when industry threatens to usurp their public running grounds—as tough to beat, perhaps, as their Pointer dogs.

English Setters

When tracing the history of dogs, all authors reach the point where they must say the true origin of a pointing breed is buried in the dim past. Then they expound on how it probably happened. So you may as well know my theory, too. It's different and, as far as I know, original. And it especially involves the Setters.

At one time, popular opinion credited Spain with originating short-haired Pointers of all types. Although a sluggish animal, the old Spanish Pointer was regarded as having super pointing instincts which he passed along in varying degrees to crossbreds in various countries. More recently, the idea has been discredited because historians discovered evidence of various Pointers popping up all over Europe at about the same time. That was around 400 years ago.

Pointing dogs have been around longer than that, however. But printing presses weren't. Gutenberg didn't invent them until the 1400's, and their widespread use came later. Johannes Caius, King Edward VI's physician, published the first dog book, *Of Englishe Dogges,* in 1570.

Before that, references were made to dogs in manuscripts such as *Le Livre de la Chasse,* written by Gaston Phoebus, Count of Foix, in 1387. He described the Chien d'Oysel, or Oysel dogs that were used with Falcons. Oysel was a term used especially when referring to pointing dogs.

The first suggestion of pointing comes to us from a much earlier time, however. The learned Roman, Pliny the Elder (Gaius Plinius Secundum), who lived from A.D. 23 or 24 to 79, authored an extensive work entitled *Natural History*. In book VIII, he discusses the faithful courage of dogs, then says, "Experience daily discovers very many other qualities in these animals, but it is in hunting that their skill and sagacity is most outstanding. A hound traces and follows footprints, dragging by its leash the tracker that accompanies it toward its quarry; and on sighting it *how silent and secret but how significant an indication is given first by the tail and then by the muzzle!* Consequently, even when they are exhausted with old age and blind and weak, men carry them in their arms sniffing at the breezes and scents and *pointing their muzzle towards cover."*

But while the Romans as far back as the time of Christ obviously had dogs that pointed, they did not have bird dogs. In fact, according to Pliny in another book of the Histories, the Romans feared and avoided quail because they thought birds sometimes picked up poisoned pebbles.

Pliny was on intimate terms with Vespasian, so he held important posts in several foreign countries. His travels, natural curiosity and studious nature combined to produce a work of wide scope covering everything from minerals to man. While he accepted some of the superstitions of the time, his personal

Ticking on an English Setter is called "belton." A Setter may be an orange or blue belton.

observations were quite detailed and accurate as is evident in existing artistic works about which he wrote. The *Natural History* was only several books out of the 160 volumes he wrote and willed to his son. And significantly, Pliny had been a procurator in Spain.

When Dr. Fred Z. White wrote *The Brittany in America,* there was nothing on the subject in English. He and Mrs. White translated the history of the breed from letters, articles and records from France. In the process they discovered a quote which the French attributed to the Romans Pliny and Sallusta, concerning dogs called "Aviaries" that their fellow travelers had found in Spain and had introduced to Italy and France.

"When the wise animal approaches the quail or any other passing bird, it seems to fascinate them by its shiny look; during this time, the bird hunter captures

his prey, by throwing a piece of meat to the bird, with the help of a kind of cage."

Although we can't accept the part about a "passing bird" being fascinated by the dog's gaze, or perhaps baiting with meat, the quote describes a dog on point. It doesn't tell us if this dog is short- or long-haired, but that's unimportant at the moment. What is important is that our first record of a pointing bird dog comes from the Romans, a people who had traveled and conquered the entire known world of the time. Had such bird dogs existed elsewhere, the Romans were in a position to know of them and would have recorded the fact.

Much later, Dr. Caius tells us, "The common sort of people call them by one general word, namely Spaniells. . . . As though these kinde of Dogges came originally and first of all out of Spaine." Dr. Caius is not describing Setters or pointing Spaniels. But in France there are Brittany Spaniels and French Pointing Spaniels, both of which point, and all of which suggests Spain for original interest in bird dogs or Aviaries. (There is more on this subject in the section on Springer Spaniels.)

Now we get to the dim past. What is the missing link?

In my opinion, the first bird dog was a shepherd. Three things have convinced me of that. First, the dogs used with nets to capture birds are said to have crept along when near birds. They crouched on point. Some flattened to the ground. A good working shepherd, such as a Border Collie, runs at his sheep, then crouches or flattens to the ground to hold them. It isn't popular, but some of today's bird dogs still crouch on point.

Secondly, sheep dogs are said to "give eye" or "fix" a flock with their eyes. Under normal circumstances the dog does not focus his eyes on a single object as we do. His eyes see a broad area at once. Only when threatening does the dog hold a fixed focus for any length of time. Crouching and holding a flock, as well as

pointing game, are times of intense fixed focus and are basically threatening postures. (It's said that pointing is the enhancement of the instinct to hesitate and precisely locate before leaping upon a victim.) Dogs' eyes at this time of intense concentration tend to show the whites, thus the "shiny look" Pliny describes.

It's assumed that man's first association with dogs developed because after the kill man threw away innards which dogs regard as first choice eating. Camp-following dogs paid their way by warning of intruders. A closer association and mutual trust brought man and dog together on the chase and kill. As man acquired herds, dogs found new uses for natural instincts. As shepherds, these instincts were honed for thousands of years before Pliny first noticed bird dogs.

Any good bird-dog man knows bird interest is instinctive and inherited. Pointer and Setter pups notice butterflies, while hound pups are smelling the ground and never see them. A shepherd dog with bird interest would soon find that quail couldn't be herded, but could be held as long as he remained crouched.

The first pointing dogs were very likely longhaired like the Setter on the left. Shorthaired Pointers came later by crossing Setters and hounds.

The next step was simply a man who also loved birds and would encourage his dog to "show eye" to quail.

The third thing that convinced me of shepherd origin was watching an English Setter in his first season. The dog slinked along and dropped his belly and showed eye at everything he saw with feathers. I remarked to my father how much this dog behaved like a shepherd. He replied that he had known another dog like this, had checked with its breeders and found the dog did, in fact, have shepherd in its ancestry. At that moment, I recalled reading that the Duke of Gordon was claimed to have used an exceptionally birdy Collie bitch in the breeding of his black and tan Gordon Setters.

Perhaps reading about the Duke of Gordon had also introduced the first seeds of thought on this subject. I don't know. At any rate in the absence of evidence to the contrary, I'll stick with my theory until proven wrong.

Was the first pointing dog a long-haired canine? Very likely. The majority of shepherds have a long, heavy coat to protect them from the elements. But

At 38 pounds, Jack Wonsover proves that it doesn't necessarily take size to make a bird dog.

that's no proof. There are also short-haired shepherds from warm climates, which is the case in much of Spain. However, since early records describe setting Spaniels, and since all Spaniels have been long haired, it's fairly safe to assume that short-haired pointing dogs came later.

In 1485, a contract was written to bind John Harris "...to keep for six months a certain spaniel to set partridges, pheasant and other game..." for a sum of ten shillings. At that time, pointing dogs were called "setting spaniels," a term which was later shortened to "setters."

Dr. Caius, in 1570, describes as follows "the Dogge called the Setter," saying that its Latin name was "Index."

"Another sort of Dogges be there, scruiceable for fowling, making no noise either with foote or with tounge, whiles they followe the game. These attend diligently vpon theyr Master and frame their conditions to such beckes, motions, and gestures, as it shall please him exhibite and make, either going forward, drawing backeward, inclining to the right hand, or yealding toward the left, (In making mencion of fowles my meaning is of the Partridge and the Quaile) when he hath founde the byrde, he keepeth sure and fast silence, he stayeth his steppes and wil proceede no further, and with a close, couert, watching eye, layeth his belly to the grounde and the place where the birde is, he layes him downe, and with a marcke of his pawes, betrayeth the place of the byrdes last abode, whereby it is supposed that this kinde of dogge is called Index, Setter, being in deede a name most consonant and agreeable to his quality. The place being knowne by the meanes of the dogge, the fowler immediately openeth and spreedeth his net, intending to take them, which being don the dogge at the accustomed becke or vsuall signe of his Master ryseth vp by and by, and draweth neerer to the fowle that by his presence they might be the authors of theyr owne insnaring, and be ready intangled in the prepared net..."

Note the description of the crouch on point and the watching eye. The name Index in Latin indicates (another related word) our pointing finger or needle of a compass, etc. Note also the emphasis on stealth as describes the shepherd-like behavior of the English Setter which Dad and I had watched.

The invention of suitable firearms for hunting changed canine requirements. Instead of working closely and quietly with nets, hunters could reach many yards ahead and take game on the wing. Faster action demanded faster dogs. Greater sport demanded the selection of dogs for snappier, more stylish standing points.

Then in 1825, Edward Laverack embarked on a hoax that was later complicated by R. Purcell-Llewellin and not corrected in the minds of most dog fanciers to this day. Laverack purchased from the Reverend A. Harrison a pair of dogs, Ponto and Old Moll, which Laverack later claimed had been bred pure for 35 years. To Laverack that meant inbreeding with no outcrosses. In his book *The Setter* (1872) he claimed his strain of dogs were all bred from Ponto and Old Moll. He admits to trying outcrosses, but implies the progeny were destroyed because they were worthless.

In a seven-generation pedigree of Countess, which Llewellin bought from Laverack and which became the first dual champion English Setter, all individuals go straight back to Old Moll and Ponto. While dramatic, it can't be true.

I'm an exponent of careful inbreeding, so I wouldn't be one to claim it impossible on grounds of inevitable crazy and deformed offspring. Laverack claims Ponto and Old Moll bore Dash and Belle. This brother and sister were then mated and their offspring subsequently brother-sister mated. The only variation of such breeding in the Countess pedigree is a father-daughter mating and farther down the line the mating of dogs that weren't litter mates. While highly improbable, I'll have to admit that with exceptionally sound stock it wouldn't be absolutely impossible. In mice, brother and sister matings were experimentally continued 200 times. They not only thrived, but by judicious selection even increased in size. But Mr. Laverack didn't know enough about color-coat genetics to cover up his false pedigree.

Old Moll was a light-blue belton and Ponto was a dark-blue belton. (Belton is a village in Northumberland England, near which Laverack hunted. He used the word to describe ticking in the color coat.) Ticking is a dominant factor. Yet the Countess pedigree lists few dogs with blue mottled coats. A recessive gene can hide under a dominant to show up later if the carrier is mated to another dog carrying this same recessive and they happen to join. In that case a few black and whites, orange and whites or tri-colors could show up. But they dominate Laverack's pedigrees when they should be rare. And ticked dogs are rare when they should be dominant.

Furthermore, inbreeding quickly doubles these recessives and brings them to the surface. If Old Moll and Ponto had been inbred themselves as claimed, these recessives would have been cut out of the strain, and they would have bred true for blue ticking.

Countess was a beauty, but we have no idea what was in her background. We do know that writers of Laverack's time had no confidence in his pedigrees. We also know that some thirty years before his book he is recorded as saying, "So highly do I value the true blood belonging to the Irish that I have visited Ireland four times for the express purpose of ascertaining

The late, great Johnny Crockett, owned by H. P. Sheely, of Denton, Texas.

where the true blood was to be found, with a view of crossing them with my Beltons."

A red setter did turn up in a litter. The pup was appropriately named Mystery, and Laverack blamed it on telegony. That's an old notion that we now know to be absolutely false. It was thought that if a bitch was mated to a sire of another breed, not only that litter, but all future litters would be mongrels.

There is also a claim by Rev. D. W. W. Horlock that Laverack mellowed under the influence of wine and told of gypsies annually hunting on a tract of ground called the Debatable Land that apparently belonged to the Earl of Carlisle in name only. Laverack had joined a group of 30 men and their dogs, one of which beat them all, including Laverack's best. Rev. Horlock claims Laverack admitted to buying the dog and breeding from it.

Laverack did inbreed, although not as extensively as he claimed, and did produce good-looking dogs. His contemporaries, however, didn't regard them as the last word in field dogs. Barclay Field, Sir Vincent Corbett and Thomas Statter apparently didn't have a need for public acclaim, but they did have a genuine interest in bird dogs. The latter two were also instrumental in English Pointer development. These men produced the stock which when crossed on his Laverack bitches gave Llewellin his start as a famous dog breeder.

Prior to that time Llewellin had been crossbreeding in an unsuccessful attempt to produce field-trial winners. In 1871, Llewellin attended a trial at Shrewsbury and bought Dan and Dick, both out of Field's Duke and Statter's Rhoebe.

Duke was a black and white dog sired by Sir F. Graham's Duke. His dam was from North of England border stock which Sir Vincent Corbett favored. Duke was respected as a bird dog, but always seemed to lack nose when entered in trials.

Rhoebe, a tri-color out of a Gordon-English cross, wasn't considered outstanding in the field and wasn't even well built. Nevertheless, Duke-Rhoebe offspring when crossed with Laveracks produced excellence in the field. That famous cross was Llewellin's foundation stock.

Dan was a highly prepotent sire and produced Gladstone, the good-looking, trial-winning dog that helped start the Llewellin rage in America. Gladstone was born in Ontario out of Petrel, a bitch that was serviced by Dan before being shipped to L. H. Smith. P. H. Bryson, of Memphis, Tennessee, received Gladstone when just a pup as a gift. The dog quickly became known as an outstanding performer and stud.

Meanwhile, Americans had been breeding dogs that became known as native Setters. The best known were Ethan Allens—excellent woodcock, grouse and snipe dogs, but widely varying in conformation; Norfords, popular orange and white dogs that bred true; Gildersleeves, orange and white, medium-sized dogs with good noses and running gear; and Campbells, the most famous in field trials.

The American natives, like their English cousins, were bred from English, Gordon, Irish and occasional Russian Setters which are now extinct, but were said to resemble large Spaniels. M.C. and George W. Campbell's strain from Springhill, Tennessee, was based on Mason's Jeff of Irish-English ancestry and Fan, a lemon and white English. Campbell's finest was Joe, Jr., a dog out of a Campbell bitch but sired by the famous imported Irish Setter Elcho whose dam was also English-Irish crossbred.

Popularity of Llewellin's dogs continued to climb in America. David Sanborn of Baltimore imported Count Noble, a great performer that excelled on prairie chickens and sired many winners out of Gladstone daughters—thirty in fact, five more than Gladstone himself.

Arnold Burges imported Druid in 1877 and became so enamored of Llewellin's dogs that he wrote to the breeder for permission to call them Llewellin Setters. Subsequent advertising and other use of the name entrenched it so deeply that for generations many people thought of Llewellin Setters as a separate breed, not a strain of English Setters.

On December 15 and 16, 1879, the natives and the Llewellins had their day of reckoning. Campbell's Joe Jr., was matched against the great Gladstone for a purse of $500 a day, the race to continue from sunup to sundown, with no score to count except bird finds. The unreasonably long contest ended with both dogs lame and sore. Joe, Jr. won with 61 birds to Gladstone's 52.

Despite the victory for the so-called natives, the well-advertised, seemingly aristocratic Llewellin breeding appealed to the American public. Llewellins became not a fashion, but a fetish. Pedigrees became more important than bird work. The dominant light-blue belton color became so prevalent among Llewellins that beginners thought all blue-ticked Setters *were* Llewellins. No one was considered a real English Setter man unless his dogs could be traced to the Duke-Rhoebe-Laverack cross.

This was happening at a time when English Setters were almost unchallenged in field trials. Count Gladstone IV won the first National Bird Dog Championship in 1896. Setters won easily every year until Manitoba Rap, a Pointer, took the honor in 1909. Setters won again for four years, but Pointers gained a dominance that has continued to this day.

Some blamed it on the Llewellin fetish which they claimed had seriously ignored ability for sake of fashionable names on pedigrees. And records do prove that Pointer men have, instead, chosen winners as their studs.

Others point out that Pointers are capable contenders in the field much earlier in life than English Setters. And records show that no Setter has won the National Derby Championship.

Not all English Setters are natural retrievers as is Peggy, owned by Ronald Palmer, of Aledo, Illinois.

W. C. Kirk, the trainer/handler who led Johnny Crockett to his sensational win of the 1970 National Championship at Grand Junction, told me there are other good Setters on the circuit that could make wins if handlers gave them the personal attention Setters need. Kirk regards Setters as more sensitive to their masters than the more independent Pointers.

Johnny Crockett, the first English Setter to win the National since Mississippi Zev in 1946, got the attention he needed before he died in 1972 by living in the Kirk household and being with his boss almost all the time.

Neither Kirk, nor H. P. Sheely, Johnny's owner, are strictly Setter men. We might be reminded of Statter and Corbett of a century ago—men who appreciated good bird work above length or wave of hair, men who could recognize and develop the mental characteristics that count in hunting dogs.

Johnny Crockett was a small 38-pound dog with a rather thin coat. He carried his frame at top speed for hours without exhausting or overheating himself. Show specimens, although among the world's most beautiful dogs, weigh 55 to 65 pounds, have long burr-attracting coats, and in comparison to field dogs are sluggish and inclined to play instead of hunting in a businesslike manner. Even the expressions are different. Show dogs look soulful, concerned, worried. Field dogs look alert and anxious.

Show strains have come to be known as Laveracks and show people call field-trial specimens Llewellins. Of course, Llewellin started his field strain on a fortunate cross with Laverack's show dogs. Llewellin then crossed an English with an Irish and got a type that came to be known as the Mallwyd show strain. So call them what you want; just make sure you know what you're buying.

A middle-of-the-road type also exists, sometimes because only a show dog and field dog happen to be available for mating, and sometimes because hunters want dogs that are slower, closer working or better looking than field-trial stock. George Bird Evans, for example, experimented and developed his Old Hemlock strain of good-looking dogs that precisely suit his hunting style.

On the average, English Setters do not mature as early as Pointers, but learn well and don't need retraining as Pointers often do. Probably most English Setters are not natural retrievers. Field trials for Setters and Pointers do not test retrieving. But Delmar Smith says dogs of the Crockett strain usually are naturals at retrieving.

The coat of the average English Setter makes him a not quite perfect hot-climate quail dog, but a fine dog to hunt any birds in the North. Setters are especially popular for ruffed grouse and woodcock hunting in the East. One of the finest days I've spent included Nelson Grove of Ohio and his English Setter, Mike. The old dog paced himself for a day's hunting and needed his collar bell the entire time. He never slowed until the hunt was completed; he never lost track of us at any time; and his points were rock solid—a good example of a good breed.

Irish Setters

If a man doesn't know another thing about Irish Setters, he'll still tell you this: "They used to be good hunting dogs. Ruined by their beauty, though, when the show people took over." And he thinks it's something brand new that just happened.

The fact is, he's right about beauty ruining the Irish. But the show vs. field contest has been a running battle for over a century. And the relatively brand new fact is that a group of dedicated breeders has made it possible to once again hunt the flaming-red dog.

Excellent hunting dogs had been developed in Ireland prior to 1600. Most were characteristically white with red patches, and by the mid-1800's Irish Setters were still that color.

Obviously, much crossbreeding was done in those days. Hunting excellence was the first aim. Poor transportation and communications ruled out breeding to the great studs as is practiced today. Perhaps the majority of hunters wouldn't have heard of the outstanding dogs. Hunting ability and availability ruled early breeding.

It is thought that Bloodhounds and black Spanish Pointers, and later, Gordon Setters were crossed into Irish Red Setters, as they were often called. This is given as the reason for rare black or black and tan pups cropping up in litters.

No doubt all those crosses were made, plus some on Clancy's sheep dog and many others. It's foolish to try to think of a dog breed as having sprung up pure. It has only been within the last century that breed standardization has become popular, with most accomplishments occurring since 1900.

Interest in the solid red dog rose in the 1800's. The white on many specimens narrowed to toes, chest and a blaze on the forehead. The first volume of the AKC stud book, then called *The National American Kennel Club Stud Book* (1878), listed Irish Setters that weren't even red. Tom (660) was lemon, Van Clark (663) was black, and Speed (650) was black and white. Others were described as red with white feet, red with white blaze, etc.

The world's first dog show was held at Town Hall, Newcastle-on-Tyne, England, in 1859, and the battle lines were drawn. Such variation in type prevailed that nobody seemed to know how an Irish Setter was supposed to be made. Each claimed his dog was the ideal.

The matter was settled in 1875 when bench judge E. Sandell recognized Ch. Palmerston's show capabilities and bought a part interest in him. Palmerston became the fashion for five years until he died and proved so prepotent and popular that he's credited with crystalizing the Irish Setter breed into a genetically distinct type.

Others credit Palmerston with being the first to destroy the breed as hunters. Irish Setters became the rage at shows, and hunting instinct diminished with beauty.

Palmerston's first owner almost drowned the dog because he didn't regard the delicately built animal as suitable for breeding. Cecil Moore of County Tyrone was chiefly a hunter. And he had Palmerston long enough to know whether the dog's field capabilities were worth passing to future generations. But T. M. Hilliard begged for the dog just as it was about to be drowned. He was given Palmerston on the condition the dog only be used on the bench. If Palmerston's 1862 whelping date is correct, the dog was already 13 when he achieved fame as a stud, living to be 18.

Elcho was the first bench champion in America. He was capable in the field as was his son, Joe, Jr., the first field champion in the United States with Irish Setter in his pedigree.

Elcho-Palmerston bloodlines were responsible for the burst of Irish Setter field and show popularity after 1880. The Law strain was the famous line to rise out at that time. Shan Law (whelped in 1901) was said to have pointing ability superior to most Irish Setters, but he lacked the range and pace of Pointers and English Setters. Many excellent shooting dogs did come out of the Law strain, however; Minnesota prairie chicken market hunters used them extensively.

By 1917, Otto Pohl announced his intention to produce beautiful field-trial-winning Irish Setters. He might have succeeded if more show people had taken an interest in the hunting capabilities of his dogs.

And so it went. Some good shooting dogs were produced, always enough to make the Irish Setter remembered as once having been a good breed. But the majority were obviously "ruined by their beauty." By the twenties, many of the show Irish were so timid

Mrs. David Hasinger, of Philadelphia, and a top field Irish of the Valli Hi strain.

Saturday Night Ed shows his "class" field-trial pose. The high tail and high-set ears were bred back into Red Setters by a scientifically planned introduction of English Setter genes.

they clamped their tails between their legs like plow-shares and seemed to try to cut a furrow as they crouched low and were dragged around the ring.

Further ruin came when show enthusiasts tried to breed an arrow-shaped dog by selecting for straight shoulders. That made the dog considerably higher at the withers than the rump. It looked beautiful, but straight shoulders prevent a dogs' front legs from having normal reach. To cover ground such dogs are forced to compensate by bounding higher like a goat. Obviously, such a gait quickly tires a dog in the field. Irish Setter standards were changed to correct these shoulders, but it's a problem that exists in the breed to this day.

Also in the twenties, Elias Vail did well with his Irish Setters in field trials. Too few joined his side of the struggle, however.

Interest dropped so low that for 26 years the Irish Setter Club of America held no field trials. They were reinstated in 1933, but by 1950 interest again dragged. The organization was, and still is, primarily show oriented.

It was also about 1950 that W. E. "Ned" LeGrande, of Douglassville, Pennsylvania, attended a trial in Indiana for Irish Setters only. The pitiful efforts he saw made him determined to do something about it. For what he did, LeGrande will undoubtedly be remembered as the father of field Irish much as R. C. Purcell-Llewellin is regarded as the father of the field-type English Setter.

The first problem was finding enough superior stock to begin a breeding program. R. C. "Rusty" Baynard, Archer Church and later Colonel Ed Schnettler, Al Bortz, John Van Alst and others joined him in the search. There were eight or ten Irish Setters in the country that could run, point and handle birds. Only three pointed with an erect tail. They were Askew's Carolina Lady, Ike Jack Kendrick (a son of Lady) and Susan. Susan was discovered to be barren.

The National Red Setter Field Trial Club sub-sequently formed by LeGrande and his friends sought aid and advice on how they could improve and expand the breed. A search for more Carolina Lady stock had proven fruitless. Earl Bond of Albert Lea, Minnesota, had maintained a strain of the old market-hunting Irish Setters for fifty years (he had bred Lady), but he left the state and couldn't be found. Lady and Ike could be inbred, and they were. But other lines had to be improved to create adequate stock. There was no recourse but to ask payment of the loan made half a century and more before.

Llewellin had crossed Irish Setters into his strain of English Setters with great success. Now the favor would be returned.   •

Ilsley Chip, a son of National Champion Mississippi Zev was mated to LeGrande's Willow Winds Smada, a bitch whose lineage could be traced through Horace Lytle's Smada Byrd and Dr. L. C. Adams' dogs to the kennels of Otto Pohl. Chip was red and white, so when crossed with a Red Setter he sired red or fawn pups with white trim.

Willow Winds Joan was the litter choice to be mated to Willow Winds Mike, a young purebred Irish with lots of fire. From that mating, Betty was bred by Rusty, producing Rita.

All of this was done without secrecy. The offspring were registered by William Brown of the Field Dog Stud Book as crossbred. One more mating to pure Irish would remove the outcross from the pedigree and make the offspring eligible to be registered as purebred. Rita was mated to Ike Jack Kendrick.

Some of the great dogs that rose from this mating were Hardtack, Mr. O'Leary, Double Jay and Willow Winds Hobo. Baynard's pure Irish, Rusty's Jinx, was also important in this early breeding. Mated with females of the outcross, Jinx was the sire of Double Jay, Willow Winds Hobo and Valli Joy Hi.

The breeding program was a success. LeGrande amassed a total of 513 wins in both open and breed trials.

Not everyone has approved of this cross. A frequent question is, "If they wanted an English Setter, why didn't they just buy one?"

Obviously, these people didn't want an English Setter. They wanted an Irish Setter, red like an Irish, with the old personality of the hunting Irish but with the running and pointing style returned that had been stolen by show breeding.

"Criticism doesn't matter," Col. Ed Schnettler told me at a Red Setter Spring Championship at Paducah, Kentucky. "Fifty years from now nobody will remember what we did. They'll only know that Irish Setters are good hunting dogs."

I don't believe history will forget what these men did for the breed. But Ed is correct in believing that fifty years from now it won't matter. The Brittany Spaniel was rebuilt much the same way about sixty years ago. I've yet to hear anyone complain about the outcrosses.

Ed's words came to mind again while I watched a young woman trying to handle an Irish of show breeding in an obedience class. That dog was interested in everything *except* his mistress. He noticed every foolish distraction, but his span of attention to anything was almost zero. It's worth a little criticism to be able to avoid that kind of breeding.

And because of the National Red Setter Field Trial Club, it won't be necessary for future hunters to complain that Irish Setters were once good but were ruined by their beauty. The organization sponsors trials to compare dogs and improve the breed, and publishes *The Flushing Whip,* a modest periodical designed to maintain communication between members and to advance the cause of the Red Setter. At this writing the editor as well as club secretary-treasurer is Bob Kerans, R.R. 1, Newton, Illinois 62448.

There are still ten times as many show Irish registered each year as there are field Irish. But most field stock is registered by the Field Dog Stud Book. This additional separation from show breeding is a further guarantee that Red Setters won't lapse ever again into oblivion.

Irish Setters respond well to gentle but firm treatment. They're intelligent and biddable, but can't be corrected in anger. As with any other breed, of course, individuals vary greatly and a few may be quite soft while a few on the other extreme are hardheaded. In selecting an Irish Setter for hunting, avoid show and so-called dual stock unless you are a failure-loving glutton for punishment. Instead, request a copy of *The Flushing Whip.* Study it. Attend a Red Setter trial. Then choose a pup from parents with the hunting style you like.

Gordon Setters

Gordon Setters aren't remembered by many hunters these days, but when they are, someone is sure to comment that they're hard to see in the field. The same thing is said about Irish Setters. Granted, a field-trial Pointer or English Setter that may be running a quarter to half of a mile away will be easier to see if white. But at the range most hunters want their gun dogs working, color doesn't matter.

We had a purebred black Irish Setter when I was a boy. They're rare. There isn't much information available on how often a genuine mutation like this occurs, but one breeder survey turned up a single black dog among almost 1200 pups. At any rate, it was many years later that I learned black dogs are supposed to be hard to see. Ours showed up well against the pale dead grass of autumn and even better in the snow. In no cover did we feel handicapped by black.

Gordon Setters were once highly popular gun dogs, especially on grouse in the East. Frank Forester, one of the very best writers on the subject of grouse hunting, couldn't praise the black and tans enough. Grouse are hunted in woods and thickets. No cover could be worse for keeping track of dogs. But the men of Forester's time somehow didn't notice any handicap.

There had to be a better reason for the Gordon's skid in popularity, and there was. In fact, there were two. The first was dog shows that began in 1859. Field and show types divided almost immediately. While it doesn't have to happen, it is a fact that when dogs are selected for appearance instead of ability, the mental faculties of the breed suffers. We can't blame show people, either. They have as much right to breed for beauty as we do for birdiness. But it happens.

Gun-dog trainer Jack Godsil has nothing against Gordons, but he's very aware of the odds for or against an individual of a breed making an acceptable bird

Gordon Setters are beautiful—in the field or on the bench. They don't have the pace, range and color for field trials, so show stock gets notoriety, field stock doesn't. It has made hunting Gordons scarce.

This show Gordon also does a good job of hunting for its owners. Such dogs are relatively rare in the breed, however, so select Gordons out of working stock.

dog. His appraisal of most of the Gordons he has seen or trained is that they're playbabies. They love to run and romp and play. If they accidently run into a bird, fine. They'll point it. But they don't go out in a businesslike manner and hunt birds.

I've seen the same thing in many Irish Setters of show breeding. They're flighty. They move as the whim strikes. They lack sufficient attention span to learn something.

The second blow to Gordon Setters was the popularity of field trials and their influence on bird dog breeding. Gordons didn't have the range, pace or color to compete successfully. Pointers and English Setters gained notoriety and public acceptance while Gordons languished.

Couple lack of interest with failure to select breeders for ability and you get the predominant picture of today's Gordons. Even some birdy individu-

als are a little too beautiful. We failed to get pictures of one working Gordon because it wasn't possible to arrange a suitable time before the show season started. After that the owner wasn't willing to risk damaging the dog's long feathering. Again, everyone has a right to his own priorities. But anyone searching for a bird-dog prospect had better know what the breeder's priorities were.

All of this doesn't mean that no field-type Gordons are available. It's simply difficult to find a breeder who has devoted himself to field Gordons long enough to have a reasonably reliable strain of dogs. One of the few long-term breeders is Hill Greer, Jr., of Brownsville, Tennessee.

Tennessee is black and tan country in hounds. It's probably no surprise that it would be one of the last strongholds in black and tan bird dogs. But Greer doesn't consider himself a stronghold. "I'm just an average farmer," Greer told me, "and I like to hunt bird dogs in the winter. I get enjoyment out of that, so I keep breeding my Gordons."

Greer usually has three bitches to breed from, plus an old dog or two, and perhaps that many young prospects coming up. "If you get too much of anything, you can't take care of it right," he says.

Greer has owned Gordons for over 40 years. His grandfather Warren Hayes Greer owned them before him. A friend of his grandfather, Gene Haggert, gave Hill Greer, Jr., a female Gordon pup when Hill was five or six years old. He grew up with the pup and has had five generations of Gordons since. He'll either line breed or buy an unrelated bitch for breeding, if he can find one that proves itself capable in the field.

I'm not trying to sell Greer's surplus dogs. But I'm using him as an example for another reason aside from the fact that there are very few others like him to choose from. According to what he tells me, I think he's doing the right thing for the breed.

I've been criticized before for advocating complete separation of show and field registries. But I see no sense in futile attempts to put the brakes on a bandwagon. If they're not playing your tune, step off and sing your own. Dog shows are highly popular. And why shouldn't they be? I think it's wonderful that something which isn't illegal, fattening or cancer causing is able to provide so much enjoyment for so many people. But when a national club that represents a field breed becomes primarily show oriented, it's time for those whose primary interests are field oriented to go their own way. That happened long ago with Pointers and English Setters with great success. The American Kennel Club registers about 2000 beauties of the two breeds annually; *The American Field's* Field Dog Stud Book registers ten times that many of hunting or field-trial strains. And Irish Setters are being brought back from the brink of extinction as field dogs in the same manner. Most members of the National Red Setter Field Trial Club register their stock with the F.D.S.B.—probably around 3000 a year. The A.K.C. registers ten times that many show dogs. In no way am I suggesting that a popularity or numbers contest be held between the A.K.C. and F.D.S.B. They're both worthwhile and necessary organizations doing a good job in representing their memberships. But the separation provides the distinction. Both memberships know where to find their kind of stock.

I'm not suggesting that all hunting breeds break away from the A.K.C. either. National clubs representing the German breeds are doing quite well within the A.K.C. registration and field-trial framework. It's only time for division when the national club representing a field breed becomes predominantly show oriented. That has been the case with Gordon Setters, so Hill Greer registers his dogs with the F.D.S.B.

The immediately noticeable difference between a show and field Gordon is size. Greer's dogs range from 45-pound females to 60-pound males. Show dogs with a height up to 27 inches for males weigh as much as 80 pounds. Females may weigh 70 pounds.

Greer seemed suspicious of outcrossing when he asked where I thought these huge dogs came from. "I've gone to Memphis to see show Gordons. Some I saw looked like tall race horses. The others were just big and clumsy."

I don't think it was necessary to outcross. Shows have a history of contributing to dog size. It seems that big dogs are more impressive. They catch the eye. And they're chosen for studs. Over a few generations the entire breed can grow.

Field dogs, of course, must be quick, agile and ambitious. They can't be lumbering dullards.

Greer describes his Gordon's working style as much like English Setters, except for range. His Gordons work closer and check in more often. They're on the move, busy, running, never puttering. An old bird-wise dog may learn where the birds live on home grounds and become a line or fence-row dog. In unfamiliar territory, or if the dog is younger, he'll quarter ahead of the hunter.

Gordons had a reputation for becoming one-man dogs, and Greer thinks they still are to a large extent. That's especially true if the dog has hunted with just one man for several years. Another may not be able to handle the dog. But Greer says a lot depends on conditioning. "Quite a few people around here get water from my farm," he said, "so there's different people coming and going quite a lot. That makes a difference. My dogs aren't usually suspicious of strangers."

Gordons also have a reputation for being natural retrievers. Greer's pups run free around the farmyard and are forever toting sticks, balls, gloves or whatever they find that's loose.

Natural retrieving is great to have in a dog, but the first thing a hunter concerns himself with in a breed like this is pointing. A man doesn't want to feed a dog for three years to find out whether it will take an interest in pointing. And that can happen with a breed that is primarily show oriented. Greer has fowl running free around the farm. "Almost as soon as they're big enough to walk, you see them stretched out on a chicken or a guinea hen," he said. "And when a pup is two or three months old and points a grasshopper, I stroke him and stack him up and really make over that dog. I make over them when they carry me a terrapin or something, too. Those kind make good dogs."

There's one Gordon Setter idiosyncrasy I'd heard of but never seen. Over the years an occasional individual reputedly circled their birds carefully as if to hold them as a shepherd would. "I had one like that," Greer said. "He'd go around and pin his bird. And when he came in to me, he'd always swing around and come back to my left side. He was a great retriever. Could bring in two birds at once. He'd try three but never did manage it."

That apparent shepherd behavior in a few rare dogs is interesting because legend has it that a black "Colley" was involved in the breed's origin.

It all started with the fourth Duke of Gordon in the late 1770's. There were said to be black-and-tan Setters in Scotland as early as 1600, and it is claimed that other wealthy breeders of the Duke's time also had black and tans, but credit for developing a genetically distinct breed apparently goes to Gordon. The dogs were called Gordon Castle Setters at that time.

One of the Duke's shepherds had a Collie named Maddy that was extremely intelligent and exceptionally birdy for such a breed. Writers of her day who had seen her didn't claim she'd point, but upon smelling game she stopped and "watched." Maddy frequently contributed to the Duke's shoots, and if legend is correct, also contributed to his strain of Setters.

Don't regard this as a taint to the Gordon purity, however. Anyone with a knowledge of dog history realizes that all breeds originated much this way. Standardization came later and with it, sometimes, rigor mortis.

Kennel responsibilities passed to the fifth Duke of Gordon, and upon his death in 1835, the Duke of Richmond, a cousin, expanded the Gordon Castle breeding. Working ability still came first. Even by 1863 when Southhill held its first field trial, there were still plenty of outstanding Gordons. They ran off with the first three places.

The first Gordons were imported to America by George Blunt and Daniel Webster in 1842. That began a popularity that only diminished when field trials selected against close-quartering dogs.

A writer of Gordon's time said they were easy to break, would back naturally, were not fast but had morning-to-night staying powers, had first-class noses and seldom false pointed. The famous Idstone said, "I have seen better setters of the black and tan than any other breed."

A century later, Greer, one of the few remaining field breeders, described his Gordons as "easy to train, they check back with me, all are natural retrievers on land and water, take briars and weather good and are mostly singles instead of covey dogs. Our coveys are maybe a mile apart. When you break them up the birds head for the thickest place they can find. That's when you need a dog like this."

We've imported a great many continental breeds to do the precise job Greer describes. And I think the properly bred Gordon is ready for a renewal of acceptance in America. But the few people like Greer will need lots of help in achieving a goal like that. If you take the notion to throw in with the Gordons, just don't buy one of show breeding and take it to a gun-dog trainer. Many are my friends, and I wouldn't be able to face them.

Brittany Spaniels

The Brittany is the only Spaniel that points. Flushing is the usual Spaniel manner of handling game. For that reason, some people regard Britts as more Setter than Spaniel and believe the breed should simply be called Brittany.

The Spaniel heritage comes through clearly and strongly, however. Like the Spaniel, the usual Brittany has easily developed quartering instincts, retrieves naturally, always seems to know just where his master is while hunting, enjoys water work, and responds to praise and encouragement better than to harsh punishment or severe reprimands.

Like other land Spaniels, Britts are expected to be without tails. If a Brittany isn't born without a tail, it's docked to under four inches. Pointer and Setter enthusiasts prefer this meter of a dog's mind to remain intact and in use; however, Brittany advocates are quick to point out the advantages of a tailless dog. For example, cups and glasses aren't whipped off the coffee table as might happen when a friend plays with an excitable tail-wagger.

Brittany Spaniels actually appear well balanced without tails. With tails, they'd look like Big Dippers. That's because Britts also have short necks and relatively small heads as a rule. And that aspect of their conformation enhances their performance as water retrievers. A short-necked, small-headed dog balances better when swimming with a duck in the mouth. A long-necked dog has trouble keeping his head high enough while carrying a payload in water. The long neck shifts more weight forward.

"Tails are docked to keep them out of car doors," Frank Kremblas says with a grin, especially if his grouse-hunting buddy Nelson Grove is within earshot. Nelson's English Setter Mike is missing some of his tail for that reason.

"I think Nelson did it on purpose," Frank told me. "He hunted with my old Bull and found out how good these Brittany Spaniels are. He wanted Mike to look like one."

Nelson just smiled. Mike is a grouse master that needs no defense. And while what we've said of Brittanies so far might make them seem all Spaniel and no Setter, watching Bull and Mike work together is enough to change that notion for anyone. When it comes to range, staunchness on point, and endurance, Bull is very much a Setter in the grouse woods.

The Setter wasn't necessary in Brittany Spaniel development, but recent history indicates that it was used. Reaching farther back in time, most authorities agree that the first bird dogs came from Spain. The Roman Pliny, who was procurator of Spain in A.D. 73, wrote that fellow Romans had taken Spanish dogs called Aviaries into France and Italy. There are more details on this in the English Setter section, but see if this quote doesn't describe a pointing dog: "When the wise animal approaches the quail or any other passing bird, it seems to fascinate them by its shiny look . . ."

It's impossible to trace the movements and developments of early dogs. We can only reason that dogs accompanied their masters on conquests and migrations and evolved according to the dictates of climate, game, and type of cover hunted. In Brittany, the northern province of France where the Brittany Spaniel developed, the human influence included Romans, Celts and Saxons, followed later by the people of Wales, Ireland and Spain, and finally the resulting Bretons themselves. Game and habitat in Brittany included woodcock thickets and duck marshes, plus hare and rabbit coverts. The dogs, like the people themselves and their horses became short, stocky and strong.

Gaston Phoebus, Count of Foix, wrote *Le Livre de la Chasse* in 1387 and included a chapter called "Du Chien d'Oysel." Du Chien means "of the dog" and Oysel refers to bird and is synonymous with falcon. The dog was described as large of body and head with a coat not too shaggy. It was probably much like the French Pointing Spaniel that has existed since at least that point in history. One European authority even claims the word Spaniel as applied to the French Spaniel is not derived from Chiens d' Espagnol, or dogs of Spain, but from the old French *s'espanir*, which means to lie down or to span.

A sudden point on a pheasant.

The Brittany Spaniel could have developed from the French Pointing Spaniel or from the same basic stock. However it came about, there did exist a type of dog in the 1600's that was much like the Brittany of today. French and Dutch artists of that time depicted the Brittany quite accurately—a little leggier than other Spaniels and often on point.

By the 1800's, more written records appear. A tailless or stub-tailed, thick-haired, long and rangy, but very unstandardized dog existed. The breed was variously called Brittany, Breton, Amorican (from an old name for the area), and Brittany Pointer.

In 1906, Major Gran-Chavin wrote in his memorandum book that while traveling through three provinces he noticed the presence of many small Spaniels. The local people boasted of their dogs' abilities on woodcock and hare. The Major describes the dogs as ". . . small spaniels . . . almost all with short tails . . . white-orange, white-chestnut, and white-black . . . excellent hunters . . . fearless . . . would point very well . . ."

With Wales across the English Channel from Brittany, it's logical to assume much trade and interbreeding of dogs occurred between the two peoples. Breeds would include both Setters and other Spaniels. Arthur Enaud is credited by most authorities, however, with recorded outcrossing to improve the breed.

In his breed book, *The Brittany in America,* Fred Z. White, M.D., quotes from a letter M. de Kermadec, an early French breeder and Brittany Spaniel historian, sent to Alan Stuyvesant in 1946. M. de Kermadec says the Viscount de Pontavice, a great hunter and Setterman had a kennel on his estate near Fourgères. One of his guards named Lulzac owned native Spaniels and was quite proud of them. Lulzac either convinced the Viscount to mate an English Setter bitch to a native stud or he took care of the matter himself. At any rate, the only pup from that mating, an orange and white bitch, was bred back to a native white and brown Spaniel. The litter was so satisfactory that the Viscount gave up his Setters.

Arthur Enaud saw the bitch hunting and also gave up his English dogs. Over a period of time Enaud outcrossed on to Italian Bracco and Braque de Bourbonnais stock, both short-haired Pointers, but the Brittany type and coat were returned by selective breeding. Better scenting ability resulted. Enaud later helped create the Club of the Breton Spaniel.

M. de Kermadec writes that at a show in 1907 a group formed the French Spaniel Club and undertook to establish the first Brittany Spaniel standard. He says they found four types in existence: the small French Spaniel, the manifestly Setter type, a small dog of a good sort but too reduced in size, and the improved type of the Viscount du Pontavice. The improved but still historic type was chosen as the standard.

In the early standards, a great deal of emphasis was

Bill Mueller, of Highland, Illinois, readies to the flush of
quail being pointed by a Brittany Spaniel.

Brittanies are usually natural retrievers and versatile. This
one retrieves cottontails but doesn't chase them.

placed on cobby bodies and naturally short tails.
Cobby is a descriptive term for horses meaning short,
stocky and strong. The Britt remains short- bodied
and compact. The naturally tailless rule was dropped
in 1933. The French club also accepted black and
white coats in that year. The color still disqualifies a
Brittany in the United States.

Louis A. Thebaud imported the first Brittanies to
the United States in the early 1930's. He had hunted
extensively in Yucatan and had attended trials in
France, where he became interested in the breed.
Others followed, and they were able to import some of
the best France had to offer.

In North America, the Brittany Spaniel has under-
gone change and still is. Americans generally ask for
more range from their dogs, and certain families of
Britts have accomplished it. Some have competed
very successfully in field trials. The vast majority of
the breed, however, doesn't range beyond the wishes of
the average hunter.

Dr. Fred Z. White told me he believes that some of
the changes noticeable in North America were due to
the short time the breed has been standardized.
Different dogs were imported to various sections of
the country where popular studs market their get. As

a result, New England Britts are often shorter than
those in the midwest.

That doesn't bother Dr. White, however. "Pointers
and Setters have been around shows and field trials
and subjected to standardizations for much longer
than Brittany Spaniels," he said. "They're still not
standardized, either."

Delmar Smith, the professional trainer from Ed-
mund, Oklahoma, adds that there are vast differences
between individual dogs of any breed, Brittanies
included. "There are two or three families of Britts
that are really outstanding gun dogs," Delmar told
me. "The rest are used for shows and pets. They lack
desire."

Delmar breeds and trains Brittany Spaniels and has
won six National Brittany Championships just to
mention the most important wins. He has worked
Brittanies in 48 states and Canada on various types of
birds, and the dogs are capable of handling all of them.

This versatility is one of the attractions making the
Brittany increasingly more popular among hunters.
Dr. White hunted Saxon, his National Amateur
Champion, on quail, pheasants, ruffed grouse, prairie
chickens, chukar and woodcock. The dog experienced
no difficulty in switching from one species to another.

(Read the section on versatile dog training for more details on this subject.)

My own Brittany retrieves cottontails in addition to birds and isn't a problem about chasing live rabbits. Delmar Smith adds doves and ducks to the retrieving list.

Add these natural inclinations to a short- to medium-range dog that is master oriented and eager to please, and we have a breed that is among the easiest for the average hunter to train.

Gun-dog trainer Jack Godsil pointed out one peculiarity of the breed that gives the amateur trainer problems. "Most Brittanies I've trained have had a temperamental streak, despite being soft," he said.

Don't try training a Britt if you have no patience. As Dr. White pointed out, "They don't force train well on retrieving or anything else."

Give lots of praise and encouragement while hunting or training a Brittany. Don't accept a bad performance or a mistake, but keep the punishment on the light side. There are exceptions, of course, but on the average, Britts will lose a great deal of hunting desire if given the flushing whip in the manner that a Pointer would take in his stride.

What it takes to train most Brittanies is firm kindness. But don't neglect to be firm because of the dog's soft nature, or his willful side will start running the show.

German Shorthaired Pointers

Gun-dog trainer Jack Godsil breeds four or five litters of pups each year. Some are Labs and Goldens, but his choice of pointing breed is the Shorthair.

"It really bothers most fellows when their dog gets out over 100 yards," Jack said. "They see the dog making mistakes that can't be corrected. They worry that the dog will range onto posted property. Neighbors often don't hunt on each other's land these days. What suits most hunters is a 60- to 70-yard dog.

"Maybe a fellow has 200 acres he can hunt on. It holds two coveys of quail. He sure doesn't need a rangy dog to find them. And once a covey is flushed, a close dog is much better at finding singles."

Jack's appraisal of today's conditions and the dog to meet them is reflected all over the Midwest, especially the northern half. Continental breeds are all popular here, but the Shorthair heads the list. Godsil's choice of German Shorthaired Pointers over other continentals is a matter of percentages, he says. The breed has been around longer, has gained wider acceptance, and has been tested and compared under field conditions more than most other continentals. The result is a higher percentage of Shorthairs capable of making bird dogs.

Other attractions of well-bred Shorthairs are natural tracking and retrieving ability. Tracking comes from introduction of Schweisshund genes when the original crosses were made back in the 1870's. English translators understood Schweisshund to mean Bloodhound. Actually, Schweiss means any kind of scent: spoor, perspiration, blood trail, or whatever. Hund means any kind of dog, not necessarily hound.

Germany had variations of the old St. Hubert hounds, originated by St. Hubert who died in A.D. 727. By the 1700's, French Talbot hounds and Bleu de Gascognes (much like American Bluetick Coonhounds) represented the more streamlined, less-wrinkled hound of the time. This type of hound influence shows in early pictures of Shorthairs, but the Bloodhound type does not. I owned a Bluetick, in fact, that could have doubled, except in color, for Woden Hektor II of 1888.

At any rate, hound inheritance gives the breed a willingness to drop its head and follow blood scent or foot trails. That characteristic also makes a good "singles" dog, but it can't be a fast, stylish covey dog at the same time. That doesn't mean the dog won't find coveys, of course. It just won't happen in the snappy, energetic manner of a Pointer.

The other breeds that went into the first crosses were Old Spanish Pointer, an old German Pointer from Baden Wurttemberg, and probably French Braques. (The word braque probably comes from the old French *braquer,* meaning to aim.)

Squabbling prevented introduction of Pointer genes until later. The English had improved the Old Spanish Pointer by crossing with fast Foxhound blood. Some of the German breeders opposed this infusion because the English version wasn't a good tracker, didn't have an adequate coat for cold-water retrieving and wasn't an especially good retriever anyway. At least as important was a sense of nationalism and rejection of anything British. The Pointer infusion did occur, however, and plenty of it.

The most notable early dog with strong Pointer characteristics was Nero 66 owned by Julius Mehlich of Berlin. While the dog had a Pointer head, critics were silenced by Nero's performances in the field and at field trials.

Breeders over the years were able to hold much of the Pointer's nose and bird-handling sense while selecting for the dense coat necessary in cold-water retrieves. Most hunters in America don't regard the Shorthair's coat as adequate for icy waters, but breed advocates point out an interesting observation. Long hair isn't necessary to insulate the body; look at the beaver or mink. Density is what counts!

In the United States, one occasionally finds a dog that must stand for tail examination to find out if it's Pointer or Shorthair. Such appearance is not proof of a Pointer outcross, but it's cause for suspicion. Crosses have been rumored, and Shorthair field-trialers have continually searched for wider, faster-running dogs. But these outcrosses are both illegal and detrimental

German breeders opposed the introduction of English Pointer genes at first, but crosses were made anyway with considerable success.

to the breed. The progeny must be covered by falsified papers, and owners of generations of dogs get a completely erroneous view of what they think is the German Shorthaired Pointer breed. More serious than that is the actual change in the dogs. These half-breeds don't fit the Pointer man's idea of a Pointer nor a Shorthair man's idea of a Shorthair.

Right about here someone will remember that I didn't criticize the early infusion of Pointer genes. Someone may have even read the section on Irish Setters where I heartily condoned an English Setter outcross. Is this different? Very!

The Irish Setter breeders carried out an honest, above-board, scientific plan to restore a breed that had degenerated into playful idiots that could no longer think or run like dogs. The man who adds Pointer to Shorthair today is doing it by stealth and simply to win field trials.

The German breeders of the 1800's weren't all-wise. The traditionalists fought to maintain rounded ears and straight profiles, regardless of the fact that this had nothing to do with performance. Humans being what they are, some men crossed onto English genes without consulting anyone. But that was almost a century ago. Since that time, selection toward a goal has eliminated unwanted Pointer characteristics. The Shorthair evolved as a breed with dense coat, good

retrieving instincts and tracking ability, as well as mental and physical propensities to hunt within range of the gun. The man who illegally outcrosses with a Pointer today stands a good chance of improving run and bird handling, but he'll very likely destroy everything else the breed has come to mean. It will take generations to again refine the results of mongrelization.

One other quality that German breeders sought in their dogs is "sharpness." In other words, they didn't want their dogs backing off from anything. The utility dog they looked for in the Shorthair had to point birds, retrieve fur or feathers from land or water, and track and sometimes dispatch wounded deer or live predators.

The sharpness test in Germany consists of sending the dog into an enclosure to kill a cat or fox. The Germans stopped allowing the public to witness this test back in the mid-1930's. This sharpness that the Germans sought is often apparent in the Shorthair's expression. And to me this is further evidence that English translators were not correct in assuming that the Bloodhound was basic in the Shorthair's background.

Around 1750 a German named Jonathan Plott emigrated to the United States, bringing with him hounds that are thought to have been of the type used to hunt boar in his homeland. Plott settled in the Smoky Mountains. There being no boar, the German and his sons soon found a worthy adversary in the black bear. Within the isolation of the mountains the Plott family is said to have continuously bred their strain of dog for 150 years before the outside world became aware of it. That local outcrosses were necessary to avoid the weakness of inbreeding is apparent, especially since no knowledge of scientific inbreeding seems to have been handed down with the dogs, yet the type remains distinct. Today's Plotts have become more standardized and somewhat houndier, but a well-bred Plott is distinguishable by its expression. It is alert, piercing, aggressive . . . in a word, sharp.

On page 25 of C. Bede Maxwell's *The New German Shorthaired Pointer* (Howell Book House) a picture of the Schweisshund of the Hanoverian Jägerei (hunting fraternity) marvelously illustrates the piercing look also common to Plotts. These hounds included all the original Plott colors that existed before the Plott Breed Club began selecting for brindles.

Below the Hanoverian Schweisshund is a picture of Treff 1010 of 1881. Mrs. Maxwell calls Treff the most solid taproot of all. "He sets his name all over, and most dogs trace to him." Treff has the same piercing expression. The color has changed by crossing and selection, but the sharpness remains.

With these German dogs the Plott family bred in isolation for so long, I think we have strong evidence of the type of hound that contributed genes to the Shorthaired Pointer.

How much the Shorthair has changed or is changing since its arrival in America is difficult to tell. Our field trials have not tested the Shorthair for the things demanded of it in Germany. In America a versatile dog is one that can point and retrieve several species of birds. A rare hunter might include retrieving, possibly even pointing, rabbits. Contributing to our shame, I think, and certainly to our waste, dogs are not or cannot be used to track wounded deer. Shorthairs in America are almost never asked to cope with predators.

Some of the early Shorthair importers did use their dogs as all-purpose hunters. Dr. Charles R. Thornton of Montana used his to point birds, retrieve ducks in icy slush, herd cattle, and even to tree game.

Others expected Shorthairs to outpoint Pointers, outfetch Labs, trail like Beagles and tree like Coonhounds—all without training. Specialists all do their assigned jobs better than the jacks-of-all-trades. As might be expected, many people were disappointed with the breed.

Sometimes the strain of Shorthair in America (or what passes for a Shorthair) has lost certain abilities because generations passed without selecting for these qualities. I tried to train a Shorthair to tree raccoons some years back, but the dog didn't have sense enough to look up when the hounds were almost in hysteria

Solid liver Shorthairs have been quite popular in Germany. This one is Gallant Rusty, owned by William Abbot, of Chicago.

over an animal they could see in the tree. Looking up is an inherited instinct of which this dog had none. Training him was not impossible, but it would have been unreasonably time consuming.

Some characteristics are contradictory, too. A well-bred bird dog has natural quartering instincts. Teaching that dog to blood trail-wounded game is one thing, but you can't teach that dog to stop quartering and questing for body scent because you decided that now is the time to hunt creek bottoms for coon tracks.

The German Shorthaired Pointer, nevertheless, was bred for versatile work. Properly trained within his capabilities, he can turn in a creditable performance. And very likely that role will become more prominent on this continent as time goes on. A very sincere, serious and enterprising group called North American Versatile Hunting Dog Association has modified European versatile dog tests to better fit North American needs. With the continued crowding of both living and hunting space, this concept can only grow—and along with it the already popular German Shorthaired Pointer.

German Wirehaired Pointers

"The breeding of a correct wire coat is the most important feature." That statement was made by the Deutsche Drahthaar Club in 1902. It remains as important today, and every bit as difficult to achieve, as it was back then. "If we get 20 percent really good coats," Don Smith told me, "it's a satisfactory litter."

Don is a Wirehair fancier and versatile dog enthusiast from West Simsbury, Connecticut. He went on to say that 30 percent may actually have poor coats. Reputable breeders refuse to register these individuals. They sell them as pets at reduced prices. Half, therefore, have acceptable coats, but breeding stock should be selected from the really good 20 percent.

That makes raising German Wirehaired Pointer pups not only difficult but expensive. It pushes prices higher than average for puppies of hunting stock, yet the litter owner isn't well compensated for his trouble. Furthermore, it tempts unscrupulous breeders into palming off culls on unsuspecting novices at quality prices. And worse yet, some show breeders, according to Don, are selecting for long-haired dogs, "then stripping the coat for the show ring. You can't tell the difference."

Why all the fuss over coat? It's the one distinguishing feature that makes the Wirehair truly more versatile than most other breeds. It's really two coats, in fact. That wiry, scraggly looking outer coat is an armor against punishment in the roughest kind of cover. Advocates also claim water shakes off of this large-diameter hair quicker than from thinner hair. The undercoat is dense and well insulating in winter, but almost disappears in warm weather, a feature that aids in cold-water retrieving, yet allows the dog to adapt to almost any climate.

I'm sure the German breeders also considered the dog's coat as part of his fighting equipment. Wirehairs were expected to trail, attack and dispatch predators. They had to trail and hold wounded big game, including the vicious boar. If a dog must fight, it's a distinct advantage if his opponent is getting a mouthful of much hair and little dog.

In North America, of course, the Wirehair is a bird dog exclusively, with the exception of a few that point and retrieve rabbits. The advantage of the wirehair coat over shorthair is in cold-water retrieves. And we're not talking about theories like the dog show women do when they ask you not to forget that their Poodles are truly retrievers.

Field Champion Herr Baron's Jo is a frequent winner in A.K.C. field trials, and Lloyd Kiechhoff hunts him hard on grouse, ducks and geese. While hunting waterfowl, Jo sits on a muskrat house until called upon to retrieve. Then he gets right back on the house, shakes off and waits for his next call to duty. Lloyd doesn't handle Jo on retrieves, just sends him once, and the dog applies his own skill, nose and memory to find the bird. He has gained such a reputation that hunters who lose a bird are told, "See the guy with the dog that looks like an Airedale. He'll find it."

Al Gallagher is one of the men who succeeded in establishing Wirehaired foundation stock in the United States during the 1950's. I was fortunate enough to see his Dual Champion Herr Schmardt's Boy Yancey work in Wisconsin during the 6th Annual GWP Pheasant Futurity sponsored by the German Wirehaired Pointer Club of America. Yancey takes hand signals and has been trained on singles, doubles and blinds. The dog loves to retrieve and has plenty of opportunities. Al lives near the Fox River in northern Illinois, where Yancey retrieves ducks for the entire season without concern for temperatures.

I found another interesting case of Wirehair retrieving in Minnesota. Don Helmeke bought his first German Wirehaired Pointer from a kennel that obviously isn't interested in maintaining quality coat standards. The dog is blond, and for some reason blond hair is always fine and silky in Wirehairs. It offers no protection in water and doesn't shake out well after the retrieve. It quickly wears off on the leading edge of the dog's legs which then rub raw, even when only hunting in dead grass. The dog was all heart for the hunt, however, and Don didn't recognize the coat problem until he had become quite fond of his Wirehair. Don solved it by outfitting the dog with a foam rubber wet suit.

We threw a dead quail into the water for a demonstration, then used the bird to provide practice for an attractively marked young dog belonging to Chuck Johnson. Everything went well until the quail became watersoaked and floated almost beneath the surface. Don sent his blond Wirehair. The dog couldn't see it, so Don began handling him, but not with the conventional stop to look, then "Over!" accompanied by a hand direction. The bird wasn't far out, so Don just quietly ordered "Left!" or "Right!" whichever was appropriate, and the dog responded like remote control.

The blond Wirehair gets plenty of practice because Don manages a hunting club, but knowing right from his left without having to be shown puts him ahead of a few people I've known who were a good deal older than this dog.

It's difficult for the novice to judge a wire coat, but blond is a color to avoid at all times. Roy Speece of Nebraska is interested in Griffons, a closely related breed, and is searching for white, off-white or light silver coated dogs that would be easier to see against the brown grass fields and brushy ditches he hunts. For that reason he is now hunting a white Italian Spinoni. But white is *not* connected with silky hair. Roy describes the soft blond hair in either breed as dirty tan or beige.

The Wirehair standard doesn't allow as many colors as Griffons, however. The acceptable colors are liver or liver-and-white spotted, ticked or roaned. Black is penalized on the bench, as is blond.

Don Smith advises a prospective pup buyer to inspect the coat by parting the hair. "The straw-colored (blond) coat is open, soft and dead," he says. "When you spread it with your finger, you see the skin. A good wire coat should lay back hard. You should

Gevevieve Capstaff shows a solid liver Wirehair. Some strains of Wirehairs are leggier than others.

Don Helmeke solved the coat problem on his dog by purchasing a wet suit.

have to part the coat with both hands in order to see the skin.

"And don't let a breeder tell you the coat will harden when the pup gets older. The coat won't change 5 percent because hair diameter doesn't change as dogs mature. You might get fooled on eyebrow and whisker length, but you can be almost 100 percent correct on length and texture of the coat when the pup is only a month old."

The Wirehair's coat is probably the feature that has prevented widespread acceptance in North America. It looks shaggy and forms a bulky outline on a body that would otherwise have the same clean flowing lines of a German Shorthair. It doesn't feel quite as nice to pet, either. The wire coat is the very thing that appeals to the practical Germans, however. The Wirehaired Pointer, called Drahthaar in Germany (draht for "wire," haar for "hair") has led registrations in the German Hunting Dog Stud Book since 1923.

The breed originated reputedly because of a squabble over breeding. The early German Wirehair Club encompassed all the wire breeds including Griffons, Pudelpointers and Stichelhaars (rough-haired dogs). But some of the breeders aroused the ire of members by outcrossing onto Deutsch Kurzhaar (German Shorthair) stock. So a separate group was formed to devote itself to German Wirehaired Pointers. This occurred around the turn of the century.

Stichelhaars were crosses of Pointers, Pudelpointers, Foxhounds and Polish Otter Hounds. Griffons were a similar mixture with a dash of Spaniel until Edward K. Korthals began selecting for type. The Pudelpointer included Poodle blood. Modern Wirehairs are a mixture of all these, plus everything that went into developing the Shorthair. One authority also claims an Airedale left its mark on coat character, shape of eyes and feet, shortened ears, and sharp temperament so appreciated by Germans. The Wirehair certainly had a broad genetic base from which to select desired characteristics.

A few Wirehairs were imported during the 1920's, but the breed was relatively obscure until the 1950's. Popularity in Illinois and Wisconsin resulted in A.K.C. registration acceptance in 1959. Haar Baron's Mike, owned by Cliff Faestel of Brookfield, Wisconsin, won the German Pointing Dog National Trial in October of 1959 and became the first Wirehair with an A.K.C. recognized field championship. His dam, Haar

Al Gallagher of River Forest, Illinois. Out front is Dual Champion Herr Schmardt's Boy Yancey.

Baron's Gremlin, won the same stake in 1960 and became a dual champion by earning her show title that same year.

In 1951, Al Gallagher of River Forest, Illinois, got first pick of a litter from a dam that had been bred in Denmark and shipped over here before whelping. That dog, Herr Schmardt v. Fox River, was mated twice to Dual Champion Haar Baron's Gremlin in the 1950's. Four dual champions and two more field champions were produced, accounting for much of today's foundation stock.

Gallagher's outstanding Dual Champion Herr Schmardt's Boy Yancey is by Field Champion Haar Baron's Mike out of Gander Mountain Asta. "I love big dogs," Al told me. "I want a dog that can bring back anything I send him for. Yancey picks up a goose and carries it like a quail. He grabs it by the shoulder to avoid getting hit by a wing if the bird's alive.

"Yancey knocked two cripples out of the air, too, just as they were lifting off the ground.

"Down at Yates' Goose Club (near Cairo, Illinois) one day, I had Yancey bringing in everybody's birds. He retrieved almost 60 geese under my handling, then 14 more for another handler."

One thing that particularly interests me about Wirehairs is their versatility. This includes Griffons.

They are equipped to retrieve with both coat and proper instincts. But ability to switch bird species and handle them is another matter. A ruffed grouse may be spooky and require the dog to lay back and point from a distance. The same practice on a pheasant may urge a pheasant to run. The dog will have to crowd the ringneck just enough, but not too much, to stop and hold the bird, or slam into it in the first place. A dog has to be highly intelligent to recognize the difference and adapt himself to the bird. If the dog adapts quickly, I'd rate him as brilliant.

I talked with quite a few Wirehair fanciers on this subject. Some were surprised. They hadn't paid attention to differences in bird behavior. Their dogs had worked satisfactorily, so they hadn't thought about it.

There may be training practices that help a dog make the switch. We'll discuss that in the section on versatile training. But most Wirehair owners simply credit their dogs with being adaptable. And after a day with Wirehair people, it becomes a common refrain: "We hunt the hell out of our dogs!" That is a tremendous help in encouraging versatility.

Al Gallagher's Yancey had the widest experience of any Wirehair I encountered. Besides ducks and geese already mentioned, Yancey hunted quail in southern Illinois, pheasants in the north and sharptail grouse in Saskatchewan, where the dog also managed several covey points on running hard-to-pin Hungarian partridge. "When we took Yancey to Ontario to hunt woodcock and ruffed grouse," Al said, "we put a bell on his collar, and he automatically shortened his range. And he never hesitated to retrieve a woodcock as some dogs do."

In searching for a characterization of the breed, I can't help but remember the old men of German extraction in my town when I was a boy in the early 1930's. Their craggy faces grew at least a heavy moustache. Eyebrows were thick. They were aloof with strangers to the point where outsiders said of our town, "All they'll give you is their hand, and they'll take that back." Yet they were affectionate and generous with their own. Practical was almost a one-word description. Yet they'd clown around with youngsters. They were so energetic and industrious that our town hardly knew the deprivations of the Great Depression.

At times their skulls seemed as thick as the triple brick walls of the homes they built. But they caught on instantly to anything they wanted to learn. They worked at any job, even seemed happy at the chance to work. When it came to trying something new, those old men seemed determined to prove to themselves and everyone concerned that they could do it. And they were rough to work for—evidence that they had needed a tough master when they were learning.

It would be hard to find a better description of the German Wirehaired Pointer.

Weimaraners

"Weimaraner Club members who have puppies to sell are asked to sell only to persons who are interested in the breed for their hunting qualities. Our dogs were bred to be hunting dogs." This is a direct quote from a leaflet distributed by the Weimaraner Club of America, Greenway Road, Sun Prairie, Wisconsin 53590. And that's a small request compared to the many strict rules of the past in Germany and North America. Perhaps no pointing breed in history has been the subject of more intensive regulations to ensure breeding better gun dogs. Yet the general hunting public continues to show little interest in Weimaraners.

The underlying reason for this seeming paradox undoubtedly has something to do with the exalted having so far to fall. And being so badly stung once, hunters are slow to make themselves vulnerable a second time. Two decades ago the breed was misrepresented and oversold. The Weimaraner reputation was destroyed. The dogs were objects of ridicule. All that remained, incredibly, was a strong-willed group of people still dedicated to the idea that originated at Weimar. They were and still are determined to see it come to pass.

Weimar is 130 miles south of Berlin; here the Grand Duke Karl August made the breed popular with his noblemen around 1810. The breed is thought to have been already identifiable by that time. A Van Dyck painting of 1631 shows a gray dog of Weimaraner appearance, but there are no other records before 1810.

Major Herber, who enforced the rules set down by the Weimaraner Club of Germany until 1939 and who is credited with forming the modern breed, published an opinion that the breed is a mutation from the black St. Hubert hound. Other guesses include combinations of various Pointers, Bloodhounds and Schweisshunds. The Hanoverian Schweisshund is a distinct breed; in general, schweisshund simply means a dog that follows scent.

The Schweisshund theory is especially interesting because Weimaraners were first used on boar and deer in Germany. As I also mentioned in the Shorthair section, a German immigrant named Jonathan Plott settled in the Smoky Mountains around 1750. The hounds he brought along were of the big game type (boar & stag) for he soon had his pack running, treeing and fighting the black bear of the region. In the isolation of the mountains, the Plott family bred these dogs for 150 years before the outside world became aware of them. They were registered by the United Kennel Club in the 1940's, and since have become somewhat more houndy in appearance, but it's possible that the old-type Plott Hound is a glimpse of the early Schweisshund that went into the making of so many German breeds.

Interestingly, gray is a rare color phase in Plotts.

It's rare because it's a dilute and recessive and also because modern Plott breeders have selected for brindle, or black and brindle. No other colors can be registered. But it's easy to select for a recessive and breed them pure in little more than three generations. No genetic experiments have been conducted on the gray in Plotts, so I can't say it *is* the same genetic gray in Weimaraners, but it makes for interesting speculation. Weimaraner puppies are born striped or brindle, but become gray in about ten days.

The old type Plott was sharper in temperament than the average hound. The Weimaraner is just sharp enough to make a watch dog. Germans selected for that trait. Both need a strong-willed master to make them mind, but the infusion of bird-dog blood left the Weimaraner by far the more trainable for obedience.

After the Grand Duke's time a private group of sportsmen attempted to develop the Weimaraner further into an all-purpose dog. By crossing existing specimens with pointing breeds, and selecting carefully, they sought to create a pointing dog that would retrieve on land or water and trail wounded game.

By 1896, German Weimaraner owners feared their unique gray breed might not survive. But they managed to get their dogs recognized as a distinct breed, and a year later organized the Weimaraner Club of Germany.

The Germans have a penchant for strict, authoritative supervision and sticking to their own rules. The Weimaraner Club reflected that attitude by allowing no one to buy a Weimaraner without joining the club.

Caesar von Heikip pointing.

Despite attention given to Weimaraner hunting ability, the breed has excelled to a greater degree in obedience competition.

And a club member had to obey the rules. A committee had to approve of the mating before dogs could be bred, otherwise the progeny couldn't be registered. Puppies were ordered destroyed if they didn't meet the high standards of the Club.

The first American permitted to join the Weimaraner Club of Germany was Howard Knight of Rhode Island in 1929. He brought a dog and a bitch to this country, but both were sterile, which surprised no one who understood how German breeders of the time guarded their creation. In 1938, however, Knight managed to import a dog and two bitches, one in whelp. The German prohibition was ended, and other dogs followed.

About a year later, Knight quit hunting and gave his dogs to Mr. and Mrs. A. F. Horn, owners of Grafmar Kennels. Howard Knight nevertheless became the first president of the Weimaraner Club of America when it was formed with twenty members in 1941. The breed was recognized by the American Kennel Club in 1943.

At the outset, the American club adopted the strict German rule: no pups to non-members, no unauth-

orized breeding or unfit pups allowed to live. But about two years after World War II imports increased, the Weimaraner Club of America launched a public relations campaign, and demand began to exceed supply. The illusion of an almost unattainable super dog was a sales pitch tailor-made for American sportsmen. Prices rose to new highs. And suddenly pups were attainable. The lure of money made it impossible for the Weimaraner Club to stop sales to non-members.

For a time the breed spread itself in every direction like a chain letter that promises great things for little effort. When the bubble burst, a great many people at great expense had come to realize not only that the Weimaraner isn't a wonder dog that outpoints Pointers, outretrieves Labs and outtrees coonhounds, but that the dog they were stuck with didn't even have the makings of a mediocre bird dog. The ones that did have ability were often unappreciated because they couldn't possibly live up to advertised claims.

It must have taken great courage at that time for members to stay in the Weimaraner Club of America. But they did. They admitted it had been a disaster for the breed, but they set out again with all the thoroughness and determination of the original German breeders.

Today's club is divided into sixteen regions with their own officers who are responsible to local members and who carry out plans and policies set down by the Executive Board of the National Club and the other elected offices.

Activities include the National Gun Dog Trial, Sectional Championship trials, the Annual Specialty Show and Obedience, the Rating Trial, and Bench and Field Futurities.

The field trials and shows compare dogs and honor winners, of course, but the rating trials are designed to raise ability level of the breed by awarding achievement titles. Prospective breeders know what the bitch or stud in question is capable of doing.

For example, NRD means Novice Retrieving Dog. This is earned by one fifty-yard land retrieve, one in water at about twenty yards and a delivery to hand or to within a six-foot area where the handler stands.

The RD, or Retrieving Dog, is qualified by retrieving a double of about twenty and sixty yards. The near bird is just into the water; the distant one is among eight decoys. Both birds are shot over.

The Retrieving Dog Excellent, RDX, gets the same test but must be steady on line until sent. The RDX must also make double blind retrieves on land and water while working to the whistle and hand signals.

The hunting tests are obviously for all bird dogs. The old all-purpose idea of pointing pheasants for Dad in the morning, running rabbits for Sonny in the afternoon, and treeing coon for Brother at night seem forgotten.

Oddly enough, with all the attention given to Weimaraner hunting ability, the breed has excelled to a greater degree in obedience competition. This says something about the intelligence and trainability of the breed. It's there. Is it possible that more Weimaraners could be better hunters if they had tougher masters who couldn't be bluffed?

"They certainly are intelligent dogs," Dave Brezina, of Lombard, Illinois, told me. "A friend of mine kept a German Shepherd in a six-foot pen with a hot-wire fence. There's nothing stupid about a German Shepherd. But then he tried to keep a Weimaraner in that pen. It didn't work.

"Weimaraners are notorious for jumping or climbing and figuring a way out. You need a pen with a top on it. My friend's dog beat the hot wire by hitting it with all four feet at once and never touching both the wire and ground at the same time."

One thing I'd examine very carefully if considering the purchase of a Weimaraner is running gear. A good bird dog should flow across the ground effortlessly if he is to hunt several hours for the gun. The Weimaraner standard calls for a conformation that indicates speed and endurance. The stifles (knees of the

rear legs) should be well angulated. And the shoulders should be well laid back. But nothing is said about angulation of the front leg. Many Weimaraners I've seen have had shoulders that were too straight up and down. To be near perfect, shoulders on a running dog should slope at 45 degrees to the ground. And when the shoulders have been right, too often the forearm isn't well angulated. The shoulder and forearm should form a 90-degree angle. Poor shoulder slope and angulation fore and aft causes poor reach, poor drive, too much hop in the gait and results in lack of endurance as well as bird flushing noisiness. That's not a condemnation of the breed, just something to watch for in buying a hunter—of any breed, for that matter.

Dave Brezina said color is one of the things he likes about the Weimaraner. "When you buy a Weimaraner, you know it hasn't been crossed with a Pointer or any other breed. Any cross would destroy the silver color.

"I like the range, too, for foot hunting. And I like the style. They're good personal hunting dogs. They behave well in the house, and aren't too independent in the field. When they shed, your wife doesn't notice it."

That about sums up what most men want in a hunting dog. And if breeders follow the advice of the Weimaraner Club of America on "destroying or spaying each animal in a litter which show serious faults such as extreme shyness, bad disposition, etc.," the Gray Ghost with the striking amber or blue-gray eyes is certain to find the place they've sought so long . . . beside the hunter.

Vizslas

The latest sporting dog to arrive on the American scene is the Vizsla, yet the breed is claimed to be among the oldest in the world. Whether the Vizsla in its present form is ancient or was developed from ancient breeds (as all dogs must be) is open to question. A tenth-century picture etched in stone shows the Magyar hunter, his falcon and a dog that might be a Vizsla. A fourteenth-century manuscript of Magyar codes contains a chapter on falconry illustrated with a dog that looks much like the Vizsla of today.

The Magyars (pronounced Madyar) were nomads of the Finno-Ugrian language group who migrated from the east. They settled in Hungary about 1000 years ago and became physically assimilated into the western peoples. Before World War I, half the population of Hungary were Magyars, and Magyar was the official language.

Falconry originated in the east, probably in China, about 2000 B.C., and gradually moved westward. The first mention of a pointing dog, however, was made by the Roman Pliny in the first century after Christ. He had seen pointing dogs in Spain. The Spanish pointing dog spread around Europe and was almost certainly the fountainhead of all pointing breeds. Somewhere in an unknown time, descendants of the Spanish dogs, possibly purebred, but more likely mixed, joined the Magyars in their sport of falconry.

Romantic historians of the breed believe the Magyars might have brought Vizslas with them from the east to Hungary. They reason that the breed was preserved because the ruling classes jealously kept hunting and hunting dogs for themselves, segregating the animals from those who might dilute the breed's purity.

From a more practical viewpoint, we'll have to admit to the Spanish basis of all pointing breeds, since there is no evidence to the contrary. Over the centuries these dogs became known by such general terms as European Pointers and Setting Spaniels. There were also a great many well known varieties named for their various districts. An example of this is the Wurttemberg strain that became an ancestor of our German Shorthairs.

What went into the Vizsla, or when, is not known. But some dispassionate observers believe the breed to be of recent origin, possibly even this century. Because the Vizsla is bred to be a so-called all-purpose, or better stated, versatile dog, it seems likely to have developed when that idea became popular elsewhere in Europe. The Weimaraner could have played a part in the breed as could have others.

The yellow or rusty gold color tells us nothing about the Vizsla background except that it carries the recessive genes for a yellow coat. In this country, Dr. Leon F. Whitney crossed an Irish Setter with a Bloodhound and mated a red male from that litter to a yellow and white Pointer bitch and developed yellow dogs that pointed. In his *How to Breed Dogs,* Dr. Whitney shows a picture of one such dog that doesn't appear much different from a Vizsla except for longer ears. After selecting for yellow for three generations, subsequent offspring can be expected to breed true for yellow almost perfectly.

All we've proven so far is that we don't know how the Vizsla originated. It is a distinctive breed, however, with its roots in Hungary. It developed on the plains of Central Hungary known as the Puszta. The area is favored with a long, hot growing season, so an abundance of grain created ideal conditions for partridge and hare. Slow, cautious and thorough dogs were selected to hunt with the man on foot. Retrieving was essential along with tracking wounded hare.

Waterfowl retrieving also entered the picture, but the Puszta region has mild winters. As a result, the Vizsla coat was never meant for ice-breaking retrieves in North America.

The breed was almost extinct after World War I and was again threatened by World War II. During the Russian invasion in 1945, a great many Hungarians fled to Austria, Germany, Czechoslovakia, Italy and Turkey. Some took their dogs. Hungarians who came to this country introduced the breed, and in 1960 it was recognized by the American Kennel Club. The present standard was approved in 1963.

In this country, Vizslas have competed successfully in limited trials which were held for the German pointing breeds. Despite the light, lean, muscular build, however, the Vizsla does not possess the pace and range of American Pointers and English Setters of field-trial strains.

Most of the dogs I've watched in trials showed signs of being pushed by their handlers. Even in foot trials, handlers move at a much faster pace than hunters could possibly maintain for any length of time. The dogs stay up front because they're trained to, and the brisk pace keeps them moving. But the movement is often too much forward just to stay ahead and too little on either side to find birds. Allowed to hunt without pressure, most of these Vizslas would have made gun dogs with very satisfactory range, however.

I confess I have by no means seen all of the field-trial Vizslas, and I don't mean the above as criticism, simply observation. The dogs are running as they were bred to run. And it's the tendency of field-trial handlers to try for just a little more from their dog. Vizslas are rarely entered in open Pointer-Setter type trials, but rather in limited A.K.C. trials, so at this point there seems to be no danger of making the breed over into short-tailed, yellow, field-trial Pointers.

Proper evaluation and comparison in field trials can serve to improve the general level of the breed, however. Better dogs are selected in the breeding program. A good example of that, I think, was Jodi of Czuki Barat, out of Czuki O'lake Catherine by F. Ch. Ripp Barat.

The stud dog questionnaire of the Vizsla Club's breed improvement committee lists Jodi's accomplishments as 25 firsts, 14 seconds, 10 thirds, and 9 fourths in field trials; winner of the 1971 Dog of the Year award for German breeds given by the Field Trial Club of Illinois; plus a best of dogs, 2 firsts, 2 seconds, and a fourth in shows; and was once the youngest Vizsla to receive Field Championship. Jodi was later beaten by his daughter Windy, owned by Phil Rosenberg, of Wheaton, Illinois. Windy was a week past her third birthday when she became a field champion. Jodi had been a little older. The point is, when dogs are exposed to the public in field trials, the best are discovered and allowed to reproduce and influence the breed. There may be many dogs of Jodi's caliber whose genes are lost by obscurity.

Jodi had enough A.K.C. points to be a field champion six times. In points, he was the number one Vizsla in the United States for 1971. Windy was number one in the puppy and derby class that year. An older offspring was number two. Critics will scoff that field trials make race horses and horizon busters out of bird dogs, and that's not what hunters want. Granted, not all hunters want or can use wide-running Pointers, but the Vizslas are not in the same league with Pointers and usually not in the same trials. Nor should they be. Pointers are generally bred to be wide ranging, hard-running covey finders to hunt in big territory with scant cover. Good ones will shorten their range in heavy cover. Vizslas are bred to be versatile gun dogs but they can stand the improvement that comes with comparison in the field.

Jodi ran a sizeable but intelligent pattern, and cast wide enough to hunt for several gunners without ever casting to the rear. But he was not wild and uncontrollable as some hunters picture field-trial dogs. In fact, Jodi was a house pet. He even slept with Lewis and Sharon Simon at their home in Antioch, Illinois. And Jodi was a bird finder.

I saw Jodi in a trial when he was almost eight. He had two finds in the thirty minutes, if my recollection is correct, but one was very impressive. He had slammed onto point thirty-five feet from a pheasant. His bracemate backed for a moment, then broke and raced past Jodi to flush and even chase the bird. The pressure of such an action is terrible for a dog to withstand, but Jodi held steady for wing and shot.

The ability of a dog like Jodi may attract new people to the breed, but sometimes it's just appearance that does it. My friend John Ingram of Dogs Unlimited admired a dog out loud and soon owned one of its offspring. We hunted ruffed grouse together in Ohio, and although the youngster is not a finished dog, he hunted at a more suitable pace and range than my Brittany.

Jim Busch, of Elk Grove, Illinois, told me he was looking for a German Shorthair when he saw his first Vizsla. "I took one look at that golden dog, and I had to have one," Jim said. Busch soon became more

The Vizsla originated on the plains of central Hungary.

The Vizsla is a retriever but its coat is not designed for swimming in low temperatures.

involved, and when I met him he was on the Board of Directors of the Vizsla Club of Illinois.

Jim is another hunter who believes field trials are helping the breed. "It took my second dog until he was two years old before he pointed," Jim said. "I just got him steady to wing and shot when he was killed in an accident. Then I bought a pup out of two Nebraska field champions. It pointed and retrieved at a year old. Another pup is doing it at six months."

In Jim's evaluation (not claiming to be an expert, but giving me a man-in-the-field viewpoint) Vizslas, on the average, are slower to mature than German Shorthairs or Brittanies. Their range has been a little too close for some hunters, but it's getting wider. Vizslas are gentle with children and learn quickly. For that reason they do well in obedience competition. And they tend to be natural retrievers. "They'll often bring back a rubber ball at seven weeks," Jim said. "If that's encouraged, they just grow up retrieving."

The Vizsla standard calls for males 22- to 24-inches tall at the withers; females, 21 to 23 inches. More than a two-inch deviation disqualifies the dog from shows. About a third of the tail is docked. While most standards call for well-angulated stifles, the Vizsla standard specifies stifles to be moderately angulated.

In temperament the breed is expected to have above average ability to take training, be demonstratively affectionate and gentle mannered yet fearless with a well-developed protective instinct. In the Magyar language, Vizsla is said to mean "responsively alert."

Wirehaired Pointing Griffons

A friend of mine said, after investing $50,000 in a fishing and camping park, "I know I'm right. There's a need for places people can go to enjoy the outdoors. I just hope I'm right before the year 2000."

That's pretty close to the way I feel about Wirehaired Pointing Griffons. It could be the hunter's breed of tomorrow—or the next day, or maybe the year 2000.

It doesn't look very promising just now. The A.K.C. registers around 200 dogs annually, placing the Griffon in the 90's among 120 breeds, lower in popularity than the black and tan Coonhound of a type that isn't even considered a hunter. And not many people fancy coonhounds that don't hunt. But I'd bet on the Griffon's future if for no other reason than the capable hands guiding its destiny.

Roy Speece, of York, Nebraska, a president of the Wirehaired Pointing Griffon Club of America, has had a lifetime ambition to hunt all the chicken-like birds of North America and a devotion to closely controlled, versatile dogs that can help him do it. Mrs. Edward (Joan) Bailey, Puslinch, Ontario, is Secretary/Treasurer and editor of *The Gun Dog Supreme,* the Griffon Club publication which the Dog Writers' Association of America in 1971 called the Best National Bulletin. In addition, one of Joan's articles won best in its category. Her husband Dr. Edward D. Bailey was elected Secretary of the North American Versatile Hunting Dog Association. Both devote a great deal of time to Griffons and the versatile dog concept.

Of course, it takes more than interested people to make a breed of dog worth owning. And the Griffon does have, I believe, features that hinder its popularity today that tomorrow will be its main attraction. First is appearance. We're used to seeing clean, sleek lines on our bird dogs. The straight-up, snap-tailed English Setter almost sends shivers up the spine when he slams into point. The muscles bulging from under the thin coat of the Pointer when he locks up on a bird intensifies the action in our mind. Then here comes a Griffon. A third to half of his tail is missing. The coat is so rough and thick we can't see the body. If muscles bulge in the tense moment of point, we can't see them. At times, the Griffon on point can appear to be just standing there. Now pet that rough-coated rascal. He'd make a good scrub brush.

But let's look at tomorrow. Nine out of ten of the dogs in our most beautiful breeds are in show business and only act the part of working dogs. I may be wrong, and I may insult some Griffon fanciers, but that scraggly, unkempt appearance should guarantee them against show-ring appeal. Like olives, Griffons take a bit of getting used to.

When a dog pleases his hunter master, however, bristles can become beautiful in a hurry. The instincts of today's sporting dogs have already become so watered down by pet and show breeding that the novice is almost sure to get stung at least once before finding good, birdy stock. Anything that keeps our dogs out of the hands of anyone but hunters will be of even greater value in the future.

Just as important in the future (even today in many places) is control. Parcels of cover not denied to hunting become smaller each year with greater demands on their produce. The bigger going dogs overrun unposted territories. The only dogs welcome under these circumstances are close–working dogs under good control. They can find those tight-holding birds, maybe rabbits as well, that their masters would walk past. The hunt can last a leisurely afternoon instead of a hard, fast hour. A lot more singles can be seen a second time after the covey is busted.

The Griffon fits these requirements. He has an immense desire to please. In fact, that's one of the principal differences between Griffons and their close

French Griffon.

relatives, the German Wirehaired Pointers. Stu Mandelkow from Minnesota has both and described them to me this way: "I believe Wirehairs are more aloof and independent. Griffons are people dogs."

Less space will make more of tomorrow's dogs full-time house pets and part-time hunters. The Griffon's strong desire for his master's approval makes him a marvelous member of the household.

Many of us are fortunate enough to own several dogs that are specialists in their fields. Less space tomorrow will reduce dog limits as well as game limits. Even today many apartment dwellers consider themselves lucky to own a single hunting dog. The more that dog can do, the more valuable he is. And that's where the Griffon shines. That's also where his coat is fully appreciated.

The Griffon won't retrieve with the drive and dash of a Labrador or point with the style and class of a Pointer, but he'll surely retrieve ducks better than a Pointer and point pheasants better than a Lab. The Griffon's dense undercoat that insulates against the cold and the outer wire coat that easily shakes free of water make the breed unique among pointers in being able to stand cold water. The only other pointing dogs in this class found in North America are German Wirehairs and the rare Pudelpointers and Spinonis. The Griffon's wire coat is just a little longer than that of the German Wirehair.

The coat that lacked appeal at first has suddenly become very practical, as is the Griffon itself. The Griffon lives happily in his master's house, works closely and carefully, trains easily to track wounded game, retrieves naturally from land or cold water and hopefully is among the least likely to be affected by show breeding. More and more, that will be the definition of tomorrow's dog.

And speaking of definitions, you've probably wondered what the word Griffon means. It would make sense if a man named Griffon originated the breed. But the credit for that goes to Edward Karel Korthals. There were hounds called Griffons dating back to antiquity, however. There still exists a Griffon Nivernais, a wild boar dog that comes to us from the Nevers region of Gallic-Roman times. And there are four versions of the Griffon Vendéen, all of different size and leg length which determines whether they hunt hare, wild boar or, in early times, wolf. The one thing alike in all these dogs is their rough, thick coat.

The Brussels Griffons are toy dogs of recent development that were originally all rough coated. Smooth coats were bred later, but the name Griffon remained.

Whether the word has a deeper root in our language than just rough, thick coat, I don't know. But it's interesting that the word griffin was spelled grifon in old French. One definition is "a close watcher, or guard." Another is a half lion/half eagle of mythology which guarded treasures. That figure was seen on ancient medals and later on coats of armor.

Anyway, the Griffons that E. K. Korthals chose for foundation stock already existed as thick-coated dogs that would point. Most authorities speculate that these dogs were the results from crosses of Setters, Spaniels and Otterhounds. One specifies Polish Otterhound. Another calls it a Polish water dog. I've found no basis for this idea, except water love in the breed. The neck also appears a bit shorter than the German Wirehair, a characteristic of good water dogs.

There is a record of Korthals buying a brown and gray Griffon bitch from O. Armand of Amsterdam in 1874. Mouche was rough coated. Then came woolly-haired Janus, a shorthair named Nunon, and Satan, Hector and Banco, all rough coated. Mouche and Janus produced Huzaar, and he mated to short-haired Junon, who whelped Trouvée. She had the hardest coat, and when bred to Banco produced Moustache I, Querida and Lina, said to be pillars of the breed.

Korthals was following the popular breeding goal prevalent in Europe at the time in trying to create the most versatile dog possible. Unlike the others, however, he didn't introduce additional hound blood (usually foxhound) to speed up his dogs. And although the existing Griffons were no doubt distinctly related to the rough-coated hounds also known as Griffons, Korthals' dogs did not take on the aloof, independent hound quality as did others to a certain extent.

Though young Korthals succeeded in breeding versatile dogs that were eager to please their masters, Korthals himself failed to please his father, a cattle breeder who regarded dogs as "insignificant animals." Disagreements apparently led to Korthals' moving to the Prince of Solms' household at Biebesheim, Germany. Here he bred Moustache I to Donna, a new bitch he bought from Heinrich Freytag in 1879. Two matings produced Augot and Clairette, who had the characteristics Korthals wanted. Another rough-haired bitch Vesta six years later did an outstanding job of whelping puppies with good coats.

Korthals promoted his type of Griffon at field trials and dog shows all over Europe. Later, while traveling as advance agent for the French Duke of Penthièvre, he experienced his best success in public acceptance of his breed. To this day the French claim it as their own and call it Korthals Griffon or simply Korthals. They claim the wirehaired Barbet, or duck dog, contributed the coat, which does seem more plausible than Otterhound.

The first Griffon registered by the American Kennel Club was Zolette, sired by Guerre, a grandson of Donna. That was in 1887. Interestingly, the dog was entered as a "Russian Setter (Griffon)."

The breed that Korthals developed in 20 years did not immediately become popular in North America, but Bob Ward and H. Kirkelie of Montana bred extensively from imported dogs in the 1920's and 1930's. Much good stock resulted, and Montana is still a strong Griffon state.

After World War II, Brigadier General Thomas Deforth Rogers brought Cisa von der Hohenlinde from Germany in 1949 and two years later started The Wirehaired Pointing Griffon Club of America. He served as secretary until 1960, after which he was president of the club until his death in 1968. General Rogers appointed Joan Bailey as acting secretary in 1967, a post she continued to fill after the 1968 election. And we've come full circle to the capable hands guiding the breed.

I think controlled enthusiasm would characterize the attitude of the Griffon people towards their dogs. They are energetically interested in providing all the information anyone cares to know about Griffons. Yet they're not evangelistic about their breed as so many fanciers are. In fact, Roy Speece, for one, fears that widespread acceptance of the breed would do more harm than good. Mrs. Bailey sends a leaflet to interested people telling them all about the good Griffon qualities and the bad as well.

Griffons do have problems. Soft coat is one. It's the same problem we discussed thoroughly in the German Wirehaired Pointer section. The second problem is size. Big studs seem to catch the eye in America, and too many Griffons exceed the standard. But the club is wisely making an effort to correct breeding instead of raising the size standard as some dog groups have. A working dog should be just big enough to do his job. The third problem is hip dysplasia that has only been recognized in the breed since about 1968. The club bulletin will not advertise dogs for sale unless dam and sire are certified for normal hips by the Orthopedic Foundation for Animals. Nothing is white-washed just because the truth might stop someone from buying a Griffon.

Field trials haven't been notably successful for Griffons. One was held near Reno, Nevada, in 1955. There wasn't another until 1968, when the Sierra Griffon Club held one near San Francisco. Most people think in terms of fast, wide dogs when field trials are discussed, and Griffons don't fit the picture.

The Quebec Griffon Club holds trials more like those in Europe. They've limited their stock to French imports or descendants of these dogs and have maintained a uniformly high quality in coat, conformation and ability.

The breed fits well into the concept of the North American Versatile Hunting Dog Association (NAVHDA) which we'll discuss further in the sections on field trials and versatile dog training. "Field trial" is actually a misnomer. Field test would be more accurate. The dogs do not compete against each other, but against a standard. No winners are "placed." All may win, or all may lose. It's a concept that is certain to gain wide acceptance among hunters.

During a natural ability trial NAVHDA held in Minnesota, the one dog that really impressed me as having the making of a bird-finding fool was a Griffon.

(So as to not offend anyone, let me point out that two courses were being run at the same time. I only saw half of the dogs.) One of the judges evaluating dogs commented that this one hadn't missed a spot where we had known a bird to be earlier.

That young dog has a great future as a hunter. I believe the breed holds the same promise.

Rare Breeds

A great variety of sporting breeds were developed through the centuries in the various districts of Europe. Fanciers of many claim theirs was the fountainhead from which other breeds sprang. Or at least they are closely related to the original hunting dogs. That may be true. Probably most are related in some way or another. It wasn't until Mendel discovered the laws of heredity that real efforts were made to standardize old breeds or create new ones.

Some of those dogs are quite unusual. The Portuguese Perdigeiro has a broad head, a very pronounced stop, a short muzzle and a short yellow-brown coat with darker hair on the ears and neck. The Mastiff influence is obvious. If you haven't seen a Mastiff, imagine hunting with a flop-eared Boxer. It is said to be a reliable pointer, and is named after the "perdiz" or cartridge, indicating its comparatively late development as a gun dog.

The French Barbet looks more like an Old English Sheep Dog than a pointing dog. This woolly dog is heavy for its size, short-muzzled like a Spaniel and has a stilted gait caused by straight legs. Besides pointing, it is outstanding on cold-water retrieves and sometimes is simply taught to flush. Barbet fanciers claim the dog hasn't changed since the 1500's and was used in forming such breeds as German Wirehaired Pointers, Pudelpointers and Griffons.

For an oddity, the Kooikerhondje rates high. The Kooiker is the man who operates the "duck decoy," an arrangement of reed fences stuck into the banks of channels and slanting toward the water. The dog walks in and out of the fencing and is only seen for brief moments. Curious ducks investigate and swim into the narrowing channel, which is then closed off, trapping the ducks. It's similar to the tolling dog of Nova Scotia that trots up and down the shore to lure nosey ducks closer to the gun. The Kooiker dog is Spaniel in type and size and has a white and red, long, well-feathered coat.

Most of the rare breeds (or perhaps we should say rare or unheard of in America) are intermediate types. The small and large Munsterlanders, for example, resemble the Brittany Spaniel but have a longer muzzle like a French Spaniel, yet with less depth of jaw. It isn't soft natured like a Brittany, either, and doesn't hesitate to attack game up to the small red deer in size. The large type is disappearing in Germany, but the small, 20-inch dog is still popular. The hair is longer than the Britt's, and the dog is allowed to keep its full tail.

The French Braque, or Pointer, is one of these breeds claimed to be the oldest in the world, antedating the Wurttemberg Pointer which was used in German Shorthaired Pointer development. Again, these come in two sizes: the 24-inch heavyweight and the more popular 42-pounder. The breed is said to have originated around the Pyrenees and spread over Europe. Many authorities call that dog the old European Pointer and consider the French Pointer a regional development, probably attained by crossing it with local hounds and shepherds. The Pyrenees are between France and Spain, and Spain is where the Roman Pliny saw a pointing dog in the first century.

The Spanish Pointer of today is large—up to 29½ inches—and rather slow, but easily trained to point and retrieve. The coat is short, smooth and either white spotted or ticked with liver or liver speckled with white. (Early Irish Setters sometimes had white speckled on their red coats, a type called "shower of hail.")

The Old Danish Pointer was a Spanish import 300 years ago. It's a heavy-bodied, heavy-headed dog with emphasis on muscle and strength and solid appearance.

The Auvergne Pointer, bred in southern France, again near the Pyrenees, is another slow dog with a heavy, deep, square muzzle. Its short coat is white with black spots and ticking. Ears are black. The only other color combination is white with dark charcoal markings.

Besides the Drahthaar (Wirehair) and Kurzhaar (Shorthair), the Germans also bred the Langhaar (Longhair) and Stichelhaar (Roughhair). Rough-haired dogs already existed during the sixteenth century, but in 1865 a Frankfurt cattle breeder named Bontant added Wurttemberg Pointer and popularized a dog that was shorter than the Griffon and had far less undercoat. It has since almost disappeared.

The German Longhair may have resulted from outcrosses with Gordon Setters which were popular in Germany about a century ago. The coat is usually solid light brown in color.

There is also a long-coated Griffon called Boulet, after the man who originated the breed. The Boulet Griffon has the head and build of a Pointer, but the coat is long, smooth, straight, silky and grey-brown in color.

The French Spaniel must also be mentioned because it's an intermediate canine that may truly have been a predecessor of more modern breeds. They are like the Springer Spaniels in head and coat, but taller (over 23½ inches preferred for dogs, 21 for bitches) and they point their game. The bushy tail is not docked. The color is tan spots on white with a small amount of ticking.

If there are specimens of these rare breeds in North America, I don't know about them. Pudelpointers exist in small numbers on this side of the Atlantic, however, and Roy Speece is hunting a Spinoni in Nebraska.

The Spinoni is so rare that we're even uncertain about the spelling. Some have spelled it Spinone. But Roy corresponded extensively with Italian kennels before importing his bitch "Spina." While the Italians did use the "e" occasionally, they spelled it Spinoni most of the time. Roy requested we use that spelling because owners prefer it, he said.

The French claim the Spinoni originated near Lyons from a probable mixture of Barbet, French Pointer and French Griffon Hound. The Italians disagree emphatically.

According to Roy, "The Italians claim the Spinoni came from the old Roman Mallossus (fighting dog in their arenas) and the common hounds of Europe. The Italians insist that the Griffon and ultimately the Pudelpointer and the Wirehair came from the Spinoni. The Germans and French do not agree, of course.

"More than anyone else, Dr. Paolo Brianzi, a veterinarian from Cremona, Italy, is responsible for the present high standards of the Spinoni. Dr. Brianzi conducted an extensive Spinoni breeding program from 1902 to 1962. The kennel is still in existence and operated by his daughter Franca. My Spina came from this kennel. Dr. Brianzi was awarded a high Italian medal of honor for his work with the breed.

"When I shopped the world market for my next dog after my great Griffon died, I had it firmly in mind that I wanted a white Griffon. 'The General,' my Griffon, had 'it all,' but color. He was hard to see in the field. I'm sure no one needs to tell you the peace of mind and restfulness of hunting a dog that can be seen. Although white is acceptable for our Griffons, none were available. No breeders had happened to see it as I do about white color. I then learned of Dr. Brianzi and his Spinoni and I also learned that Dr. Brianzi had purposefully developed the white Spinoni. It might be interesting to you to know that the Spinoni of northern Italy are grizzled grey much like most Griffons that we see.

"So, the southern Italy Spinoni run to mostly white with orange ears and some orange spots. The northern dogs run from white to dirty white to grizzled grey. The northern dogs are reported to be larger but even the Spinoni from southern Italy are big enough. My Spina weighs 70 pounds now and she is in good shape to slightly heavy. He might hunt best at 65 pounds; from my friends who have them I believe these figures would be average."

The Spinoni's coat like the Griffon's is hard, dry and stiff, the undercoat downy. Eyes are light brown, not yellow. Tails are docked to half length.

Spina has hunted with Roy for three seasons: her maiden year, as a yearling and as a two-year-old.

Roy Speece of York, Nebraska, hunts with an Italian Spinoni called Spina.

During that time they bagged valley quail in southern California, blue grouse in Idaho, Mearns' quail in Arizona, and bob-white, pheasant, sharptail grouse and waterfowl in Nebraska. Roy bagged nearly 150 birds per season over Spina, not counting waterfowl.

"I'm a nut on control," Roy said, "but I believe from my reading and from my friends who have them that in some way Dr. Brianzi bred human sociability into these dogs. He may have selected for it. At any rate, because I am a nut on it I have broken this Spinoni to hunt my way. She loves it. She is my legs and my nose—I am her guide."

Italy has a second pointing breed, the Bracco. While it appears to be somewhere between the Pointer and a hound, it is not nervous like a Pointer nor independent like a hound. The coat is short. Colors are white, white and orange, white and brown, or white ticked with orange or brown. Like the Spinoni, they are rather large.

North America's best known Pudelpointer devotee is Sigbot (Bodo) Winterhelt of Orono, Ontario. He and H. D. Hume imported eight specimens beginning with Catti v. Waldhof in 1956. In 1960, the Pudelpointer Club of Canada was formed and patterned after the objectives of the Pudelpointer Club of Germany.

Winterhelt credits Baron Von Zedlitz, writing under the nom de plume of Hegewald, with creating the breed. In 1881, Hegewald wrote his theory on using the English Pointer as the basis of a superior versatile breed:

"His outstanding nose, his fiery temperament combined with a highly developed searching instinct and his lightning action—this is what we need. He is, however, purely a field specialist and we require greater versatility. The way to attain this is through actual addition of the blood of the Pudel—the most intelligent and easiest to train of all dogs. Our high ideals and objectives should bring about, through rational breeding, the creation of a Wirehaired Pointer that differs from English Pointers only by having a more practical color, more practical hair and a cropped tail. One would get, in addition to the outstanding nose, stamina and speed of the Pointer, the intelligence, obedience, loyalty, courage and love of water of the Pudel."

Soon afterward, Walter of Wolfsdorf, a forester from Silesia, under Hegewald's direction bred Tell, an English Pointer owned by Kaiser Frederick III, to a Pudel bitch named Molly. Six Wolfsdorfer Pudelpointers were registered in the Utility Dog Stud Book that was started in 1892.

Twelve strains were created by Pudel/Pointer crosses made by Jägers (professional hunters) under Hegewald's direction. Following Hegewald's theory, these half-Pudel, half-Pointer dogs were bred back to Pointers creating three-quarter Pointer stock while selecting for desired coat and temperament. Against 12 Pudel crosses, 87 were made with Pointers.

In 1897, Hegewald and a wealthy manufacturer named Oberländer organized the German Pudelpointer Club. The purpose was to form a governing body to continue their aims. Selection of breeders would be made on the basis of performance and efficiency in searching, pointing, tracking and retrieving from land and water. Breeding would be from original stock, unless authorized by the Breeding Committee. (Only two times has Pointer blood been reintroduced in Germany when world wars reduced stock to dangerous levels.) And finally, the Club would lay emphasis on strong mother lines and strengthen the existing stock by highly selective inbreeding.

Today's sportsmen may grin at the idea of crossing Poodles into hunting dogs, but the Pudel of the time—as it was developed in Germany and later used in France—was a competent waterfowl retriever. J. H. Walsh, who wrote under the name Stonehenge in the 1850's, said:

"With more intelligence than falls to the lot of any other dog, he unites great fidelity to his master, and a strong love of approbation, so that he may readily be induced to attempt any trick which is shown him.... He fetches and carries very readily, swims well, and has a good nose, but has no particular fondness for hunting game..." and later, "A large wide head, rising sharply at the forehead, long falling ears clothed with thick hair...square muzzle....A well-formed pointer-like body, but covered with thick closely curling hair, hanging down in ringlets below."

Stonehenge described the standard Poodle as it was then and still is today.

Obviously, all was not ideal with the cross. Lack of pointing and no desire to hunt in the Pudel could combine with the Pointer's independence and create a deer chasing wire-haired hound that loved to retrieve ducks. But intelligent selection and careful inbreeding could weed out those unwanted characteristics and enhance nose, pointing, will to hunt, intelligence, birdability, waterlove and eagerness to retrieve.

In the process of breeding for these qualities, the Germans created a medium-size (23-inch, 55-pound) dog with a solid brown coat. The color and texture varies from light to dark and smooth to rough, but the ideal is dense and wiry.

In Germany, when the two modern Pointer crosses were made, all offspring were blocked from breeding until carefully tested. If they were approved, their progeny experienced the same restriction. This practice was carried through three generations. A third such Pointer cross was made in Canada with the permission of the German Pudelpointer Club and Stud Book. American registrations are now made in the Field Dog Stud Book, however.

Bodo Winterhelt, also a president of the North American Versatile Hunting Dog Association, admits that it has been a long, difficult and sometimes disappointing task to develop a top-notch strain of Pudelpointers. A few dogs have had what they've been selecting for, however, and Winterhelt feels an adequate genetic pool will soon be a reality. In the future, he believes Pudelpointers will play a significant part in American hunting.

Pudelpointers originated in Germany from a carefully planned breeding program of crossing Pudels to English Pointer stock.

3/The Retrieving Breeds

Labrador Retriever

If you're looking for a dog that breaks all the rules and makes you love it, pick a Labrador Retriever. Popularity destroys the temperament of a breed. Look at the record. It has happened over and over. But Labs have been in the top ten of A.K.C. registrations for years. Over 35,000 Lab pups are registered annually. And they all find homes, not because Lab is the fad name, but because these dogs are many things to many people.

Breeding for show points has been almost universally destructive to hunting instincts. And there is no dearth of Labs in shows, but while I'd still pick a pup from hunting parents even in Labs, it's hard to find a prima donna Lab that doesn't enjoy working if given a chance.

Hunters tend to be critical and suspicious of field trial stock. Often it's without basis, but there is a bit of truth in the idea that excessive control of the dog in trials doesn't test a retriever's instincts to search and find, but rather tests the trainer and the training. Be that as it may, the Lab remains our easiest-to-train hunting dog. A rank amateur can do it, almost despite himself.

The Lab wasn't made to run, either. He's a swimmer. The breed originated with Newfoundland fisher-men. When netting along the shoreline, it was dangerous for small boats to carry lines to the beach. So Labs (called the St. John's Newfoundland at that time) swam the lines to men ashore who hauled in the nets. Anything that fell overboard was the dog's job to fetch. Even fish were retrieved.

But run? Labs are built too heavy and stocky. Their shorter necks help them balance better while swimming with a duck in the mouth. A longer-necked dog balances better when running. But just ask them to run. Show a Lab you expect him to run in front of you, zig zag across the field to teach him to quarter, shoot a few birds, and he'll soon be a flush dog with plenty of will to run.

The average Lab loves to retrieve so much that he'll fetch a dummy time after time and pant excitedly over the chance of getting to do it one more time. He's so eager for birds that he'll probably see a duck flying before the hunter does. He'll quiver with anticipation. And if the shot is true, he'll coil like a steel spring in eagerness to be sent.

Rule of thumb tells us that dogs with this kind of tense enthusiasm will be nervous and excitable. They'll run their pens endlessly. In the house, they'll forget and knock over everything in sight. Not the Lab. When the retrieve is completed, he'll march to the back of the blind and calmly wait hours if necessary for his next call to duty. When practice or play sessions are over at home, he'll be patient until the next time. A Lab may make a few suggestions by bringing you objects he thinks might be turned into a game of throw and fetch, but he doesn't become a pest.

With thievery at an all-time high in the United States, we all understand the character of crime. It's selfishness personified from any viewpoint. And the Labrador Retriever is a kleptomaniac. He's compelled to pick up every loose object and carry it to his nest. Experience tells us that criminals have an insatiable desire to possess objects. They'll even struggle to avoid losing these objects if the victim catches them. To the Labrador Retriever, the most loved of all objects is a dead bird, which that kleptomaniac delivers eagerly and tenderly to our hand.

Intelligence is another aspect of dogdom that sometimes creates trouble. We want dogs that catch on quickly so they can be easily trained. But the truly smart ones begin outwitting us. They find a way to get out of the pen. They pursue their own interests. They do things their way. The Lab manages to maintain a high degree of intelligence without being willful.

The Lab's best description might be intelligently adaptable with a strong desire to please. Whatever the job, they can learn it and are willing and eager to do so. How the early breeders managed to get all this inside of a dog hide is unknown. The Labs were already established as a breed by the early 1800's.

Colonel Peter Hawker saw the dogs of Newfoundland in 1814 and later recounted their details. The dog we moderns know as the Newfoundland, Hawker described as "very high." The other he called the St. John's Newfoundland, which he said was "by far the best for any kind of shooting . . . generally black . . . no bigger than a pointer, very fine in legs, with short, smooth hair and does not carry his tail so much curled as the other; is extremely quick, running, swimming and fighting . . . in finding wounded game there is not a living equal in the canine race."

In 1822 another traveler reported "small water dogs that are admirably trained as retrievers in fowling, and are otherwise useful . . . . The smooth or short-haired dog is preferred because in frosty weather the long-haired kind become encumbered with ice on coming out of the water."

About the same time in history, some of these dogs were visiting England on cod boats from Newfoundland. The second Earl of Malmesbury bought one of these dogs at the port of Poole. Much later, in a letter dated 1870, he said, "We always call mine Labrador dogs, and I have kept the breed as pure as I could from the first I had from Poole, at that time carrying on a brisk trade with Newfoundland. The real breed may be known by its close coat which turns the water off like oil and, above all, a tail like an otter."

The Duke of Buccleuch, Lord John Scott and others joined the Earl of Malmesbury in breeding Labradors, as did his son, the third Earl of Malmes-

bury. The Duke kept a stud book which makes it possible to trace pedigrees as far back as 1878. The dogs thought to be most instrumental in founding the breed are Major Portal's Flapper and Mr. A. C. Butter's Peter of Faskally. An earlier known mating of 1885 would trace all Labs of today to Lord Malmesbury's Tramp by way of his offspring from the Duke of Buccleuch's Avon.

The breed died out in Newfoundland. England's new quarantine laws ended export profits and with it the incentive to breed dogs. A heavy dog tax at home eliminated the desire to keep a few for pleasure.

How completely extinct Labs were in Newfoundland is illustrated by an experience of Hon. A. Holland-Hibbert, the Lord Knutsford. He had become one of the breed's strongest advocates and decided to visit Newfoundland in search of any remaining native stock. When inquiring about such possible dogs with a local dog breeder, the man told him, "Go over to England and try to get one from a man called Holland-Hibbert."

It is thought that outcrosses were made onto other retriever breeds between the time of early imports and 1903, when Labs were officially recognized by the English Kennel Club. Because an occasional Lab will point, some writers believe pointing breeds were in-

Yellow coat is a recessive genetic characteristic.

Chocolate is also a recessive genetic characteristic and therefore more rare.

cluded in the mixture. It's impossible to tell because Labrador characteristics were and are dominant. Crosses almost always exhibit Lab features and behavior patterns.

Lady Howe's kennel, Banchory Labradors of Lorna, was the greatest producer of dual-purpose dogs. In England, a Labrador cannot be made a bench champion unless the dog has earned a working certificate, a practice which United States breeders have not had the dedication to emulate.

Labradors were introduced in America in the early 1900's but didn't achieve popularity immediately. Locally bred dogs were entrenched in hunters' affections—the Chesapeake Bay Retriever in the East and the American Water Spaniel in parts of the Midwest. The curly-coated imports were also popular in certain areas. Labs didn't really catch on until they started winning the A.K.C. recognized trials which began in 1931. The Arden Kennels of Averell Harriman and the Wingan Kennels of J. F. Carlisle furnished America's best foundation stock.

The last year in which more Chessies were registered than Labs was in 1935. There were 178 Chessies and 126 Labs recorded that year. Today there are only about 2000 Chessies registered annually, compared to more than 18 times that many Labs.

While occasional superior dogs of other breeds win retriever trials, they're overwhelmed by the onslaught of Labs. Apparently, the percentage of dogs having

Ken Wappler, of Milwaukee, Wisconsin, is about to accept delivery of a pheasant from his chocolate Lab, Flor-Loral Farful, otherwise answering to "Far".

field trial potential runs better in Labs than in other breeds. Good ones of other breeds, Chessies in particular, win more than their share for their number of entries, but handlers can't seem to come up with enough superior dogs to make a dent in the Labrador stronghold.

When it comes to picking an individual Lab, color has no bearing on ability and doesn't affect the coat density in any way. In general, however, one might cast an extra critical eye when choosing a yellow or chocolate Lab. Blacks are dominant and by far the most numerous. Chocolates are recessive to black, and yellow is recessive to chocolate. These colors being relatively rare, it's a temptation to breed for color and forget ability.

One chocolate owner told me, "I don't care what color a Lab is, but if this chocolate dog shows himself to be superior in field trials, he'll be more valuable to me. If he's not good I won't have him long."

That's holding color in the proper perspective. Anyway, most of us don't regard the Labrador as a great beauty. Its attractiveness as a breed is in eagerness to please, courage to face the rigors of hunting, intelligence to learn quickly, adaptability to learn a variety of jobs, a coat for protection in any climate, patience to wait without pestering and power to go and keep going when called upon.

Golden Retriever

The second most popular retriever in the United States is one of the least water-loving. But don't take that as a criticism of the breed. The Golden has good and sufficient cause to be popular.

The Golden lags behind the Lab in registrations, but is far ahead of the third most popular retriever, the Chesapeake Bay. The average Golden can't compete with Labs in field trials because very few are tough enough for that. And Chessies have field-trial Goldens beat in the ratio of winners to numbers of dogs entered. But the Goldens are versatile and the most tractable of all retrievers, two qualities that make the breed a favorite among people with widely varied interests.

Walt Scherer, Jr., of Ottowa, Illinois, for example, loves to hunt pheasants and ducks. He became interested in the breed a decade ago when he saw a Golden work during a duck hunt. Since then, Walt has also acquired Labs and an interest in field trials. But for a man who uses his dog in upland hunting as well as waterfowl retrieving, the Golden is an excellent choice.

This is especially true for the average hunter who guns pheasants, quail and rabbits much more often and with greater success than he hunts ducks or geese. Upland hunting can be enjoyed any time during the season. Duck hunting requires much sitting and bird

watching just to be on hand when the big flights occur. If seasons aren't coordinated with the weather or if work and other duties prevent the sportsman from hunting on the right days, retrieving ducks can be a very minor part of a dog's life.

Land work is superior to water work among Goldens because land dogs were used in the breed's development. Lord Tweedmouth (Sir Dudley Marjoribanks) originated the breed, but what kind of land dogs went into Golden ancestry wasn't revealed until modern times. The mid-1800's saw the awakening of animal husbandry. Knowledgeable breeders were learning that inbreeding or line breeding could set a type or even a breed. (A favorite method was breeding a good sire to his granddaughter.) Men were gaining reputations and sometimes wealth for the breeds they developed. And they didn't care to discuss secrets. For that reason or as a grand practical joke, a legend was authored that gave Golden origin a great exotic appeal.

Sir Dudley was supposed to have been very impressed with a troupe of dogs he saw perform in a circus at Brighton-by-the-Sea. He wanted a pair but the owner wouldn't split up the group, so Sir Dudley bought all eight, mostly to get the one named Nous. All the elements of a preposterous joke were included—the dogs were shepherds but were called Russian Trackers out of which Tweedmouth intended to breed retrievers—but people accepted it as truth. The story was published repeatedly until 1952, when the sixth Lord Ilchester made public his great-uncle's breeding records.

A Golden Retriever.

We don't know if Sir Dudley made up the story (although I'm sure he enjoyed it), but we do know he made up the breed. And there was, in fact, a dog called Nous. He was also purchased in Brighton, but from a cobbler who had taken the dog in settlement of a debt. The breeder was Lord Chichester. Nous (meaning wisdom) was the single yellow pup in a litter of black Wavy-Coats (later called Flat-Coats).

Sir Dudley's estate was on the Tweed River in southeast Scotland where there existed the now extinct Tweed Water Spaniels. Stonehenge said they were small. Dalziel, 1881 author of *British Dogs,* said the breed's close curls were light liver, ears were heavy and hard like a hound's, tails were long, forelegs feathered, hind legs smooth, hips pendulous and the head conical. (As an aside, read that description, refine the dog a bit in your mind, then look at a picture of the American Water Spaniel, whose origin is unknown.)

Nous, whelped in 1864 and purchased in 1868, was mated to Belle, a Tweed Water Spaniel of Ladykirk breeding that was whelped in 1863. Four yellow pups resulted from the 1868 mating: Ada, Cowslip, Crocus and Primrose.

According to his studbook covering the years 1868 to 1890 (now preserved by the Kennel Club Library in London), Sir Dudley line bred extensively to his original mating. To maintain hardiness and possibly to add desired traits, he also outcrossed onto one of Sir Henry Mieux's black Flat-Coats, another Tweed Water Spaniel, an Irish Setter and a tan Bloodhound. Line breeding was the instrument that made them breed true to type at an early date.

Out of this, Sir Dudley created one of the most gentle, human-oriented dogs of all time. Wanting to please is the Golden's goal; working for approval is his occupation. The dog looks big and formidable, but is useless as a watch dog because to him anything a human does is right. He's trustworthy among children as well as adults no matter how he's treated. The Golden's expression shows complete trust.

He isn't aggressive with other dogs, either. And I don't know anyone who has had a Golden he considered hard mouthed. In fact, the average Golden shouldn't be sent to dispatch or retrieve a varmint that might have been wounded during a day's hunt. It's quite possible that the dog would endure a severe biting rather than kill the animal before retrieving.

If Sir Dudley made a mistake, it was in coat. While it does insulate the dog, it absorbs and holds a large amount of water that must be shaken out in the blind or boat while duck hunting. It also causes drag while swimming. I must admit, however, that the coat is adequate for what the British call a day's rough shoot. That doesn't mean difficult hunting. It means taking the game as it comes on land or water. It's no problem to the hunter if the dog shakes out on the bank after a retrieve during the course of jump shooting ducks.

As I said earlier, the Golden is probably more

Sir Dudley Marjoribanks originated the Goldens by breeding a yellow Flat-Coat to a Tweed Water Spaniel, now extinct.

capable as a retriever on land than in water; perhaps Lord Tweedmouth intended it that way. The Flat-Coat achieved its greatest use as a land retriever. That may have been the greater use for a retriever at the time and place. And that's the case in many parts of the United States today. But again, the long silky coat is a bit of a problem because it collects more than its share of burrs in the uplands.

The Golden's gentle, human-loving nature also makes it a superb house dog. His quiet, Spaniel-like softness and unexcitable nature make him a perfect pet—except, again, for coat. Long hair must be combed frequently by anyone who dislikes the sight of dog hair on the floor, furniture and trouser legs.

The Golden's coat was probably responsible for delayed achievement of breed status, too. Goldens were considered a color phase of the Flat-Coated

Jack Godsil and Milo, a dog elected to the Golden Retriever Hall of Fame for its achievements in obedience.

In 1939, Rip, owned by Paul Bakewell III, of St. Louis, became the first field trial champion of the Golden breed. He was also named outstanding retriever for that year and the next. Then the first National Championship was held in 1941 and was won by King Midas of Woodend, owned by E. N. Dodge, of Wayzata, Minnesota. Popularity rose. Sheltercove Beauty won the National in 1944; Beautywood's Tamarack in 1950. Charles Morgan handled both dogs for Dr. L. M. Evans. The last Golden to win the National was Ready Always of Marianhill, owned by Mahlon B. Wallace, Jr., of St. Louis, and handled by William Wunderlick in 1951.

While the Golden hasn't been able to keep up with Labradors in wins, it is the only breed able to wrest a National Championship away from the black dogs. And field trial enthusiasts like Walt Scherer, Jr., keep searching for that great one.

But as we said at the outset, Goldens are versatile. They want to please and are willing to try to do it in any way they can understand. Trainers of dogs for the blind are experiencing a low reject rate among Goldens. Goldens are popular at shows. They're wonderful family pets. They're competent retrievers in the uplands and lowlands. But the Golden really excels when allowed to participate in the hobby of people like gun-dog trainer Jack Godsil.

Jack's avocation is a busman's holiday. He enjoys obedience trials, and Goldens are naturals for the task. Jack's training made Milo of Ben's Major, U.D., owned by Frank Holmay, formerly of Chesterfield, Missouri, the highest–scoring Golden in obedience work in the U.S. during 1968, '69, '70 and '71. In the '69-'70 season, Milo was the highest-scoring sporting dog in obedience. He was elected to the Golden Hall of Fame for obedience. "He was the steadiest in obedience of any animal ever handled," Jack told me. "Out of the 46 times he was entered, he placed 43 times."

Trainability seems to be a combination of intelligence and desire to please. One without the other makes the trainer's job difficult, sometimes impossible. A high degree of both is what makes the Golden outstanding in obedience work.

That same quality makes the Golden a good choice for the amateur trainer. It takes very little effort to get acceptable performance out of a Golden. It's also a good choice for women hunters or field-trial aspirants. Older men who need a slower, closer dog but still demand performance find Goldens made to order. Their noses are excellent as a rule, sometimes winding game fifty yards away. And while the coat picks up burrs, it also allows the dog to tackle any kind of cover.

Goldens in the U.S. and Canada are to be colored exactly as their name suggests. Mahogany like an Irish Setter is undesirable. So is the opposite end of hue range: cream. Or it's undesirable over here. It's now acceptable in Great Britain. If you're buying a

Retrievers until 1913. And in truth, it must be admitted that Flat-Coats were used in Golden breeding by others than Sir Dudley. The Earl of Ilchester bred Ada of the 1868 litter to both Flat-Coats (called Wavy-Coats at the time) and Labradors. Ingestre and Culham kept no records, although many of today's Goldens can be traced to their stock.

In 1913, the British Kennel Club recognized the dogs as a separate type and called them Yellow, or Golden, Retrievers. The word yellow was dropped in 1920. From that time and through the 1930's, interest in showing the breed grew rapidly in England.

The Canadians recognized the breed in 1927, but the American Kennel Club took five more years. Even then, Goldens had a tough time competing for popularity against home-bred Chessies and the no-nonsense, fast-working Labradors.

Golden pup and want to be sure it will grow up to fit the color standard, look at the ears. Puppies are often light colored, but their ears change little in hue as they age. The color of a Golden pup's ears will closely approximate its entire coat color when mature.

If color doesn't matter and the coat won't be a problem, there's only one more thing to consider before acquiring a Golden pup. That's you. If you're short on patience and tend to get really rough with a dog that makes a mistake, consider a Chesapeake Bay Retriever. If you're patient, easy going and tend to be a little soft on dogs, get a Golden. He'll work his heart out for you.

Chesapeake Bay Retriever

It's an undeniable fact that a dog or child is happier when he knows his limits and boundaries. Uncertainty created by an inconsistent master is the root of much nervous apprehension and many mistakes. It's also an undeniable fact that some learn limits by suggestion and praise while others need a heavy hand. In retrieverdom, the first extreme is the Golden; the latter is the traditional Chesapeake Bay Retriever.

Elsewhere in this book I've said trainability is the combination of high intelligence with a desire to please. The Chessie got more than his share of the former and little of the latter. He is the toughest to train of all retrievers. Yet once he's trained, he retains it without refreshers. And he has a way of coping with retrieving situations that seem to border on exercising the power of reason. A child begins to create problems when he starts thinking for himself. At times, that seems to be what makes the Chesapeake difficult.

Most creatures, including the majority of dogs and many humans, always take the path of least resistance.Yet, with an easily retrieved duck or two dead on the water, a Chesapeake will swim through them to follow a cripple, as if he were able to reason which was in danger of escaping.

Maybe we're giving the dog too much credit. It's claimed that coonhound was part of the Chesapeake's origin, and hounds have a strong instinct for chasing whatever moves.

And still, many retrievers become confused when the current carries a duck out of sight. Unless highly experienced, many have difficulty in realizing that the game moved beyond where it was last seen. It's a natural tendency. I've seen human hunters trigger off a late shot, aiming exactly where a rabbit entered taller cover and not calculating how much farther the rabbit ran after it was last seen. Yet the Chesapeake will swim resolutely on as if he understands the laws of motion and can calculate where to expect the duck. A hound in this situation on land would run to where he last sighted game, then resort to his nose to follow the trail.

A tendency to be swaybacked has been a breed trait, possibly dating back to the alleged Virginia black and tan hound in the Chessie's origin.

Further evidence of the Chesapeake's intelligence is in the number of falls he can mark and handle without direction. Doubles and triples are easy. He'll retrieve a cripple while remembering exactly where he saw the dead ones fall. I recall one hunter who thought whistle training was unimportant except for field-trial dogs. It was rare if his dogs needed handling because they always knew where the birds fell. When a cripple got out of sight, his dogs seemed to know where the bird went better than the hunters did. His dogs were Chesapeakes.

It's a little frustrating to know a dog has that kind of intelligence, yet seems to have trouble learning simple obedience lessons. But again, it stems from an independence that could easily be credited to the alleged hound in the Chessie's genes. Hounds are terribly slow and uninterested in learning obedience. They want to do things their way and certainly must when hunting. No handler is around to put a hound back on the trail with hand signals. This hound-like independence of the Chessie, while making him difficult to teach, is the very trait that makes him think for himself when making a long difficult retrieve without a handler's help.

And Chesapeake fanciers shouldn't be angered by this reference to hound characteristics in their favorite dogs. The word hound has been used in a lot of insults, but not by houndsmen. At least, before you get insulted, follow the hounds long enough to learn how courageous and tenacious they can be and how fast they can learn the things they want to do.

In fact, that last phrase is the secret to training a Chesapeake, according to William Walters, of West Bend, Wisconsin. I met Bill at a field trial. We began talking about Chessie traits, one of which is hard headedness. "I had no trouble obedience training my dog," Walters said. "Chesapeakes have more of a mind of their own than Labs, it's true. They'll quit if they don't want to do something. *But if you can make a Chesapeake want to, he'll do anything!*"

An often-quoted observation on that subject was made by Mrs. Eloise Heller about her FTC, AFTC, Can. FTC Nelgard's Baron, C.D.:

"I was told when I bought this seven-year-old dog, he was as tough as they come. He had been violently beaten, shot with shotguns and generally mistreated . . . a month of living in my house, really becoming *my* dog, made all the difference in the world . . . and [he] was doing his best to please me. It wasn't at all necessary to hit him, for if he disobeyed in a handling test I could just walk out in the field and scold him. If I said 'Shame, shame on you,' I could drop him to the ground with dejection. I praised him when he did well, scolded him when he didn't and he gave me his all."

Obviously, Mrs. Heller had found the way to make her dog "want to." To pass the Companion Dog Obedience test and win frequently in field trials is unusual for a Chesapeake.

Perhaps the Chessie's hardheadedness is too well advertised. Perhaps too many of us begin a Chesapeake's training with the belief that severe punishment right from the start is the only way to win what is certain to be a difficult contest of wills. With any dog, it's wise to first gain his confidence as Mrs. Heller did. Next, teach obedience firmly but without losing patience. After the dog has been at it long enough to know what's expected of him, then discipline him to whatever degree is necessary to stop flagrant disobedience.

Like children, dogs will try their masters at times, Chessies just a little more often. The important thing with this type of dog is to administer punishment in a manner that's understood. Don't nag or the dog will stop paying attention. Don't hit half-heartedly or he'll regard it as roughhousing. And don't punish often. When all else fails and it comes down to a licking, make that dog think he's not going to come out of it

alive. Then you and dog have a firm understanding, and the need for punishment will arise much less frequently.

Bill Walters feels that if an amateur trainer like himself can teach a Chesapeake, maybe there's a little too much fuss over the subject. Certainly it's not a factor that should enter into making a breed choice. As a matter of fact, the Chessie is a perfect choice for the fellow who isn't overendowed with patience. He won't cower a Chesapeake.

What Walters does consider an important factor is coat. "I hunt the Horicon marsh every Saturday and Sunday and twice during the week," he said. "When the channels and potholes freeze up, my dog and I might break through twenty yards of ice to reach open water. And then we hunt in it. When my dog makes a retrieve in that ice water and comes back panting, I know he's enjoying himself instead of suffering and I've picked a dog with the right coat."

It's a fact that the Chesapeake has a coat superior to any other retriever. The outer coat is thick, harsh and fairly short, not over 1½ inches long anywhere. The undercoat is dense, fine, woolly, and almost impenetrable by water. The outer coat may appear rough or have a tight wave or even tendency to curl, although the latter is frowned upon. Oil on the outer coat keeps water away from the body just as it does for ducks. And oil prevents the coat from holding water. When the dog shakes, the hair is left moist, not wet.

The coat is obviously nothing like that of the hound we mentioned being part of the Chesapeake's genetic base. In truth, the hound played very little in the development of this uniquely American dog.

According to an 1845 letter unearthed by Elmer M. Jackson, Jr., editor of the Annapolis *Evening Capitol*, it all started with two shipwrecked dogs saved by a Maryland importer named George Law.

"In the fall of 1807," Law wrote, "I was aboard the ship *Canton*, belonging to my uncle, the late Hugh Thompson of Baltimore, when we fell in, at sea near the termination of a very heavy equinoctial gale, with an English brig in a sinking condition and took off the crew.

"I boarded her, in command of a boat from the *Canton*, the brig's boats having been all swept away. I found on board of her two Newfoundland pups, male and female, which I saved, and subsequently on our landing, purchased from the captain for a guinea apiece."

The Newfoundland dogs which Law bought were not of the huge breed we know today. They were of a type the British called the St. John's Newfoundland, which was later refined and developed in England, where it became known as the Labrador Retriever.

Law named the black female Canton, after the rescuing ship. The dingy red male was already named Sailor.

General Ferdinand Latrobe, a former mayor of

The Chesapeake Bay Retriever has an unsurpassed coat for cold-water retrieving.

Baltimore, was associated for nearly thirty years with the Carroll's Island Club, the group largely credited with Chesapeake development. He said Sailor and Canton were bred to black-and-tan coonhounds to improve nose and stamina.

Obviously, other breeds were used in the admixture. From what we've been able to learn, the coat of the St. John's Newfoundland was much like that of today's Lab. Crossing it with a hound coat will not produce the Chessie type. Latrobe believed the hound also lightened the Chesapeake color. Perhaps. The hound that was popular in Maryland and Virginia at the time was genetically similar to today's Bloodhound in color and coat. Most were tan with a black saddle. The tan varied from red to the color of straw. Some are solid red or yellow. But dark brown or liver is extremely rare in hounds.

The Chesapeake coat, in genetic terms, is bb (all-brown) modified by one of three or more types of C genes to determine hue which can vary from straw to dark brown. The Irish Water Spaniel carries the same color genes. The Curly-Coat has bb genes for brown (liver) but no recessives to modify hue. Either breed could have contributed to tight waves, sometimes even curls, on the Chessie's coat.

The Chesapeake was also noted for sway back which was common in the old Virginia hound. Modern breeders seem to be trying to avoid that. They're also trying for more amiable dogs. Soft Chesapeakes used to be rare. They're still not common, but out of two trainers I visited recently, I found two soft Chessies.

This trend could result in an easier-to-train dog for field trials and obedience competition, but it will no longer be a Chesapeake as its originators intended. The Chesapeake, more than any other breed, is a waterfowl specialist. He isn't good doing double duty on upland game. He's not showman enough to compete with most people's idea of a field-trial dog. But nothing closer to a duck-retrieving machine has ever been bred.

The Chesapeake Bay Retriever originated where salt water gets down to 27 degrees before it freezes. And these tough Eastern Shore waterfowlers needed a strong swimmer that could fight cross winds and choppy seas, not for one duck but maybe a raft, because some were market hunters using young cannons.

Big, bold, powerful, self-confident and independent enough to do this job in the water, the Chesapeake can't suddenly convert to a mouse on land. He's inclined to be aggressive with other dogs. And a thief expecting to carry off a fine sporting dog will more likely run off sporting a fine dog bite.

The breed began to show up in the Mississippi flyway shortly after the Civil War. Dead grass became a favorite color because hunters of the flyway believed it helped if ducks couldn't see the dog. That's very debatable. So is the Chessie's appearance. Some hope the dogs are too ugly to become popular in shows and as pets.

I had to acquire that notion by being told. The first Chesapeake I saw was at Batchtown, a popular duck hunting area on the Illinois River. This big powerful dog walked past like a fellow who knew where he was going, what he would do when he got there and expected no interference along the way. His tight waved coat was the closest to olive I've ever seen on a dog. The sight almost took my breath away.

Curly-Coated Retriever

Like the Flat-Coat, the Curly-Coated Retriever is a breed we could have neglected with hardly anyone noticing. But the Curly-Coat is simply treading water just now and we'd hate to see the breed sink any lower. These dogs are ignored because they're misunderstood, and we hope they're still around when their time of popularity returns. While most hunters wouldn't mourn the Curly-Coat's demise, keep in mind that earlier in this century a group of people thought they would have to take measures to prevent extinction of the Poodle. Now it's number one in general popularity and has been for a decade. The public is fickle concerning its dogs.

One wonders, in fact, if the average hunter's attitude toward Poodles doesn't have something to do with the Curly-Coat's lack of popularity. A mental picture of a Paris fashion model with a delicately clipped Poodle on leash lent a "sissy" connotation to the breed. As far back as a century ago, writers were commenting that the Poodle had no interest in the hunt. And a superficial glance at a Curly-Coat does suggest Poodle.

The coat, of course, is what looks like a Poodle, and it causes all kinds of undesirable first impressions. Poodle hair keeps growing and requiring frequent cuts and grooming. A day with beggar lice and cockleburrs would probably end with shaving the Poodle's coat to the skin, unless it was trimmed very short. Even during a swim for a duck, the Poodle's coat looks as if it would pick up every bit of small rubbish the water had to offer. The impression carries over to the Curly-Coat, and we envision endless hours caring for the coat before, during, and after the hunt. But first impressions are often wrong impressions.

N. Dale Detweiler, of Wind Gap, Pennsylvania, is one of the few Curly-Coat enthusiasts in the United States, and probably the most knowledgeable. Dale tells me, "The Curly-Coat *does not* require extra attention to their coat when working upland game. Sure, they acquire stickers but these "free up" far more easily than in Setters, Goldens, etc."

Dale insists that burrs will work out in a day or two by themselves if the hunter doesn't have time or is too tired to do it himself. And, of course, the dog will groom himself.

I thought however, I might find a less biased opinion in *Dogs—Modern Grooming Techniques,* published by Arco. It was written by Hilary Harmar, a respected dog authority, especially in show circles where grooming is regarded as a pleasure rather than a chore. Hilary says, "The coat, surprisingly, is extremely easy to manage."

She continues (and bear in mind she's talking about preparing a Curly-Coat for a show, not simply keeping a hunting dog presentable):

"Many breeders prefer to use hand massage on the body, and the coat is only brushed occasionally. It should, however, be brushed down to the skin when the puppy coat is changing. In fact, the less done to the coat the better."

Hilary discusses scissoring the tail and curls on the head for show purposes, but not the body coat. She even notes that many people do not advocate bathing unless really necessary as it softens the coat. The Curlie's coat should be a tight mass of crisp curls.

This coat that turns out to be easily cared for also enables the Curly to withstand icy water and enjoy it. A quick shake leaves it no more than moist. No retriever except the Chesapeake Bay, has a better protective coat, and chances are strong that the Curly-Coat contributed its genes in the crossbreeding that eventually became the Chessie.

The Curly-Coat is one of the earliest retrievers mentioned in literature, but the type as we know it probably wasn't established until the mid-1800's when early bench shows began to stabilize the various breeds through standards.

According to *The Sportsmen's Cabinet* in 1803, the Curly-Coats were ". . . exceedingly singular in their appearance, and most probably derive their origin from the Greenland dog, blended with some particular race of our own."

The "race of our own" is what history leaves to conjecture. The existence of dogs renowned for their water work was recorded before 1500. But poor transportation and communication isolated various districts where different names were given to what could have been essentially the same dogs. Or they may have been crossed with other local dogs to create minor differences. The situation is something on the order of fishes in the United States. Is this fish a Papermouth, Speck, Calico Bass or Crappie? If it's called by one name in your district, did you recognize the others?

These early retrievers were variously called Old Water Dogs, Old English Water Spaniels, common English Retrievers, Water Spaniels, English Water Poodles, and maybe others. The Poodle that became well known as a French Duck Retriever was really developed in Germany, where it was called a Pudel. At any rate, there were retrievers dating into antiquity that may have lent their coats to the Curly through crossbreeding, probably on the St. John's Newfound-

The coat on a Curly does not require the grooming one might expect at first glance.

This Curly shows the proper conformation.

land that was refined into today's Labrador Retrievers.

Stonehenge wrote in 1860 that the Curly-Coat was "... always a cross between the St. John's Newfoundland and the water spaniel, which is generally Irish." The Irish has a top-knot that invariably shows up in crosses, so we have to take that speculation with a grain of salt. But what other Water Spaniels could he have meant? We don't know. There was a Tweed Water Spaniel, but it's extinct. The only Water Spaniels remaining today are the Irish and the American. The American, like the old Tweed, doesn't have a top-knot.

Whatever the ancestry, the Curly-Coated Retriever became a distinctive, unusual and capable breed that seems destined to remain obscure unless more promotional-minded individuals begin extolling its virtues. It can be done. Ed Bruske of Illinois and Dale Detweiler began calling attention to the breed in 1965, and 133 were registered in the next seven years,

compared to only 122 in all the years from 1933 through 1964.

An unusual virtue which makes the breed more versatile than the average retriever is an inclination to point "... not with the style of Pointers and Setters," Dale says, "but nevertheless a rocklike point."

Detweiler has visited breeders in the United Kingdom and has corresponded with Curly-Coat owners both in America and abroad. He finds this tendency to point not at all uncommon. A Texas Curlie was backing Pointers on quail at four months of age and shortly afterward pointed singles on his own.

Field trialers won't be enthusiastic over this trait perhaps, but it's a new approach to versatile hunting. It did, in fact, lose a trial for Pamika Gypsy Moth, Australia's number-one-bench Curly, owned by V. Richardson. It was Richardson's first time to handle Gypsy in a field trial. His brother and father shoot over the dog, but he does the showing. The trial consisted of a water retrieve, a retrieve from the opposite shore in cover, and a half-mile land retrieve in a minimum of six feet of cover. The dogs are rarely seen during a retrieve in Australia's almost impenetrable cover, so they're on their own to do the job with their noses.

Gypsy made her water retrieves, but on her land retrieve "froze on point for a rabbit." Richardson excused his bitch because she had worked on rabbits all through the Easter holidays and rarely worked birds other than quail on land.

An occasional Labrador Retriever has learned to point, but the tendency is not strong. Detweiler believes any Curly can be easily taught to be steady on point. In New Zealand, he says, Curlies are used extensively to point California quail.

Although the Curly is the tallest of our retrievers (the standard calls for 24 to 28 inches and 70 to 100 pounds for males; 23 to 26 inches and 60 to 80 pounds for females) he is a naturally close-working dog. His long legs allow him to hunt many hours with ease, and his coat lets him penetrate the most punishing cover. The game he jumps, when trained as a flush dog, is almost always within shotgun range.

The black or liver, dark-eyed dogs seem good at marking falls on land or water and persistent in tracking runners. They've even been used to track kangaroos.

They were bred for water work, so that's where they're best. Most are capable of diving repeatedly for crippled ducks. A Florida Curly named Lark loves to retrieve from the ocean, and will dive if any thrown object sinks. When Lark's master tires of throwing, the dog dives for rocks, shells or seaweeds in an effort to revive the game.

Curlies also seem to love jumping. Kook hunts pheasants and ducks for H. A. Southard in Iowa. Kook jumped four-foot fences carrying ducks or pheasants when not fully grown, just 60 pounds. And he did it with ease. According to Southard, "Kook won't climb over anything if it looks like he can jump it."

Curly-Coats aren't especially sociable among other dogs or strangers, but this possessiveness toward family and home can be genuinely useful at times. Lark, the dog we mentioned earlier, woke the family at 3 a.m. by barking, growling ferociously and charging at a screened window. An intruder was seen leaping the fence, and the screen had been slightly cut. Curlies don't bark excessively as a rule, but won't hesitate when they recognize something is wrong.

The search for something different, something rare, often leads to breeds that aren't popular because they seriously lack ability. That isn't the case with the Curly-Coat, but they certainly are rare. In recent times, the A.K.C. has registered from 19 to 40 pups a year. Detweiler estimates there are less than 200 in the United States and about 350 in the United Kingdom.

In training, Curlies are very tractable, but they're so smart they'll likely "try" their trainers. Corrective measures are necessary, of course, but seldom do they have to be strong.

Detweiler says he wanted a waterfowl retriever that would double as an upland hunter, have natural inherent instincts, be tractable, be rugged but gentle, have a family disposition, and not be commonplace. That, he claims, describes the Curly-Coated Retriever.

Flat-Coated Retriever

When a breed comes in 104th to 108th in a field of 120, as the Flat-Coated Retriever has in recent years, it's safe to say that Americans regard such dogs with almost total lack of interest. I really wouldn't be remiss if I excluded these dogs from my descriptions of acknowledged hunters. But I am including the Flat-Coat for what I think are good and sufficient reasons.

First, the dog achieved its greatest popularity among English game keepers. A dog has to do something right to please a professional. What he did, and how it might fit into America's future hunting picture, I'll discuss in a moment.

Secondly, dog popularity, as nearly everything else, is greatly influenced by advertising, whether paid or free.

The Labrador Retriever is clearly more popular than other retrievers for two reasons. He's a marvelously intelligent and trainable dog that deserves to be popular. But his manner of handling and working also makes him superior in field trials. The resulting notoriety and breeding makes the Labrador available. I won't say it's a fact, but it's a possibility that if more hunters were given a free and even choice, the Flat-Coat might be chosen far more than he is today.

A superficial glance at a Curly-Coat suggests Poodle, but the Curly is a hard-going Retriever.

The Flat-Coat can't begin to compete in field trials. He's simply too slow, too phlegmatic. But he's a natural retriever and easily controlled. He doesn't get excited, so he can live with the family without fear of tearing the house apart, despite his 60- to 70-pound size. And his calm nature makes him perfectly at home with children. Although he's reserved toward people outside of the family, he's not antagonistic. Your friends don't have to be afraid to bring their children along when they visit.

Oddly enough, the Flat-Coat didn't attain its highest following as a waterfowl retriever. While he's a natural in water, he was put to greatest use on upland game. The game keepers of England's estates and moors were sometimes requested to harvest game for the table. It made sense for them to hunt the margins of their employer's holdings. This game might be on the neighbor's estate tomorrow if poachers don't steal it from the edges today. And this practice left the main habitat untouched for the employer's shooting sport.

The Flat-Coat was evidently the perfect dog for this workmanlike job. He was easily controlled and worked close, so there was never the problem of trespassing or interfering with neighboring game keepers. The dog had the instincts and coat to make land retrieves in any cover and water retrieves in any weather.

Some British advocates claim the Flat-Coat can be trained to search for and even point game. That would be very difficult compared to training dogs that were bred to point. The Flat-Coat, it seems, is best suited as a non-slip retriever or a close working dog to flush and retrieve.

We have already reached the point in this country where hunting is limited in many areas. Trespassing is a problem. Some hunters have chosen closer-working breeds of pointing dogs; others are using retrievers to jump game and fetch it. The hunter whose stamping grounds are small and who is forced to stop at the boundary line might one day appreciate a Flat-Coated Retriever, especially if he likes a big, amiable companion around the house.

As with most breeds, where the Flat-Coat came from is subject to speculation. The first record of the breed was an 1860 entry into a dog show at Birmingham, England. R. Braisford exhibited a dog named Wyndham and evidently caused considerable interest. Retrievers were not plentiful at the time, and this one was very different.

Those who wrote about him later said Wyndham

It is thought that Gordon and Irish Setters were crossed to achieve the desired flat coat.

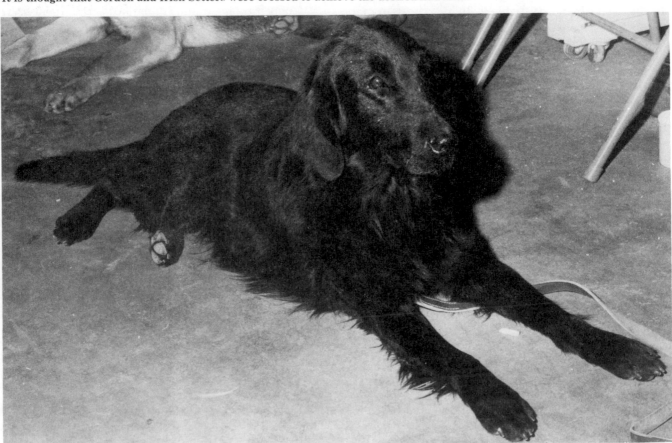

was of Labrador Retriever type in color and conformation but not in coat. Its black hair was much longer and exhibited enough wave that the breed was actually called Wavy-Coated at one time. Wyndham was also slightly larger than a Labrador Retriever.

Labrador Retrievers did not become established until the 1870's, but foundation stock called the St. John's Newfoundland had been coming to England on cod boats for some time. That early type is thought to have been crossed with Gordon and Irish Setters to achieve the desired coat.

Some also speculate a Collie cross to improve the more popular flat coat. Perhaps, but I even tend to doubt the Gordon cross because I can't find evidence of it in the face. Labs have always been dominant in crosses, and it is in this one. But I can see Irish in the head. I owned an Irish-Lab cross, and he looked much like a Flat-Coat. Of course, this is all meaningless speculation. The Flat-Coat has long been established and standardized as a pure breed with a character of its own.

There were probably others like Wyndham around the English countryside at the time because Flat-Coats became popular quite fast. Only four years after Wyndham's debut, in 1864 an all-breed show at Ashburnham Hall, Chelsea, included classes for Flat-Coats.

Major credit for development is given to Dr. Bond Moore of Wolverhampton. He destroyed all pups that weren't completely black and rigidly selected for Lab conformation. His strict culling program was probably motivated by the confusion others were causing by outcrosses. One such wild scheme to "improve" the breed was infusion of Borzoi blood because someone thought Flat-Coats needed longer jaws to retrieve hares. Dr. Moore was a stabilizing influence.

Other Englishmen who devoted much of themselves to the breed were Reginald Cook, of Shropshire, Mr. Shirley, of Warwickshire, and Ellis Ashton, of Derbyshire.

Blackdale Ben of Wingan, imported by Jay F. Carlisle, was America's best known Flat-Coat. He did well in field trials and sired Dr. H. I. Hoen's Black Royal, another good field dog. Star Lea Solitaire, trained by Bill Gladwin, was a daughter of Blackdale Ben. Black Ben Benjamin was an outstanding grandson. Most Flat-Coated Retrievers in America can trace their ancestry to Blackdale Ben.

The present standard was written in 1923 and reflects the strong interest its authors had in the hunt. The Flat-Coated Retriever should show "power without lumber and raciness without weediness." The eyes should have an intelligent expression and "the jaws should be long and strong, with a capacity of carrying a hare or pheasant. The neck should be obliquely placed in shoulders running well into the back to allow of easily seeking for the trail."

Few Flat-Coated Retrievers exist in America today;

The jaws of a Flat-Coat should be long and strong with a capacity for carrying a hare or pheasant.

fewer hunt. But his big chance may yet come with hunters who need a slow, close, easily handled dog. I hope he's still around when the time comes.

Irish Water Spaniels

The Irish Water Spaniel, it would seem, may be a little too smart for his own good. Or perhaps he's a little too Irish for his own good. He takes direction unless it doesn't sound reasonable to him. Then he does it his own way. He'll do his job in a workmanlike manner—unless he gets a laugh. Then he may deliberately blunder again just to hear the mirth. These qualities, while fun, don't endear him in field trials where handlers are dead serious.

In the field, however, it can be useful to have a dog that thinks for himself. Tom Marshall, of Southport, Connecticut, recalls a day in the '30's when his Irish Water, Jiggs, did a lot of thinking for himself. Tom had joined three friends who were sitting in the rocks of a breakwater shooting over scoter decoys. The hunters dropped a couple of surf scoters in the Sound, and Jiggs, true to training and field-trial manners, remained steady until sent, and then retrieved the birds. As a joke to confuse the dog, one of the hunters dropped a scoter on the other side of the breakwater. Jiggs couldn't see the fall, but he finally found the bird anyway and delivered it back over the rocks.

When the next scoter fell on the wrong side of the breakwater, Jiggs apparently decided it was foolish to work against a handicap like that. He remained on top of the rocks where he could see both sides.

Scoters started streaming over the rocks and Tom's friends really got busy. As many as six birds were on the water at once. The tide was going out and a sandbar had appeared behind the breakwater, so now Jiggs didn't even bring the birds to the rocks. He'd go for the distant bird or a cripple first. One sharp bite on the neck quieted the birds and all were piled on the bar.

After the flight was over, Jiggs returned to the pile of birds, picked them up two at a time by the necks and delivered them to Tom.

This kind of intelligence and adaptability is treasured by hunters, but figuring out an original way of doing things doesn't win field trials. And field trialing is what promotes and maintains popularity of a breed.

Irish Water Spaniels learn quickly and are well suited to obedience trials, but as Tom says, "The Irish are inclined to be clowns." And they do present a comical appearance, so people sometimes laugh at them. At a time like that, likely as not the Irish Water will deliberately make a mistake like jumping the hurdle twice while retrieving a dumbbell, just to get another laugh.

Tom recalls Irish Singer who'd clown in field trials as well. He could be ahead after five series, mark his bird, take direction and look like a sure winner—then stop and play with feathers on the water.

Singer would also act like he forgot he had hind legs while swimming. Tom was expected to walk along and hold up his tail until he got his rear end in motion.

Oddly enough, besides preferring to do his own thinking and preferring a laugh above praise—plus being headstrong—the Irish Water Spaniel has easily hurt feelings. Harsh treatment dulls his bird sense and interest. For that reason, Marshall advises gentle but firm treatment. Lead them. Encourage them. Work gradually. Irish Water Spaniels mature slowly. If a professional will train your Irish Water, pick one that has had experience with Spaniels.

How the Irish Water Spaniel acquired his characteristics isn't known. Water dogs, or dogs with a propensity for water, are claimed to have been mentioned in Persian manuscripts dating back to 4000 B.C. Babylonians and Assyrians had a type of Poodle perhaps hundreds of years before Christ. Some regard the French Barbet as the prototype of all European water retrievers. Irish law mentions a Spaniel in A.D. 17. In France at the time of Francis I (1494–1547), restrictive measures were taken against stray dogs, but it was recommended that farmers keep ". . . hounds and Water Spaniels to search for whatever occasionally entered their fields."

Two types of Water Spaniels existed in Ireland by the early 1800's. The northern variety had a parti-colored, wavy coat. It was small, like a similar variety in England. A larger curly-coated Water Spaniel was used in the bogs around the River Shannon in southern Ireland. The latter type was apparently the basis of the Irish Water Spaniel as we know it.

Justin McCarthy is really the father of today's Irish Water. He began experiments in the 1850's. Like so many in the 1800's who learned the secret of establishing type by inbreeding or line breeding, he did

The Irish Water Spaniel is a true Irishman. He takes direction . . . unless it doesn't sound reasonable to him.

Irish Water Spaniel owned by Charles and Dorothy Goodnow, of South Sudbury, Massachusetts.

The Retrieving Breeds/**61**

not divulge it. That McCarthy inbred in some manner is a foregone conclusion. What he used to cross with the South Country Spaniel before inbreeding is not so easy to determine. The Irish Water Spaniel does, however, bear a striking resemblance to the Standard Poodle. Both have non-shedding, dense, harsh, crisp ringlets. Both have the top-knot. Both are highly intelligent. The mystery is the very short hair on the far three-quarters of the Irish Water's tail. Where such a heavy-coated dog got a Pointer-like tail McCarthy wouldn't say.

Tom Marshall said he had Irish that would point, but he discouraged it because he wanted flushing dogs. An actual Pointer cross seems unlikely in view of the coat texture, but that tail came from somewhere. Some writers have also doubted the possibility of Pointer or Poodle crosses on the grounds that other colors would have been introduced. Many German dogs of the period were solid liver, however. And since liver is a recessive characteristic, fewer generations of color selection are necessary before the dogs breed true than if a dominant color is desired.

The Curly-Coat also comes in liver as did the now-extinct Tweed Water Spaniel of the Scottish-English border country. The Chesapeake Bay Retriever is well known to have started with red and black dogs. Outcrosses introduced liver which, in its varying degrees, is the color of the Chessie. So it's highly possible and very probable that Curlies (which also frequently point), Poodles and the St. John's Newfoundland could have lent genes to the Irish Water, either before or during McCarthy's breeding experiments.

The distinctive smooth tail also could have been a "sport" (mutation) which, if recessive, could easily have been established by inbreeding. If we ever figure

Irish Water Spaniels tend to be soft natured with easily hurt feelings. They should be treated and trained as Spaniels, not as Retrievers, as far as temperament is concerned.

out the tail's origin, then we can go to work on another unusual Irish Water characteristic: its distinctive gait. Marshall describes it as being like a single-footing horse. However he did it and whatever he used, Justin McCarthy developed a dog that has bred true for a century.

The Irish Water Spaniel didn't take long to find America. He was mentioned in books of the 1860's. The first volume of the Stud Book of the National American Kennel Club (which later became the A.K.C.) registered 12 dogs and 11 Irish Water bitches in 1878. No Labs or Goldens and only two Chessies were recorded that year. The first registered Irish Water was Bob, number 1352, owned by Richard Tuttle, of Chicago. It had been bred in the Mississippi flyway by J. H. Whitman.

The breed caught on fast along the Mississippi River. For almost two decades the Irish was a Midwest dog. Then they migrated east to Cape Cod and Long Island. Irish Waters were extremely popular into the 1920's. In 1922, the Field Dog Stud Book's number-one retriever was the Irish.

Tom Marshall points out that as far back as the 20's "Jay Carlisle and Roland Harriman were importing Labradors from England and Scotland along with such trainers as Dave Elliot.

"For the little amateurs like myself, it was impossible to beat any of them," he said. "The Labrador has gone ahead because most every breeding combination was a good one. . . . The entire calibre of this breed had gone so far ahead."

In my correspondence with Tom Marshall, I've found him often modest, always objective and never breeds blind by any stretch of the imagination. Of a half-dozen Irish Water Spaniels that placed well in

Litter of Irish Water Spaniels at the Goodnow's Princess Colleen Kennels.

field trials during the 1930's, Tom owned two: Black Water Bog and Bog's Jiggs. And he bred Step and Singer. Bog was the first Irish Water to win his CDX (Companion Dog Excellent). Yet, Tom regarded himself as a poor handler who "could not remain cool."

I judged the Labrador Trial four years in a row. I think the main reason I was asked to judge was because I did not own a Lab." At the urging of veteran show woman Mrs. Henry Hall, of Sudbury, Massachusetts, Marshall started the Irish Water Spaniel Club of America with 15 members scattered around the country. (The club still exists, with Mrs. Marion Hopkins, of Bradford, New Hampshire, as secretary.) And Tom says he still likes the Irish " . . . but they are just too much dog for me now." He has switched to the smaller American Water Spaniel.

With this background, I think Marshall can be relied upon to give an objective comparison of breeds as well as the Irish Water character: "A Labrador always beat me and my Irish always beat the Chesapeake," he says. "So far as their nose was concerned, I never saw a Labrador, Chesapeake or Golden with a nose as good. They were outstanding on trailing a crippled pheasant or duck . . . but I do not think they compare with a topnotch Lab in marking." And he adds, "They did not always take direction as well as a professionally handled Labrador.

Tom trained his dogs to hunt like Springer Spaniels and used them on pheasants, woodcock, Hungarian partridges and chukars as well as ducks and geese during waterfowl season. While he found the coat impervious in briars, Tom said it was sometimes a handicap in icy water. It gave them more protection than a short-haired dog, of course, but "the dog would finally get iced up if the shooting was fast. You could end up with a dog with half of each ear an ice cake and a huge ice cake from the back of his neck to the base of his tail. If you had time to throw a blanket over him he would thaw out."

Irish Water Spaniels in America have grown more leg than they had in Ireland. "When my wife and I were in Ireland we saw tighter coats and shorter legs," Tom said. "Over there they were hunting their Irish every day on anything that flew or ran. This included partridge, snipe and large hares . . ." Shorter legs are probably preferred for hunting game on land while longer legs apparently have been more satisfactory in America's marshes.

Learning from experience and solving problems on his own are the Irish Water's strongest points. Marshall hunts in marshes on strong tidal creeks. The fall may be several hundred feet away with the bird floating in a strong current. An Irish Water might make a mistake until he learned which way the water was flowing, but after that, "You would see the Irish in the water just waiting for the bird to float down to him."

Tom Marshall was particularly impressed with how both Bog and Jiggs could handle the difficult rail (sora). "In those days I used to kill over 250 birds in a ten-day period," he said. "My son was an active shooter and pusher at the time. It was common (with taking turns pushing) to come home with the limit of fifty birds. Both dogs could find crippled rail which is unusual as they are great divers and swimmers and have very little scent. Except for an American Water Spaniel, I have never had any other retrievers that would do this."

Irish Water Spaniels are eligible for field trials, but they're rarely entered. And since most of the dogs are in the hands of people with show interests, not many hunters notice them. To the credit of the Irish Water Spaniel Club of America, however, a dog must earn a working certificate before he's eligible for bench championship. The Irish Water is a breed just treading water, waiting (and deserving) to be rediscovered.

American Water Spaniels

American Water Spaniels, I believe, are like the citizens of the first 13 colonies—American by birth, but English by genetics. Some rather fanciful tales have been told about the American Water's origin but they all run contrary to common sense.

Breeds have had their beginnings in several ways, but none as magical as the American. Districts which were relatively isolated over long periods of time gradually evolved general types of dogs simply because of availability and a few exceptional studs in the area. Even these general types dating from antiquity required the efforts of someone to standardize them because men always crossbred.

Most dogs originated from the breeding or by the influence of a great man. That could have been the Grand Duke Karl August making the Weimaraner popular among his noblemen, the Duke of Gordon developing the black and tan Gordon Setter, Edward Korthals creating the Wirehaired Pointing Griffon, or Edward Laverack developing his blue belton English Setters.

The third way man has directly influenced dog evolution is by group efforts. That approach became popular during the 1800's, particularly in Germany where a group that later became the Klub Kurzhaar developed the German Shorthair. Similar groups developed the German Shepherd and German Wirehair. Modern breed clubs strive for perfection and standardization.

There is no evidence that any of these influences were applied to the American Water Spaniel. Great men aren't noted for hiding their achievements from public view. They seldom could if they wanted to. No one man is linked with the breed except Dr. F. J. Pfeifer, through whose efforts the American Water became recognized by the A.K.C. And, as is quite natural, he is well known to American Water fanciers.

When even loosely organized people work together in a group, there are records if only in the memories of various men involved and their descendents. There was obviously no group action to originate or promote the breed until the American Water Spaniel Club was formed in the mid-1930's.

The Wolf and Fox River region of east-central Wisconsin is credited with developing the American Water. But the area was not settled by immigrants and then isolated for the great period of time it would take to create a breed through natural selection.

It seems as if the breed suddenly appeared in the late 1800's, perhaps 1880, and within a few years was breeding true to type—miraculously with no help from an individual, group or long natural selection. And the theory of the crosses that went in the American Water's genetic base does nothing to make it sound plausible that the dogs could breed true in a decade or two.

According to the generally repeated, if not entirely accepted, story, waterfowlers of the Wolf/Fox River Valley needed a skiff dog. Other retrievers were too large. These men reached their haunts by boat, sometimes hunted from the skiff, and the heartiest might have stayed the night in his small craft. He needed a small dog that could stand the water and the cold of a day or days in the marshes.

Supposedly, old English Water Spaniels, now extinct, were imported by hunters searching for a suitable small dog. The English Spaniel couldn't take the cold, so Irish Water Spaniels and Curly-Coated Retrievers, both popular at the time, were crossed in to achieve a better insulated coat.

When you go to breeding small dogs with large dogs you don't get some of each in the litter. You get medium-sized dogs. If you mated brothers and sisters from many such litters, most of their offspring would be medium dogs, a very few would equal the original small and large dogs in size, and an extremely rare individual would be smaller or larger than those in the initial cross. You can see how difficult it is to get back to small size.

If you're a quick thinker, you've already decided these breeders could have mated a Spaniel/Curly or Irish cross back to the English Water Spaniel. A three-quarters Spaniel would be smaller. True. But then we'd have coat problems. That was the purpose of all this in the first place. Dr. Leon F. Whitney found straight hair partially dominant over curly. If a breeder were lucky enough to get curly coated pups in the first cross, his chances would be even less when crossing back to a Spaniel.

I'm not saying it's impossible, just difficult. It would require a great many litters, much time and effort, and no little amount of money. Yet, no eminent personage or dedicated group left a trace of any great effort. The American Water Spaniel simply stabilized itself in size and coat type.

If you're still able to swallow a pill of that size, consider color. Curly-Coats come in liver or black. Never mind what color the Spaniel was. Liver is recessive, another characteristic that would have required careful selection to breed true. It's not difficult to select for liver, of course, but coupling it with coat type and size greatly decreases the odds of finding one

American Water Spaniel Mickthea Little Red Robinson, CD, enters the water for a retrieve.

pup in many that happened to be blessed with all of these qualities.

So, forget the Curly-Coat. The Irish Water is liver. Breed it to a liver Spaniel, and the color problem is solved. Yes, it is, but another problem is created. The top-knot on the Irish Water's forehead is dominant in crossbreds. It shows up in pups when an Irish is mated with an American, too. And the Irish Water's head is narrow and high of dome compared to the broad, flat skull of the American.

We also have the opinion of Dr. F. J. Pfeifer that Irish Water Spaniels were not part of the American's genetic base. Dr. Pfeifer began practicing in New London, Wisconsin, in 1909, but had acquired his first American Water Spaniel in 1894. They were variously called Water Spaniels, American Brown Water Spaniels and American Water Spaniels. Dr. Pfeifer noticed that these dogs bred true to type and had as long as he could remember, so he thought they deserved recognition as a breed.

The United Kennel Club accepted "Curly Pfeifer"

The author believes American Water Spaniels originated from Tweed Water Spaniels.

in their registry in 1920. By 1924, Dr. Pfeifer could trace lineage back seven generations and was awarded Purple Ribbon breeding status. The doctor bred extensively and sold over 100 pups a year, mostly to states in the Mississippi flyway. His Wolf River Kennels housed as many as 132 Americans at one time.

Without question, Dr. Pfeifer was the all-time largest breeder of Americans. And he had a knowledge of the breed from an early date. He always insisted that Irish Water Spaniels were not introduced until after the American had been registered. In fact, he culled many top-knotted pups from matings with dogs outside of his own kennels. All of his dogs and those he knew to be purebred had the characteristic broad, flat, smooth forehead.

Dr. Pfeifer believed the American Water Spaniel originated from a Curly-Coat/Field Spaniel cross. I think we can accept Dr. Pfeifer's opinion on top-knots. They're dominant and immediately obvious in a litter of crossbreds. But the study of dog genetics had hardly begun when the doctor was active in breeding. He couldn't be expected to know that the flat coat of the Field Spaniel would be dominant to the curly coat, nor would he realize the other complications of breed evolution.

What then? Is there no answer? It's quite possible that man may have obscured the American's history, as with so many other things, by giving it a different name in every locality. We've mentioned this elsewhere, but before travel became easy and communication became almost instantaneous, a northern bluegill fisherman hearing about bream in the south would probably believe it to be an exotic species. And when someone says "Spaniel," we think of a small dog with long and flat or wavy hair. And the old English Water Spaniel very likely was flat-coated. It seems so from the records I've read.

But O.D. Foulks, writing in *The American Sportsman* after the Civil War, mentions crossing Newfoundlands with English Water Poodles. What is an English Water Poodle! It reminds me of the time I asked my grandfather if any of the family had fought in the Civil War. "What war was that?" he asked.

"You know. The one between the states. In the 1860's."

"Oh," he said, "you mean Lincoln's war!"

It so happens that there's another breed in another region that could pass for American Water Spaniels. Bluegill or bream? This time it's Boykin or American. The breed is small like the American which stands 15 to 18 inches at the withers and weighs 25 to 45 pounds. It's also brown and has a coat of tight, tiered waves or curls. Whit Boykin was one of the principal breeders, so they're called Boykin Spaniels. And they're from Boykin, South Carolina. Mrs. William A. Boykin bred them at Wannah Plantation as late as 1953.

Naturally, the Boykin is thought to be a cross

between a Spaniel and a water dog. The idea that essentially the same dog could be evolved in two parts of the country simultaneously is more than I can believe.

Both dogs came from the same fountainhead, I maintain. And I think the secret of their origin lies in what the Wisconsin waterfowlers meant when they said English Water Spaniel.

When kennel records came to light and established the Golden Retriever's origin as beginning from a yellow Flat Coated Retriever/Tweed Water Spaniel cross, interest developed in the latter. It was apparently an extinct breed. But what did it look like? Stonehenge had written that they resembled small ordinary English Retrievers. What were small ordinary retrievers to the people of his time?

Hugh Dalziel, in *British Dogs,* written in 1881, was more explicit. He said they were light liver in color and so close in curl as to give the impression there had been a cross with a smooth-haired dog. Would that be the marcel-like wave or curls of the American? The tail was long, ears were heavy in flesh like a hound's but slightly feathered, forelegs were feathered but hind legs smooth, head was conical, and the lips were slightly pendulous. Refine that dog a bit, and it sounds more like the American than any of the imagined crosses could have produced.

Was the English Water Spaniel, so-called in Wisconsin, the same dog that was called the Tweed Water Spaniel in the English-Scottish border country? Certainly Americans would think of such a dog as English. Some might call it a Poodle. To others, it might be a water Spaniel. I see no reason why Tweed Water Spaniels couldn't have reached these shores. Neither do I believe that the Tweed has to be the American's ancestor. But I'll be satisfied with this theory until a better one comes along. And it will certainly have to be more plausible than anything advanced so far.

I can't believe, either, that the word Spaniel was just tacked onto the American Water because he happened to be small. The breed is a bit sharper than other Spaniels, but a Spaniel he is. He takes to quartering naturally, is easily trained and has a strong desire to please. He retains his training, but may sulk if treated roughly.

Joe and Sharon Tryba, of Neenah, Wisconsin, use their Americans to hunt pheasant, quail, woodcock, partridge, duck, geese, rabbit and even squirrel. "The American Water Spaniel is a meat dog," Joe says, "and will retrieve fur as well as feather. The same animal may hunt pheasant in the morning, rabbit in the afternoon and partridge in the evening hours. I have never seen them leave a pheasant track (if it's hot) to take a rabbit unless the rabbit runs in front of their nose."

Tryba also has a game farm and adds, "One of the things that makes them so well liked here is that if any of our birds get out of the pen we can send a dog after

American Water Spaniels were first used by waterfowlers who needed smaller dogs.

it, and the dog will bring it back without a scratch. We just put it back in the pen. Our dogs will yip on a hot pheasant track and sound exactly like they were running a rabbit. They will also point a bird that is sitting tight."

Tom Marshall, of Southport, Connecticut, started the Irish Water Spaniel breed club, but later switched to the American because the bigger dog became too much to handle. Tom once wrote me that his American had retrieved over 50 rails in five days, ". . . mostly sora mixed with a few clappers and Virginias. This is the hardest kind of work for a dog. He cannot swim or walk, but must elbow his way through broken-down rice and sedge grass. This year the rice has been over the gunner's head so my dog marks the flush, but sometimes cannot see the fall. There is nothing harder to find than a crippled rail as it has little scent and can dive if not badly shot. My dog Bog several times found a rail that had been down for ten minutes. He also made real 'double' retrieves, coming in with a pair of feet sticking out of each side of his mouth."

This grand little hunting breed was recognized by the Field Dog Stud Book in 1938 and by the A.K.C. in 1940. He may not retrieve with the dash of a Lab, spring game with the snap of an English Springer Spaniel or show as pretty as the Setters, but he's an acknowledged worker. And it doesn't matter if you and I differ on where he came from, because he's just like the rest of us now—all American!

4/The Flushing Breeds

English Springer Spaniels

In the section on English Setters, I expressed the opinion that pointing breeds evolved from shepherd stock or from crosses with shepherds. Dropping and showing eye to hold sheep seems akin to early pointing behavior. Where then does the Spaniel come from? Where could we find a canine that quarters naturally? And in that same shepherd stock?

And, further back than that we can look to wolves for both instincts. Pointing, showing eye, etc., is the hesitation before attack while the wolf zeros in on his prey. This is the canine manner of hunting small animals and birds. Wolves have also been observed rounding up groups of herding animals before they cut out victims. Running back and forth in a quartering pattern moves the herd or holds them together. The instincts are all there—herding, pointing and quartering. They only required man to selectively breed for these qualities. And man did, as soon as he had the need.

It may be that I'm wrong about pointing and quartering instincts being selected out of shepherd breeds. Pointers, Setters and Spaniels may have developed simultaneously with shepherds. It's hard to determine, but history has recorded shepherd dogs long before bird dogs. There are drawings on cave walls showing the use of dogs in hunting that are much earlier than man's domestications of livestock, but these pictures invariably show the chase and kill of big game. There are no records of dogs used to hunt birds until around the time of Christ.

A reference in Irish laws of A.D. 17 mentions Spaniels. The Irish people *(Gails)* had evolved from a Celtic-speaking tribe who originally came from what is now northern France.

Greece and Rome of classical times had a type of poodle but did not have dogs to hunt birds. However, Romans recorded the existence of dogs in Spain called "Aviaries," a name that obviously refers to dogs being used to hunt birds. They even described the dog on point which might indicate that pointing and flushing Spaniels could have developed side by side.

The Greek Oppian, in the early part of the third century, wrote of dogs belonging to the wild tribes of painted Britons, or Brythons, another Celtic-speaking tribe that had moved from the north of France, or Gaul, as the Romans called it then. These dogs were skinny, dull of eye and about the size of the Romans' small house pets. Oppien called the breed "Agassaeus" and claimed their scenting powers to be easily superior to all other dogs. "Since it is very clever at finding the track of those creatures that walk the earth," Oppian wrote, *"it is also able to indicate with accuracy even the scent which is carried through the air."*

The eastern field-trial circuit didn't recognize the midwestern trials until Cliff Wallace, of Wadsworth, Illinois, and his dogs proved almost unbeatable.

The italics are mine to emphasize the suggestion of pointing, whether it be on birds or land game. The Agassaeus has variously been called the ancestor of the Basset, Beagle, and Brittany Spaniel as well as the Terriers. And it could have been involved in all of them. But here we have a long-haired dog that lived along the coast of Brittany in northern France at a much earlier time than Oppien's century. And the peoples of a sister tribe had called a dog "Spaniel" in A.D. 17. The Agassaeus was evidently capable of hunting birds. And the English choice of name, "Hispaniolus" or French "Espagnol" (later written in English as Spanyell, Spagnell or Spainell) points to Spain as the origin of bird-hunting dogs. All of this could mean that bird dogs may have been in use much earlier than the time of Christ and had spread northward.

How far back could it go? Earlier I said that pointing and quartering (part of herding behavior patterns) were instincts derived from the wolf. And some shepherds have prick ears like northern wolves, while others have flop ears and shorter muzzles like the mastiff group that seems to have developed from a wild canine (probably Tibetan wolf) in Tibet. Selective breeding from crosses of these animals might have produced the ancestors of our bird dogs. The earliest

proof of this is a dog skeleton from 3000 B.C. discovered at a Neolithic site called Windmill Hill. The dog resembled a Greyhound in its deep chest, rangy build, long straight tail and tuck-up at the abdomen. Unlike the Greyhound and like the mastiff group, the dog had a relatively short muzzle, a definite stop and the wide nasal openings of a scent hound. It probably was a hound, but not unlike our Pointers in type. And it illustrates at what an early time dogs of modern type existed.

Spaniel history becomes clearer as the veil of mystery is lifted by the written word of Gaston de Foix, a French nobleman who had a thousand dogs in his kennels at one time. In his famous *Le Livre de la Chasse* written in 1387, he tells of using hounds or Spaniels with hawks. The Oysel Dogs (a term applied to long-haired and short-haired, but especially reserved for long-haired dogs) were so called because they were bird dogs and because they hunted with a bird, the falcon. Gaston Phoebus, Count of Foix, described them as large of body and head with a beautiful, not too shaggy mauve coat. He praised their ability in water, especially at retrieving diving ducks, and told how on land they quartered before their masters, sometimes so energetically that they led the hounds astray.

The Springer Spaniel is the perfect pheasant dog.

Dr. Johannes Caius, a graduate of Cambridge University, whose English name was probably John Key or Kees, wrote England's first dog book, *Of English Dogges,* in 1570. "... of the Dogges which came of a gentle kind, and of those which serve for fowling ... there be two sortes: The first findeth game on the land. The other findeth game on the water.

"Such as delight on the land, play their parties, eyther by swiftnesse of foote, or by often questing, to search out and to spying the byrde for further hope of aduauntage, or else by some secrete signe and priuy token betray the place where they fall.
"The first kinde of

Such serue   The Hauke,

"The seconde,   The net, or traine,

"The first kind haue no peculier names assigned vnto them, saue only that they be denominated after the byrde which by natural appointment he is alotted to take, for the which consideration.
"Some be called ⎧ For the Falcon ⎫
                 ⎨ The Phesant   ⎬ and such like,
Dogges,   ⎩ The Partridge ⎭

"The common sort of people call them by one generall word, namely spaniells. As though these kinde of Dogges came originally and first of all out of Spaine, the most part of their skynnes are white, and if they be marcked with any spottes, they are commonly red, and somewhat great therewithall, the hears not growing in such thicknesse but that the mixture of them may easely be perceaued. Othersome of the mixture of them be reddishe and blackishe, but of that sorte there be but a very few. There is also at this day among vs a newe kinde of dogge brought out of Fraunce (for we Englishe men are maruailous greedy gaping gluttons after nouelties, and couetous coruorauntes of things that be seldom, rare, straunge, and hard to get.) And they bee speckled all ouer with white and black, which mingled colours incline to be a marble blewe, which bewtifyeth their skinnes and affordeth a seemely show of comlynesse. These are called French dogges as is aboue declared already."

The gentle Spaniel character was echoed by William Shakespeare just a few years later when he wrote "... as likeable as a spaniel whimpering on the doorstep for its master."

Before 1400, Geoffrey Chaucer, in *The Wife of Bathe,* wrote, "For as a Spaynel sche wol on him lepe."

And the likeable Spaniel continued to leap into British affection until, regardless of origin, it evolved a distinct type there "... with floppy ears, the chest, belly and feet white," as Aldrovandus wrote in 1637. By the 1800's the divisions by duty that Dr. Caius described were reinforced by divisions of size. Spaniels over 28 pounds were called Springer, Field or English

Springers "hup," or sit, to flush, shot, voice, whistle, and when delivering a bird.

Spaniels. Those from 14 to 28 pounds were considered Cocker Spaniels. Those under 14 pounds were comforters or lap Spaniels, or as Dame Juliana Berners had said in her *Boke of St. Albans* (1486) "... smale ladies popis that beere a way the flees and dyveris smale fawlis."

The hunting Spaniels lasted longer out of need, thank goodness, than those used to decoy small vermin from milady's person. Around 1810 the Norfolk Spaniel had become very much like the Springer of today. Beginning in 1813, the Boughey family of Aqualate, Shropshire, bred and kept a stud book of their pure line of Springers. Mop and Frisk, two Spaniels that many of today's Springers trace back to, became famous at that time.

Oddly enough, despite the early and widespread use of Spaniels, they did not immediately become popular in shows. These dogs that King Henry IV of France prohibited for a time under penalties of fines, banishment and death because he feared they would destroy all the game in the countryside were apparently thought of as too common for shows. The Brittany Spaniel had been regarded that same way in French shows. While Pointers and Setters were shown as early as 1859, Springers didn't get much attention in England until 1903.

Field trials for Spaniels also lagged behind those for pointing breeds. The Sporting Spaniel Club started the competition with its first trial on January 3, 1899,

on the estate of William Arkwright of Sutton Scarsdale. Another was held on December 12, 1899, on B. J. Warwick's estate. Springers failed to place in the top three at both trials.

It didn't take long, however, for the bigger, faster dogs to eclipse the Clumbers and Cockers. The Kennel Club granted a separate classification in 1902, and Englishmen scoured the country for dogs that looked like Springers.

For a time there was so little standardization in looks and size that Springers and Cockers could be born in the same litter. Even the first bench champion, Beechgrove Will, sired offspring that were registered as other breeds.

The Boughey family continued to breed Springers until the 1930's. Sir Thomas Boughey's Field Trial Champion Velox Powder, whelped in 1903 and winner of 20 field trials, had a pedigree that reached back to a bitch born in 1812. Velox Powder, along with Horsford Honour, Dash of Hagley, Sam, Rivington Sam, and Bruce became the fountainheads of today's American and Canadian field and bench champions. That seems even more unusual in light of the great differences in general appearance, size and coat length of field and bench Springers.

Sportsmen searching for hunting prospects must keep in mind the fact that field and show dogs within this breed are two different creatures, yet are all registered by the A.K.C. as one breed. Show dogs are

D.J., owned by Dr. James E. Prickett, is considered to be the finest specimen of show-type English Springer Spaniel. Note the differences between coat and size in show and field springers.

frequently bigger than the standard, have longer hair and much greater feathering. Good field Springers have leg conformation and angulation that allows them to flow across the gound at great speed with a minimum of lost motion. Show Springers, while they are certainly beautiful animals, often have a lumbering hobbyhorse gait. In this breed, beware of anyone with show champion stock who claims his dogs are dual (field and show) Springers. There were once great English dual champions like Flint of Arendale and Horsford Hetman that influenced American Springers, but the dual concept is now a thing of the past.

According to historian G. Mourt, a Spaniel was brought to Jamestown Colony in the early 1600's. Springers became popular in the United States before the Civil War, but then lost favor to the wide-running pointing breeds that were necessary to hunt open spaces of the Midwest, West, and South. Spaniels have never been very popular for use on quail.

The Springer's fortunes began to change in the 1920's. Imported pheasants prospered in the northern states and were highly sought after wherever they thrived. Rangy dogs of the pointing breeds had trouble holding the running ringnecks. By the time gunners arrived, the pheasants had slipped off, leaving the dogs with empty points. But Springers proved to be perfect on pheasants. They weren't attempting to hold birds in the distance. Springers quartered their ground before the hunter and drove the gaudy Chinese bird out of its cover within range of the gun. Whether the ringneck was in stubble, corn, briars, rice or alders didn't matter; the flushing dog could move him.

Thousands of the perfect pheasant dogs were imported during the 1920's. Probably the largest importer/trainer/salesman was Eudore Chevrier, of Winnipeg, Manitoba. The A.K.C. recognized Springer Spaniels in 1924.

Field trials began in 1924 after Freeman Lloyd instigated organization of the English Springer Spaniel Field Trial Association. Aughrim Flash won that first trial at Fisher's Island. The first field-trial champions were Aughrim Flash and Tedwin's Trex, already an English field-trial champion.

Another field-trial circuit was organized in the Midwest, but the eastern group did not recognize their events as qualifiers for national championship competition. By 1935, however, the midwesterners couldn't be ignored. From then until 1946, they were unbeatable. Solo Event, imported and owned by James Simpson, Jr., was the greatest of the dogs. Clifford Wallace, of Wadsworth, Illinois, one of the world's great dog trainers of all time, regardless of breed, was Solo's trainer/handler.

The great pheasant dogs also went west to California's rice fields and spread through the Pacific coastal states. Springer field trials have gained a foothold in the West, and western dogs are strong contenders in the annual national championship.

The well-trained Springer Spaniel is expected to quarter before the hunter in a windshield–wiper pattern, never more than about 25 yards from the gun. That gives the shooter time to swing into action before the bird is out of range. On flush, the Springer should instantly sit (termed "hup" by Springer trainers) and remain steady to shot. The dog should mark the bird well, but wait to retrieve until given the order. That gives the gunner time to reload in case another bird is in the vicinity and flushes when the dog resumes movement. The Springer should also "hup" to shot when he hasn't flushed the bird. That nicely aids the dog in marking, allows the hunters to reload and eliminates interference with a possible bracemate.

A well-educated Springer is a delight to hunt. Yet an untrained Springer doesn't ruin the day as would an undisciplined Pointer or Setter. Spaniels are little trouble to keep within gun range; they quarter naturally and even the untrained dog's nose is better than the hunter's at finding fallen birds.

I'll never forget the observation of a friend of mine who had hunted with a Springer for the first time. His brother-in-law had just purchased the dog, and it had no formal education whatsoever. Just as though he had been doing it all of his life, the dog ran up and down the line of three hunters, always within gun range, flushing rabbits, quail and pheasants for the shooters. "I don't know how the dog knew to do that," my friend told me. "I wouldn't have thought of it myself!"

Cocker Spaniels

Cocker Spaniels separated from other Spaniels as a distinct type during the nineteenth century. The Kennel Club of England made it official by recognition in 1892. Size was the criterion. Under 28 pounds made the Spaniel a Cocker.

The fact that they were called Cockers, however, is an indication that these smaller dogs were also selected for a different purpose than Springers. Cockers could get their lighter bulk under and through heavy, bushy cover that would exhaust a larger dog that had to struggle through or over. That's the kind of cover woodcocks love, so the small dogs were chosen for the job of cocking and became known as Cockers. Naming Spaniels for the job they do was an ancient practice in England. Dr. Caius described it in 1570.

These were all English Cockers, obviously, and resembled English Springer Spaniels except for size. They still do, and should. At one time, Springers and Cockers occurred in the same litter. Losing or gaining weight actually allowed some individuals to switch breeds and enter trial and show classes for either Springers or Cockers at different times. American Cockers orginated in England but underwent great changes after they arrived.

James Farrow's Obo, bred from English imports Fred and Betty, is credited with being the foundation of modern Cockers. Obo, born on June 14, 1879, grew

This is a merry Cocker of the old type of twenty and more years ago. Although not widely used, they were great little hunters.

The English Cocker Spaniel has remained fairly well suited for hunting.

to 10 inches and weighed 22 pounds. He was first shown in 1883 at Manchester, New Hampshire. His descendants were many on both sides of the Atlantic.

Hunting with any kind of Spaniel had ceased to be popular in the United States by the time of Obo. The American Spaniel Club was organized in 1881 to popularize field Cockers, but failed. It wasn't until 1924 that the first championship field trial was held for Cocker Spaniels. Trials prospered for a time, and Cockers were again hunting, especially on the east and west coasts and northern parts of the Midwest.

But the Cocker in America began to change. Skulls became more rounded, muzzles shorter. A sloping back line came in vogue, and dogs were often selected for the straight shoulders that makes withers higher than the rump. Cockers became more beautiful to the eye, more favored on the bench and more loved as pets. The merry little dog was America's number-one choice from 1940 to 1956. Bandwagon breeding destroyed the merry temperament, however. Shy, often hysterical, snappy specimens were bred because they were bench champions. It cost the breed its public favor and presented a problem that conscientious breeders are still fighting.

Fanciers of the old type English Cocker Spaniel were more aware of the change than was the public. For a time their dogs were just a little larger—28 to 34 pounds—but they insisted on separate registration. They organized the English Cocker Spaniel Club of America in 1935 and immediately began discouraging interbreeding of the two types. They claimed their dogs were related to Springers, while American importers had favored dogs that had branched away from the mother breed. Field or Cocker Spaniels (field meaning hunting) had divided into Sussex, Field and Cocker Spaniels in the 19th century. Cockers were

Modern American Cocker Spaniels have too much coat to be practical in the field.

under 25 pounds and often black. At the same time there existed a small, red and white, short-nosed Spaniel of probable Chinese origin that John Churchill, the first Duke of Marlborough, began breeding around 1700. It later became the English Toy Spaniel. Dr. Caius described a similar dog as "Spaniel Gentle, otherwise called the Comforter."

The English Cocker fanciers believed the American Cocker traits to be a combination of those two lines.

The English Cocker Spaniel was recognized as a separate breed by the Canadian Kennel Club in 1940. The American Kennel Club accepted this decision in 1946 and began separate registrations in January 1947.

This action had followed an exhaustive pedigree search to determine which lines were English and which were of American type dating back to 1892, the beginning of Cocker registration in England. Only those without American admixture were qualified to register as English.

At the time it seemed to many like a great fuss over practically nothing. What's a little difference in size? Today, however, it's much easier to see what the English Cocker breeders saw then. The American strongly shows the traits of the two lines described above.

Today's American Cocker is the victim or beneficiary of (depending upon hunting or show viewpoint) typey breeding. That's the practice of selecting for exaggerated characteristics, as a cartoon artist does when he enlarges on obvious traits to make a caricature. We began to have Cockers that looked more like Cockers than Cockers do.

Typey breeding resulted in a very pronounced stop, a high-domed skull, long ears, prominent eyes and an extremely long coat. For a show-minded individual

Modern English Cocker Spaniels belonging to W. F. Whittall, of West Vancouver, British Columbia.

who doesn't mind grooming, the American is the most beautiful of Spaniels. To the hunter, everything is wrong. The long coat catches everything and drags most of it home. Long ears get in the way. Bug eyes are exposed to injury. Excessive dome in the skull seems to invite more problems with water on the brain. And in the process of breeding for type, temperament went from the merry hunter to the miserable hellion.

To the credit of today's breeders, American Cockers are becoming easier to get along with, but a sportsman looking for a hunter from American Cocker stock really has his neck stuck out. A friend of mine owned a hunting cocker some years ago and wanted another. A western breeder told him he not only had hunting stock, but that they were cheaper because these weren't in as great demand as show Cockers. What my friend got was a show Cocker not of show quality. It ran under the table when I talked to it and threatened to snap when I extended my hand to make friends.

American Cockers *could* make flush dogs, but they have to do it despite many characteristics rather than because of them. There is almost no interest in hunting them or even talking about it.

English Cocker Spaniels are being hunted in this country, however. They represent the only logical choice for an American wanting to hunt a small Spaniel. Welsh Springers are larger and too independent to train. Clumbers and Sussex Spaniels are too slow. The Field Spaniel is very rare and also suffered by breeding exaggerations at one time. The German Spaniel is really the only other hunting choice, and he's as large as a Brittany Spaniel. In fact, the German looks like a Brown Britt with its high-set ears. Anyway, the breed is rare in North America.

W. F. Whittall, M.B.E., of West Vancouver, British Columbia, has been using English Cockers in the field for over 45 years. He regards them as the smallest *practical* bird dogs at about 30 pounds and 16 inches at the shoulder.

Why pick the smallest possible dog? Whittall says there are always those in any endeavor who delight in using something smaller but more skillfully to get a job done. That might be bringing game down cleanly with a 20 gauge instead of a 12, fighting a lunker bass on light tackle rather than horsing him in with heavy line and rod, or using an English Cocker against game in heavy cover.

Gladys F. Harriman, from across the continent in Arden, New York, echoes this pride in the small dog mastering his jobs. She and her husband E. Roland

Harriman have been hunting over 40 years and would have no other breed. "They can do anything a Springer can," she says.

Mrs. Harriman adds that their height makes them suited to heavy cover, "I have never seen a briar patch that they would not enter."

Professor Douglass C. North of the University of Washington at Seattle regards Cocker size as the perfect compromise for the family man who lives in the city and likes to hunt in the fall.

Beth McKinney, of Redmond, Washington, breeds English Cockers and says that people who have bought her pups for hunting have all had prior experience with Cockers and knew what they wanted from their dogs. She finds they are people looking for something different, attractive and smaller.

"Most people seem to feel that hardly any real training is necessary, except some basic obedience," Mrs. McKinney said. Oddly enough most of her pups were sold to duck hunters.

Douglass North said his first Cocker retrieved its first duck at five months of age. It was the first time he had seen one fall into water. "There was absolutely no training that preceded it," North said, "and my present Cocker took just three hours to learn what quail hunting is all about when she was eleven months old. I have typically tried to train them in basic obedience and in hand signals for the directions they are to hunt, but beyond that the rest came automatically."

W.F. Whittall said much the same thing. "I have never consciously had to 'train' any of my English Cockers for hunting—their instinct is to hunt close, therefore no problem of one disappearing over the horizon. Again because of their naturally intense desire to follow your bidding, there is no difficulty in controlling them; a spoken command or even wave of the arm is enough—they seem to know what you want them to do.

"A pup can be taken out at four to six months old. For the first few times, he will just follow his elders without seeming to understand what it is all about and then suddenly, as though a light switch has been flicked on, he will connect."

Ruby and H. C. "Dan" McGrew, now of Mesa, Arizona, owners of Dual Ch. Camio Boy and National F.T. Ch. Camio's Cheetah, point out that these dogs used for hunting have lighter coats than show dogs. Beth McKinney gets around the heavy coat problem of some individuals by stripping them before hunting season. "We have lots of burrs and foxtails," she said, "which are hard to spot in long hair, even though many of these dogs are much less heavily coated than those seen in the show ring."

As Gladys Harriman points out, English Cockers, like dogs of any breed, are individuals. Some are bolder than others. Some hunt with noses on the ground. Some "breast" scent. Some are quicker at figuring things out. As a general breed characteristic, however, English Cockers are not quarrelsome. They're full of fun and energy when it pleases you, but know when to lie quietly in a corner. They don't yap, but they'll announce the approach of a stranger. Children can tug and pull on them without the dog snapping.

Whittall points out an unusual characteristic: the Cocker was originally bred to hunt woodcock in thick patches of cover, the hunter remaining outside, the little dog penetrating and giving a short, sharp bark when putting up a bird. This distinctive bark, the only sound a good Cocker should make in the field, is quite obviously a warning signal. On open ground within sight of its master, it will not utter the bark.

Whittall concludes that above all is the English Cocker's inborn desire to please. That's what makes the breed so easy to train for obedience or the field.

North phrases it even stronger: "The English Cockers I have hunted with have always been natural hunters from the beginning, so the question of whether they will make good hunting dogs is already answered."

The large and sometimes bulging eyes of modern American Cockers makes them susceptible to injury in the field.

5/Making the Choice

Choosing a Breed

Maybe you read all about the hunting breeds before you reached this page. Or maybe you skipped to this section to shortcut the task of studying all the breeds before making a choice of dog. It doesn't matter what approach you take. Either way, this is the perfect time to study *you!*

There are breeders in this world who would subject you to a personality test before they'd allow you to buy one of their pups, but that's not what I have in mind. I mean you have to know yourself before you can know what kind of dog is suitable.

If you think living with yourself for all these years is an adequate basis of understanding, consider the man who recently told me of his intention to buy backwoods property in Colorado. He carried on at length about the joys of using such land to get completely away from people for extended periods each year. I suggested he be sure he knows himself before parting with any money. The first question: how important is it to get away from people? Very, he thought. All right, there are ample opportunities to get completely away from people right here. How much of your time do you actually spend enjoying privacy now? I knew that all of his free time is spent in the company of friends and frequently in a crowd, the bigger the better. But he was surprised at the revelation.

Truck-camper salesmen quickly caught on to a similar way people have of fooling themselves. A man goes in to buy a truck for camping. The salesman wisely asks what percentage of the use will be for camping so a correct choice can be made. The buyer is invariably surprised to learn that probably 80 percent of his truck driving will be to work and back or running errands, not camping!

How do you fool yourself about a dog? Suppose you're gung ho on ruffed grouse. The challenge really grabs you. A pansy can't take the leg work to find them. A poor shot or a slow shot can't put a pattern on those woods wizards darting through trees and behind brush. The crazy anticipation of never knowing how the next bird will behave ties you up in knots. And when you do scratch ol' ruff out of the sky, you can't help but fan his tail, look at the dark band and wonder at the rest of his suit—so well camouflaged at a distance, so colorful close up. But never gaudy—dressed in the best of taste, you think. And the best of taste when cooked, too! It's too bad you live 300 miles from good grouse country, but you usually manage two trips a year. And right now you're dreaming of a traditional English Setter to lock down, tail up and tense, on your favorite of all feathers.

What do you hunt the rest of the year? Ducks. Sometimes geese. Almost every weekend of the season. You live right on the flyway.

Do you fool yourself and hunt a Setter on grouse twice a year and hunt waterfowl dogless for the entire season? It would be better to compromise, and the choices are many.

The first choice of duck hunters is the Labrador Retriever. The Lab is easily trained and can be used as a nonslip retriever on upland game as well as waterfowl. They don't give up easily on crippled birds in either case. Or better yet, teach the Lab to quarter like a Springer Spaniel when hunting on land.

If you live in a temperate part of the flyway, a Springer Spaniel might be a better compromise. Springers retrieve naturally, although they aren't as rugged in water as Retrievers. And they're great at flushing and retrieving upland game.

The Golden Retriever is another good choice for doing double duty on land and water. In fact, the Golden is superior to other retrievers on land. The American Water Spaniel also knows how to be a retriever or flush dog.

Yet I wouldn't blame you if none of these breeds fits your image of a grouse dog. Seeing a dog on point in the grouse woods may mean more than all the retrieves of an entire season. But if you must have an English Setter, look for one from a family of natural retrievers. Not all Setters are outstanding at retrieving. And don't subject a Setter to long waits while soaking wet in freezing temperatures.

There are better choices of pointing breeds that will double as waterfowl retrievers, however. Although his coat isn't as protective as that of a Lab, the Brittany Spaniel is usually a natural retriever and is a superb ruffed grouse dog. The German Shorthair does double duty fairly well, too, if water conditions aren't too severe. All of these dogs have much white on them which makes them easy to see while hunting on land.

First choice of quail hunters in big country is the Pointer. Pointers are also capable on grouse, and individuals make good pheasant dogs. They're not the best retrievers.

Any dog that retrieves is a good bet to take along dove hunting. They'll find the birds you can't and get practice for the coming hunting season.

Some hunters object to easily seen colors on water-fowl retrievers, but the ducks don't seem to mind. While educated ducks flare at the slightest sign of a human, they rarely pay attention to a dog, even when it is sitting outside the blind.

If you insist on a camouflaged coat for a waterfowl retriever and happen to live where dogs break ice to retrieve, but still insist on a pointing breed for your grouse hunting, you're in luck. There are two choices: German Wirehaired Pointers and Wirehaired Pointing Griffons. Both have adequate coats for northern water work and accept the task with pleasure. And both are close-working pointing dogs that do a good job on ruffed grouse.

Which of the two you choose becomes a personality contest. The German is more aloof than the people-loving Griffon. If you're short on patience, the German Wirehair will take rougher handling without folding up. If you're a little on the easy side and prefer to train by encouragement and praise, pick the Griffon.

And that brings us into a whole new aspect of breed choice. These dogs do have personalities. Every one is an individual. Yet the majority (not all) have characteristics common to their breed. If the breed you choose doesn't complement your own personality, you're in trouble. I can tell you from experience that if you despise a dog your children will respond by defending the "underdog" and make it difficult, if not impossible, to get rid of the irritating or useless animal. Your wife will probably fight against keeping the dog in the house and will complain about it regularly—until you discover the dog is not your type. Then she's in love with it, and it's a family pet. That seems to be human nature. Study breed characteristics, and be sure from the start that the dog will suit your personality and hunting needs. If you're rough and impatient don't pick a soft Springer Spaniel. If your wife has to discipline your children, don't pick a Chesapeake Bay Retriever because you'll just have one more boss.

The Pointer, or English Pointer, is king in bobwhite country. For stylish points, wide-ranging endurance and ability to learn his trade at an early age, field trials have proven that Pointers lead by a wide margin. Next in line is the English Setter for those who prefer long hair and dogs that might take longer to learn, but don't have to be "tuned up" regularly. The Brittany Spaniel isn't far behind, especially for those who prefer a shorter-ranging dog. Today's hunters in the northern reaches of bobwhite country are using German Shorthaired Pointers for the same reason.

Ruffed grouse specialists in the East are partial to English Setters. Eastern grouse dogs are bigger and have heavier coats than some of the same breed used in quail country, but they're agile, hard-working dogs that can maintain a running pace through the entire day if kept in hunting condition. Don't confuse field and show Setters. They are two different breeds, and most show Setters are next to worthless in the field.

As with quail hunters, the Brittany Spaniel is working its way into the affections of the grouse-hunting fraternity. The better ones range as far as their bells can be heard and are capable of outstanding work on ruffed grouse.

In other parts of the country, grouse hunters are less often specialists. Close-working continental breeds, Springer Spaniels and Retrievers are all used successfully on ruffed grouse. Most English Pointers range too far, although some do quite well, especially in milder climates.

Pheasant hunting specialists have a made-to-order dog in the Springer Spaniel. In *Recreations in Shooting,* written by Craven in 1842, the author says of Cockers, and the same applies to Springers, "If taught to keep always within half a gunshot, they are the best dogs in existence." Pheasants like to sneak away and run ahead of pointing dogs. There is no such problem with a close-working flush dog cutting a windshield-wiper pattern before the gun.

English Setters are the number two choice for quail, number one for ruffed grouse in the East; some strains retrieve naturally without force training. This dog is midway between a show and a field-trial setter in appearance, although inclining more toward the former.

Some pheasant hunters insist upon using pointing breeds for esthetic reasons. Two types of dogs are successful. Fast dogs that slam into pheasants suddenly catch the birds unaware and afraid to move for fear of being caught. The other type of pheasant dog is slower, closer working and very careful. These dogs learn to follow pheasants each time they run, but don't crowd the birds enough to make them fly. The pheasant will finally stop running and hold for the dog. Both types of dogs can be found within the same breeds such as Brittany Spaniels and German Short-haired Pointers. German Wirehaired Pointers, Wirehaired Pointing Griffons, Weimaraners, and Vizslas are usually among the slower-working dogs, but all are used to hunt pheasants. Fast-moving Pointers,

English Setters and some strains of field Irish can also handle pheasants, but they are used less frequently because wide-ranging dogs are hardpressed to hold ringnecks until the hunter can catch up.

Waterfowl specialists—usually duck hunters with an occasional bonus goose—choose Labrador Retrievers in numbers probably equalling at least the total of all other retriever breeds. In simple registration numbers (many will be pets, not hunters, of course) breeders recorded twice the number of Labs as the sum total of other breeds in 1975.

Goldens are a little easier for the amateur to train in obedience, but they're also softer. Labs are seldom ruined by overzealous training. Both double quite well in the uplands.

Brittany Spaniels are the only pointing Spaniels and are growing in popularity. Most are medium-range hunters and natural retrievers, quite versatile and easily trained.

The wildfowler who hunts under the most severe weather conditions and doesn't care at all for upland hunting will want a Chesapeake Bay Retriever. They're a little harder to train, as a rule, but no dog is better dressed for cold weather.

Dove hunters are rarely specialists. And since dogs are only used to retrieve—sometimes only to find the bird—the job goes to any dog that's handy. Some hunters use their pointing breeds just to give them something to do. Retrievers get practice for the coming season. I even used a young hound one time when no other dog was handy. If we couldn't find the bird ourselves, we led the hound on a leash to the vicinity of the fall and let it nose around. It didn't retrieve, of course, and we had to be quick to keep the hound from gulping the bird, but we didn't lose any doves, either.

If you're not a specialist, you certainly have preferences. Most men hunt one species a great deal and others only occasionally. In that case, decide which bird is your favorite, and study the breeds that excel in hunting it. You'll find that some dogs are also capable of hunting birds that you regard as secondary.

Many of these secondary capabilities are bred into the versatile breeds. They are not expected to out-point Pointers or outretrieve Labs, but they do a

Shall it be a Labrador Retriever? Most are easily trained.

Golden Retrievers excel in land retrieves.

workmanlike job if properly trained. Pointing, retrieving and tracking crippled game comes naturally to German Shorthaired Pointers, Brittany Spaniels, Vizlas, Weimaraners, German Wirehaired Pointers and Wirehaired Pointing Griffons.

If in doubt about what dog to use on such game as rare western quail or chukar that doesn't hold well for dogs, never hesitate to take along a well-trained Retriever. In fact, a Retriever that can be controlled is valuable on any kind of bird hunt. Much the same could be said for the Springer Spaniel, but not for the pointing breeds since their range can destroy hunting for species that run or fly before the hunter can get near.

When you pick a breed, determine the game you'll use it on, whether you prefer or need a pointing, flushing, retrieving or versatile dog, where the dog will live and how he'll fit in and, most importantly, how it matches your personality.

One more thing. And we left it for last in the hope that it will make a lasting impression. We've discussed characteristics common to the average dogs of various breeds. There are dullards in every breed that never learn a thing. And there are exceptions in every breed that are more capable than any of us anticipated.

There are sometimes wider differences between dogs within a breed than the differences between breeds. Don't complain if you pick the exception to the rule. Buy a grown or trained dog in the field where you can witness his capabilities. If you're buying a pup, look for further advice in the next section.

Choosing a Pup

My son-in-law Ron Palmer told my daughter Beverly, "A fellow is coming to look at the pups this afternoon. Get the best female and put it in the house. I want your dad to have it."

"How will I know which one it is?" Beverly asked.

"Just watch them a while. You'll be able to tell."

With that simple suggestion, Beverly picked out one little bitch from a litter of all black Labs. That afternoon two fellows showed up. They watched the pups for a time, then the buyer said, "The way to pick a pup from a litter is close your eyes and grab one." Which he promptly did! He got a male, so he was satisfied.

When I arrived much later, I asked which pup was mine. "Take your choice," Ron said.

The Chesapeake Bay Retriever is probably the number-one choice for the waterfowl specialist who uses a dog for very little else. The Chessie's coat is unsurpassed for retrieving in extremely cold weather.

The Vizsla is another close-working dog. These dogs retrieve naturally as a rule, but their thin coats are not suited to cold-water fetching.

I watched the pups for a few minutes and picked out the same one Beverly had taken into the house which had also been Ron's choice of the litter. The pup has since proven us correct.

Obviously, the grab bag approach is no way to pick a pup, but many people just haven't heard of any other method. Even when they're told how to do it, many scoff and say, "There's no way to know for sure how a pup will turn out."

That's a fact. We can't be 100 percent certain. But we surely can cut down the odds of picking an absolute dud by changing our guesses from wild to calculated.

The best way to begin is by owning the litter. The fellow with the litter has several weeks to watch his puppies for superior qualities. The single pup buyer has to make his decision in minutes.

If you don't own a bitch, you've probably tuned me out already. But don't give up the idea. There's one other way. Maybe a friend of yours, even an acquaintance, has a good bitch of the breed you prefer. Why not offer to pay the stud fee and share the pups?

But notice I said *good* bitch, not just available bitch. The dam supplies her pups with 50 percent of their genes, just as the sire does. Be very careful when you choose, because dam and sire selection is really the first step in intelligent pup selection.

If there's no way for you to own the litter, be just as careful in choosing dam and sire. If the sire has made a name for himself in field trials, his background, breeding, ability and achievements are easy to learn, but don't stop there. What kind of pups has he sired? Are they becoming winners? Is his influence strong, or do pups from some bitches make good and those from others do nothing? If the dog's genes seem to "nick" well with a certain bitch or bitches, try to get a pup from one of those matings. Intelligent breeders usually repeat proven crosses.

Avoid show stock like the plague. Dogs registered by the Field Dog Stud Book are almost always hunters. When the designation "Ch." shows before a name in the pedigree, that means those dogs were field champions. Dogs registered by the American Kennel Club *may* be

German Shorthaired Pointers have replaced Pointers in much of the Midwest because today's hunters believe they have a more practical range. They are good retrievers and of the pointing breeds with short hair have the best coat for water retrieving.

hunters. "Ch." on A.K.C. papers means show champion. If many Ch. dogs are in the pedigree and few or no "F.T.Ch." (field-trial champions), avoid those pups like you would a hive of bees because, friend, you're about to be stung.

Show breeders will tell you they improve hunting dogs because they select for "sound" stock. Unfortunately, they seldom know what "sound" means in field terms. If good-looking legs made a runner, all of our track stars would be women. When show breeders do select for the right physical attributes, they still fail to breed for desire, interest and will to hunt. How can they select for it when they haven't seen the dogs hunt, much less matched them against other hunters?

There can be dual champions (field and show) among some of the continental breeds. That's also true of Brittany Spaniels, in case you don't regard that breed as a continental.

Some breed clubs do insist on maintaining the old field standards that were developed when men commonly understood how the structure of a horse af-

fected its various gaits. Many old horsemen's terms are used in the standards. And they still hold true for dogs. Many breed standards were changed to suit fashions among show breeders, however, and their dogs were ruined for field work in the process. Read the section on Irish Setters for an example.

Springer Spaniel show breeders haven't changed the standard; they and the judges just ignore it. So we have beautiful Springer champions that don't meet the standard, and useful field Springers that do. Show fanciers have every right to breed for beautiful dogs. I don't argue with that. In fact, I thoroughly enjoy looking at them. Just don't get stuck with one when you're looking for a field performer.

Maybe somebody told you "papers don't point birds," so you weren't planning to bother with background and pedigree. Don't believe it. That's an easy slogan repeated by people who are mentally lazy and don't want to be bothered with having to reason out the probable results of a mating. Demand the proof of ancestry. Even if you don't recognize your pup's

The pup that consistently shows the most interest in anything new is a good choice.

ancestors now, you probably will later. And you'll be able to continue a lineage should you decide to breed your dog.

Let's look at one more pitfall in breed or pup selection before we get down to picking the individual pup. That's color. It's so easily recognizable that we often tend to equate it with other things. A fellow who had a good black-and-white Pointer when he was a boy gets an idea that black-and-white Pointers are good. He's looking for black and white when he sees a litter of pups instead of watching for the true indicators of ability.

The next fellow learns there are good Pointers in every color and will not pay attention to color in any breed. As usual, the truth is not in either extreme.

We're getting into rather fine points of pup selection now, but that's the purpose of this section. If we don't consider everything, you may as well close your eyes and grab. Color does not make a dog good or bad. But color can *accompany* good or bad. For example, some people have noticed bad tempers among the golden shades of yellow in Cockers. How does yellow make a Cocker snappy? It doesn't. Neither does the snappy temperament make the coat yellow.

I'm not saying it did, but here's a very simple way it can happen. Somebody wants golden yellow dogs. An available yellow bitch isn't the best in temperament, but she's bred anyway. Yellow is a recessive, so by

selecting for yellow over three generations, the dogs will breed fairly pure for color. A little inbreeding or line breeding will speed up the process. Selecting for color without regard for temperament, and possibly intensifying the bad temper by inbreeding is the easiest way in the world to get beautifully golden, bad-natured dogs.

Brittany Spaniels are another example. Early in this century one of the founders of modern Britt strains was convinced orange and white made the better field dog. His influence caused liver and whites to be rare. More recently, some liver and whites have been apparently bred for color with less regard for ability. As a result the liver-and-white dogs have not excelled in field trials despite the fact that color itself has no direct bearing on ability.

Chocolate Labs have not been outstanding in field trials, either. Perhaps it's because there are so few to compete. And maybe, because there are so few, breeders may have selected for color, perhaps subconsciously, instead of ability.

Learn what color means to a breed through rarity, or through the influence of a famous stud or an influential breeder. Don't form judgments based on old wives' tales.

When you have found or bred a suitable litter from which to select, the next step will eliminate roughly half of the choices. Will you choose male or female?

I incline toward females myself, because good ones are so hard to find. Great sires are abundant in every breed. And they can reproduce themselves hundreds of times whereas females are limited to a few litters. If you own a good female, it's no problem to find a suitable mate to breed worthwhile offspring.

On the other hand, I wouldn't pass up the best pup in the litter just because it's a male. In fact, I enjoy my male dogs more than my bitches.

Most writers claim females are milder natured, more affectionate and more eager to please, therefore easier to train. I think they're confusing motherhood with dogs. I find males more affectionate and eager to please, therefore more trainable. It's a clear-cut case of everyone being out of step but me. But I do have a theory to support my observations.

Dogs have very basic motivations and behavior patterns, nearly all of which are directly tied to hunger and sex. Pay attention to the expressions dogs use. The one most closely tied to what we're discussing here is the agreeable look. On a human it would be an ingratiating smile, but the dog doesn't move his lips in this expression. He just opens his mouth and holds it open. He probably pants, too, regardless of the temperature.

Both males and females use the agreeable expression, of course. But watch which uses it most and why. Notice that a male almost never fights a sexually mature female. He's rowdy and may get too playful. If so, the female nips him. He smiles as ingratiatingly as a dog can. If she gets too rowdy, he doesn't nip. He smiles again as if to say, "Come on, Honey, be good."

Most important, he chases her around every six months with the agreeable look plastered all over his face. He's sexually prepared to be agreeable at any time. The bitch can be aloof to the dog if she chooses and often is all year, becoming as willing to please as the male only briefly during her season. This behavior is instinctive, of course. But being programmed to be sexually agreeable at all times, I believe, is what makes the male by nature more eager to please in all relationships.

If you doubt this, pay closer attention next time you pet a male dog. He will exhibit evidence besides the agreeable look that he is being aroused sexually.

Please don't attach human moral concepts to either the bitch's or the dog's behavior patterns. They're animals behaving instinctively. Use your knowledge to make your choice of male or female. It may help while training your dog, too.

It's easy to be strongly influenced by a pup's soulful look, but don't make the choice on that basis.

This is the agreeable look the author believes he sees more frequently on males than females.

Picking a pup is a hard choice. But don't close your eyes and grab one.

I'd almost forgotten the reason most people choose males over females. It is a little trouble to confine or watch over a female in heat. If she's kept in the house you'll probably want to use one of those new diaper affairs to protect the rug.

It's all worked out right down to the sex. Now to pick the individual pup. Someone said the titman (last born) is always best. Old wives' tale. Another said, pick the runt. He probably picked the biggest one time, and it was worthless.

How about the litter leader? The agressive one. That's easy. The litter boss is the biggest, if male, or the loudest barker, if female. Either way they're on top by bullying the others, not necessarily by using intelligence.

Maybe your wife or one of the youngsters fell in love with the cute, shy little pup shivering in the corner. Break their hearts now. It's easier than it will be later when they're really attached and you have to get rid of the worthless mutt.

Look for the bold pup that isn't afraid to move out on its own and investigate surroundings when you turn the litter loose in the yard. But make sure the pup moderates his boldness with sense. If the pup shows no interest in your whereabouts, he may be a field-trial prospect, but probably isn't master-oriented enough to suit a hunter.

What I watch most in a pup is how he reacts to a new experience. If I drop an empty water bucket, I expect a sensible pup to run. But the pup I want is the one that will come back to see what all the commotion was about.

I shot a crow one time when I thought two young pups were a block away at the clubhouse. The male went screaming for safety. The female followed for a few feet, then turned around and came running to me to see what was going on. You know which pup had the makings of a hunter. But don't try that method. It can easily cause a gun-shy dog.

Pups change from moment to moment. A pup that seems lazy this minute may be a fireball the next. He may be sleepy or have a full belly. That's why it pays to own the litter. You can watch them all for seven weeks before making a choice. By that time, if you're observant, you'll know which pup responds most intelligently to anything new.

Why seven weeks? Many breeders sell pups when shots can be given at twelve weeks. Isn't it better to wait and get your money's worth? Isn't it risky to take a pup at that age? And if you own the litter, is there any need to make an early choice?

The answer is, wait as long as necessary *if* the pups are separated at seven weeks. Under no circumstances should the litter remain together beyond that age.

A detailed study of dog behavior and inheritance was conducted at the Hamilton Station of the Jackson Laboratory at Bar Harbor, Maine, under the leadership of Dr. J. Paul Scott. The idea was to learn more about the effects of inheritance and environment on human social behavior, but the benefits to dog owners have been immense.

Dr. Scott found that pups become aware of the world at four weeks. By seven weeks the brain is physically matured, but impressions on it are few. At that point the pup begins to be an individual and the struggle starts. The biggest male or the loudest female rules the litter. Intelligent pups may figure a way to get their share. If they're weaker, they learn to get out of the way. Top dog to underdog stratification is soon accomplished within the group. Each pup forms an opinion of himself and his status that stays with him for life.

A pup receives certain genetic capabilities from his parents. But these are modified permanently by experience. If taken from the litter at seven weeks, however, he can grow up regarding himself as important. He can reach the full capabilities of his inheritance.

I've seen enough litters handled both ways that I'd never accept a pup past seven weeks if it had remained in the litter. There are times when whole litters make good if separated, while only one or two amount to anything when kept together.

Suppose you're offered a young dog of, say, nine months. You don't know whether he was separated from the litter at seven weeks. He may or may not reach full genetic capability. What should you do?

At that age he's old enough to take out and test for natural ability. If he satisfies you, it doesn't matter that he could have been better. You know what you're buying, whereas a twelve-week-old pup can be a pig in a poke. There are many things to consider in selecting the right pup. But don't throw up your hands and base the choice on emotional impulse. We pick mates that way, and a third of us end up in the divorce court.

This is a better method of selection. Maybe the pup with the bird isn't the best of the litter, but it couldn't be a bad choice. And if a pup must be chosen quickly, I can't imagine a hunter picking any pup but this one.

6/Training

Puppy Play

This is, and should be, a fun time for both you and your new pup. Like the grandparent who can enjoy a child and not worry about its discipline, you can enjoy your pup and worry about making it mind later. Many of the things you do now will lead into obedience later, but you're not burdened by enforcing it.

Remember, however, that whatever you do with your dog will condition its responses. And recognize that this little animal is a dog with dog's behavior patterns. His instincts can't change. They don't have to, either. It's a marvelous fact that they treat us just as they do others of their own kind and make delightful additions to our society in the process. We, of course, are more adaptable. We can recognize characteristic dog behavior and use it to advantage by slightly adjusting *our* behavior.

Ever notice how some people can walk right up and pet a dog and have them respond with immediate affection while other people make dogs cower? It has nothing at all to do with dogs' likes or dislikes. It's a matter of adjusting our behavior to get the desired response from dogs.

One fellow barges right up to the dog, leans over and brings his heavy hand down on top of the dog's head. However gentle the man may pet the dog's head, the dog cowers. It cowers even before the hand arrives.

The man who knows dogs will squat to canine level, bring his hand forward, palm up, and stroke the dog under its chin. The dog waggles with delight.

While we might not see much difference in the two approaches, dogs do. Discipline always came from above for pups. It may have been a nip from the dam. Or if the pup misbehaved seriously, the mother may have picked it up and shook it. When dogs test each other for superiority, one brings a paw down onto the other's neck. And when a strange dog approaches deliberately and rapidly without overtures of friendliness, the other dog considers it an attack until proven differently. If he doesn't regard himself capable of winning, he cowers submissively to avoid a fight. And so dogs cower when our hands come from above.

Playful invitations, however, come from eye level or lower. One pup may bow its head low and rear end high, encouraging another to romp and wrestle. If we squat to their level, dogs recognize the promise of fun and come running.

Petting under the chin is no accident, either. Petting is pleasurable to dogs because they experience it from their earliest moments when they're being stroked by their mothers' tongues. When a little older they reach up and lick their dam (sire, too, among wild canines) about the face. It's partly begging for regurgitated food. (In nature, the canine hunts and eats prey, then returns and regurgitates food for the pups.

It's their first food other than milk, a transition between milk and solids.) The action also shows how the pup looks up to the adult. Later in life that same action is no longer begging for food but symbolic of great adulation.

Many dogs are deeply overcome when we show them adulation by stroking under the chin. They respond with short, tentative licks which bring the tongue barely beyond the lips in another expression of deep affection. Their eyes tell the rest of the story.

We begin to see how our actions if modified to fit canine behavior patterns can elicit desired responses from our dogs. Why put a rope on a puppy and drag him across the lawn repeatedly to teach him to come? Squat, and he will come. Say "come" every time you squat so he begins to associate the command with his action. Later on, when it's time to teach obedience, the dog will learn "come" means "must come." For now, it's play time. Don't get upset by inconsistent response. You're building for the future. You want a young dog with complete confidence in himself. To achieve that, the pup must be 100 percent sure of your love. He must be a consistent winner in what he tries. Whenever possible, set him up to be a winner. And praise him so he knows he did it right.

If you took the advice in the section on choosing a pup, the dog was acquired at seven weeks. In the Bar Harbor experiments, Dr. J. Paul Scott learned that this is the critical period to begin socialization with humans. Dogs that aren't handled by humans before they're fourteen weeks old are forever wild and timid. I once acquired a Beagle that hadn't been socialized, and no amount of affectionate handling was able to overcome her fear of humans. Fortunately, this is the time in a puppy's life when it's so appealing that we can't let it alone. Just make sure you *have* the pup during that seven- to fourteen-week period. And make it fun, never serious.

Early physical development is also important. Take the puppy with you whenever possible. Those little legs will have to work to keep up, but hunting dogs' muscles don't develop while curled up in a corner. Romps in the back yard are great. A walk in the country is better, but stop before the pup is exhausted.

It's easy to teach a pup to sit months before formal obedience training begins. But it's an introduction. Keep it play. Don't insist on perfect performance.

Children should play with pups. It's good socialization for both— but children should not attempt to train pups.

Squat and the pup will come almost automatically. Say "come" every time you do this, and the pup will understand the command long before obedience begins.

Call for attention and step backwards away from the pup when he picks up a bird. He'll follow. Let him catch up. Praise him and take the bird. He's learning to retrieve.

Most of my newly acquired pups have been brought home in an automobile, and none that I got at seven weeks ever suffered from car sickness. I put the pup in a cardboard box for its first ride and place it on the seat beside me. It can't see over the top and get motion sickness from watching objects whiz by. My wife and I talk to the pup and pet him during the entire ride. By taking them along frequently as they grow older, pups accept automobiles early and learn to regard riding as a pleasant part of life.

I've had other dogs acquired later in their lives that never got used to riding, despite being eager to go because they loved to hunt. I recall three that drooled through every trip. One piddled. Another relieved her bowels every last time I took her hunting, and it didn't matter how much I exercised her ahead of time.

At some time as the pup grows older, he'll venture farther than you want or into an area where he doesn't belong. Before this he came rather consistently when you'd squat and call. But now he's too full of enthusiasm. And he's too far away. He'd rather not. It's still not time to bear down for strict obedience, but his precocious behavior has placed him in a possibly dangerous position.

What do you do? Let him get away with it and hope for the best, or run him down and scorch his hide?

Neither. Just remember he's a dog, and dogs are programmed to chase what runs. Call his name to get attention. Run, not away, but across the dog's line of vision so he can recognize your movement. He'll come running. As he nears you, turn away to encourage chase. When he's very close, run in a tightening spiral, and grab his collar when he catches up with you.

Your impulse will be to beat the tar out of him for not coming in the first place. Don't. Roughhouse with him a bit. Praise him for coming. Make him feel rewarded for what he did. *Never* punish a dog when he has come to you, regardless of the reason. If you do, the dog gets the notion that the way to get punished is to come to you; the way to avoid punishment is to avoid you. This is important at any time, but especially important to the pup whose complete confidence you must gain if you expect to develop his full potential.

The chasing instinct can also be used to advantage in early retrieving lessons during puppy play. Toss a dummy. The puppy will chase and grab it. Call him when he picks it up. Maybe he'll bring it to you. But he'll probably want to run off with the dummy. And he hopes you'll chase him. What a great game!

Don't do it. When he picks up the dummy, start running backward. He'll chase you. Clap your hands

Let the growing pup watch an older dog perform. It may join the fun.

Bill Kepler, of Oneida, Wisconsin, interests a pup in birds.

and call, if necessary, to get his attention. When he catches up with you, take the dummy from his mouth gently (don't yank it out and cause a distasteful experience), then praise the pup for the grand job he did.

One of the main things you're doing in this puppy play is introducing the youngster to new experiences. If he succeeds in these experiences, he'll tackle new tasks with interest and ambition. If he fails in a few, he'll begin to accept failure as a way of life. As he grows older, his pessimism will make him give up the hunt before it starts. So be very careful not to introduce him to failure. Don't throw the first dummy very far—just a few feet. Don't insist that the puppy enter water until he wants to. Cross a fence where you know he can get through. Don't take the pup out with an old dog when he's too little to keep up. And don't nag, nag, nag. If you feel like repeating something, make it praise—lots of it.

While you're playing with the new pup, don't hesitate to call it by name. Bird-dog pups are sharp. They usually know who they are in a couple of days if allowed the company of their "people pack." Whenever you can, use his name. After he knows it, use it with every command. Duke, come; Duke, fetch. Duke, no!

That last one's a surprise. He'll catch on to the different tone in your voice when you say that one,

and he'll probably stop what he's doing. Don't make a fetish of this command, but use it enough so he learns it. Don't get rough, but make him stop whatever he's doing wrong. It's not too early to teach "sit," either. Hold his chin up with your right hand and gently press down his hindquarters while saying "Duke, sit." Flatter his ego over a job so well done.

If the puppy is of a pointing breed, don't teach him to sit. Instead, croon "Duke, whoa-a-a." Stroke him and continue crooning. Pull gently and steadily on his tail. He'll resist and lean forward looking bold and anxious. Stop after a few moments and tell him how pretty he is.

A puppy forgets easily and quickly, of course, so don't get steamed up if he sits or stands well today and doesn't tomorrow. Just show him again tomorrow and pour on the praise.

Whenever you're putting the dog into something—cage, car, kennel, the house, etc.—say the command. Trainers say, "Kennel." You may prefer, "Duke, get in." The important thing is that the puppy hears it and gradually learns its meaning.

If you have a treat to feed him, and you will, make use of it to reinforce commands. Give it to him if he comes when called or sits or whoas when told. A treat can also be used to teach "down." Hold it to his nose for a sniff, then drop your hand to the floor. If he drops

Tie a pigeon's wings and put it with the pups.

to the floor with it, fine, you're off to a perfect start. He'll probably just drop his head. As his head goes down, give the command. With your hand on his back, press down and away to bring him to the floor. Pushing straight down on the shoulders will be resisted by his rigid front legs. By pushing back and down, he's taken off balance.

You won't use food reinforcement during serious training later on, but much of the work is already accomplished if the pup grows up knowing the meaning of various commands. And the work is easier if the pup associates the command with pleasant experiences.

Make no effort at this stage to teach heeling, especially with pointing and flushing breeds. Don't give them the notion that their station in life is at your feet. Forget the command entirely until the pup has learned the joys of hunting and no longer has to be encouraged to leave you. That may be many months away. In the meantime, it's no big deal to have to use a leash when the dog must remain near you.

Let your pup run around the yard for a while with the leash snapped to his collar. He'll become used to it and lose his fear or suspicion of it. Then begin to restrain him with it. Avoid a hassle whenever possible.

Puppies can be started on pigeons to develop bird interest even before they leave the dam. Gun-dog trainer George Vuillemot, of Beecher, Illinois, raises a few litters of German Shorthairs and has his pups retrieving live pigeons before they're fully weaned. He ties the pigeons' wings in an upward position so they

If done early and often enough to be fun, pups grow up with a bold bird interest.

Give the pup plenty of chance to run and develop its growing muscles.

attract attention, but the birds can't strike a pup with the leading edge of a wing. Then he places a bird on the floor with his pups. The pigeon tries to walk away. But it can't move too quickly for puppy attention span, and one is sure to notice and follow. In no time at all the puppies begin chasing the pigeon and dragging it back to the nest.

If you try that method, make sure the wings are tied. A good rap on the nose could destroy a pup's bird interest for a long time.

Those who don't have pigeons handy may want to start their bird dog pups with the more conventional wing and fishing pole method. The bird wing is attached to a short line. Toss it out for the pup's attention. He'll run and pounce at it. Jerk it from under his nose. He'll chase. Stand in one spot, and keep turning and jerking the wing ahead of the pup. When he learns he can't catch it, he'll try to stalk it. Finally, he'll point. Praise him. If he becomes lax, twitch the wing. He'll stiffen again. Once he is pointing the wing, it's usually wise to stop this puppy play and advance to live birds. Pointing a wing is not his life's work.

Never tease a puppy. You'll make him want to bite, and he's denied that privilege, or should be. The teased pup is always the loser of the game. We're teaching our pup to be a winner.

A great deal of training can have its roots in these very early weeks. Sometimes the only thing left to teach is "must." And we've done it while the puppy was too little to cause much trouble. Best of all, we accomplished it at a time when it's pure fun for puppy and master alike.

Fun in the Field

A friend likes to hunt birds, but more than that he loves obedience competition. Most of his dog training is spent perfecting discipline. The dog is accustomed to strict control when in crowds. As a result, my friend's English Setter is afraid to leave his side when there are other people in the field. He can hunt by himself, but even then the Setter tends to disbelieve that his freedom will last. So every now and then the dog bolts and is gone for hours on a wild binge of self-hunting.

My friend is willing to put up with that kind of field behavior because his first love is obedience training. But I think it's safe to assume you're not. If you want to avoid it, *do not* put your dog through strict obedience training before he learns the joys of hunting. Training a bird dog is the delicate process of gradually bringing the youngster under firm control while not at all dulling the edge of his desire and spirit. The 1955 National (Retriever) Champion Cork of Oakwood Lane is said to have left a bitch he was to service when a pheasant escaped. After retrieving the

Helping dogs across fences makes them dependent. They must learn to do it themselves.

ringneck, he returned to mating. Your chances of getting that kind of superior hunting desire in a dog aren't very great, but strive for it in every way you can.

Take your young dog to the country for walks as early and often as possible. When the pup is little, try to avoid problems. Don't let a wide creek get between you. Cross the fences where you know the pup will have no problems. But don't help him across. If you do it once, you'll have it to do each time. And he must learn self-reliance.

If possible, let the puppy see livestock and become accustomed to farm animals early. If he's used to them, he won't chase and harass them later. But watch so the pup doesn't walk up to a horse, cow or pig to make friends and get kicked or nipped. This is especially important when farm animals have young.

Don't keep the puppy in the field until exhausted. Quit while he's still having fun. You want him to grow up feeling it's impossible to get too much hunting.

At this point, don't worry too much about modifying the dog's range. Let the pup run as he will, but keep track of him. When he comes to you, don't yell at

After a few successful tries, they soon know how to handle fences.

him for hanging around. Don't encourage it by petting him when he comes in, either. As the puppy grows a few months older and gets some leg length and stamina, he'll show you his natural range. That's the time to disapprove if he checks in too often or doesn't reach out far enough. If he's too wide and too independent for your style of hunting, praise when he's within easy voice range and pet him when he comes to you. That's why you didn't order him away from you when he was little. Now he's willing to come to you when it's important.

If you have a really wide-ranging dog and you fear he may be too wide for you, be careful that coming to you doesn't come to mean getting put on the leash. Pet or praise each time he checks in, and send him out again. Don't leash him and quit until he has been praised and sent on several times and has run the edge off of his energy. If every time he comes close to you it's the end of his field run, he'll learn to stay out until he's good and ready to quit.

Actually, hunters often worry about range far more than necessary when starting pups of pointing breeds. Strict obedience training later on will reduce range somewhat, and if you're not careful the dog will be hunting much too close. Good rapport between you and the dog and lots of hunting experience will also encourage practical hunting range.

With Springer or Cocker Spaniels, it's a different matter. You don't want range. But you do want desire, so let that puppy run and have fun.

Don't hesitate to let a retriever enjoy some field fun, too. If his future includes flushing game, it's essential.

The purpose at this point is to build bird interest. If we can lay additional groundwork to make future training easier, fine, but we shouldn't do anything that might dilute his bold desire to hunt. As he grows bigger, we don't bother to find easy places to cross a fence. He finds his own! Creeks, briars and brush are all taken in stride very quickly without our help. But we must avoid setting up rules that make the youngster feel this great outdoors is fighting him. Sure, you want him to point staunchly. Maybe you plan for him to be steady to wing and shot. But we didn't solve algebra problems in the first grade, either. Don't yell when he chases every bird he sees instead of pointing them. Let him have all the fun he wants in kindergarten if you don't want a drop-out when the going gets tough later.

This doesn't mean the pup should have his way with every whim that strikes him. If he disrupts the household, stop him. Teach him what "no" means. And make it stick. But now is not the time for him to relate "no" with birds. Be thankful if he chases birds. He's interested. Let him chase to his heart's content. You don't want him to get the notion he's not supposed to bother birds.

Some trainers believe it's best never to let dogs chase birds. Then they don't have to be broken from the habit. This may be practical if one of two things can be guaranteed: the dog makes it as an outstanding hunter or he's put out of his misery. If you can't be that dispassionate, if the family loves the pup and you're stuck with him for better or worse, you'd better let the young dog improve his odds of becoming a bird hunter by chasing feathers all he wants.

While he's learning to love birds with a passion, we can lay the groundwork for an intelligent running pattern. Don't just turn the dog loose and walk behind him in a straight line. Zigzag. Introduce the whistle if you like. When you change direction, blow a long note to get the dog's attention. Extend your arm in the direction you're going, and start walking. The dog will catch on after a few times. Some grasp it immediately. You have begun to teach quartering and the use of whistle and hand signals almost without trying.

I prefer a long whistle note for turning the dog because a youngster may not respond immediately. You can continue the long note without getting angry. A short, sharp note implies expectations of instant response and obedience. I feel that way, and dogs sense it, too. So I save that sharp blast for stopping dogs. It can mean "whoa" to pointing dogs, "sit" to retrievers and flushing dogs or "stop" no

Gary Arbergast clipped some of the primary wing feathers before throwing the pigeon. The additional flutter caused by the bird's increased efforts to stay aloft is a great attraction for a young retriever.

matter what any of them are doing. A tat-tat-tat-tat staccato note implies urgency, and I have better luck calling my dogs in with it than with other notes. If a professional trainer teaches your dog a different set of whistle commands, however, don't argue with him about it. Whatever works for the individual trainer (or dog) is the thing to use.

Exuberant young dogs often run away from you in a straight line, sometimes down a corn row or field road. Then they remember it's a big world and you are the guide. They turn, look for you, and come running back. When the dog looks, change direction and give a hand signal so the dog casts into new cover. There are no birds where he already ran. Zigzag. Use the whistle if necessary. Get him to quarter on his way back.

This is especially important in learning to work downwind. Dogs work into the wind naturally and

Praise the dog when he returns with the bird, but don't demand such things as sitting before giving up the bird. Just make it evident that you're pleased, as Dotti Arbergast is doing here.

John Ingram of Dogs Unlimited likes the Retriev-R-Trainer to introduce gunfire with retrieving fun.

The Retriev-R-Trainer uses a .22 blank to propel the dummy. John has added feathers to provide a little bird smell.

obviously can't smell scent that's being blown away from them. But you can't always be walking into the wind. The dog can compensate for this, however, by quartering back to you after making a downwind run.

When you're teaching the dog to quarter, try to turn him when an object (fallen tree, clump of cover, pile of brush, fence row, etc.) will further encourage him to take the direction you're suggesting. It will serve to reinforce your command and teach the dog that interesting things happen when he follows your orders.

The big difference between teaching pointing and flushing breeds to quarter is range and precision. The Pointer or Setter may be zigzagging half a quarter away while the Springer Spaniel should be within half a gunshot. At this point, however, you're only suggesting, not demanding. Let the Springer range if he wants, especially if it gets him into birds to chase.

Retrievers that are being taught to flush game will not learn quartering as easily as Springers. Some stay too close while others range too far. They all generally tend to run straight lines instead of quartering.

The dog is probably five or six months old now. Start banging feed pans and water buckets more frequently and noisily than you had been around the kennel. If he shows any indication toward noise shyness, do the noisemaking while he's eating or while you're petting him. Teach him that noise doesn't hurt. Then take a .22 pistol or rifle along on your field trips. When he's off at a distance, running and enjoying himself—or, perhaps, chasing a bird—fire a blank. If it distracts him from what he's doing, discontinue shooting until the next trip. But pay no attention whatever to his concern.

When he no longer reacts to the .22, shoot progressively closer to him. After this fire a small-gauge shotgun, again beginning at a distance. If you don't have or can't borrow a .410 or even a 20 gauge, I know you're not going to buy a special gun to train the dog. If you must use a 12 gauge, try to precede it with blanks in a large-caliber revolver. Failing that, use the lightest 12-gauge loads you can buy or handload. Begin from a great distance, and point the shotgun away from the dog. Be sure to fire only when the dog is having a good time.

We're making a big fuss over accustoming the dog to gunfire when the chances are great that it won't bother him a bit, but it's by far the easiest and safest

The unit is fired from the back end by means of a spring-loaded pin.

Distance can be adjusted by elevation of aim or choice of light or long-range charges. Much longer retrieves are possible than with hand-thrown dummies.

practice. Curing gun shyness is a terribly long, drawn-out difficult chore, one that most average amateur trainers will probably never accomplish. The best cure, by far, is never to let it happen.

While you're making field trips, watch the young pointing dog carefully for independence and bird interest. The shy dog may require more age, more times in the field and more encouragement. The bold dog will show it much earlier. But you have to recognize this interest. That's when your dog is ready for more formal discipline. Don't hurry him or you'll wind up with a mediocre, mechanically working dog. And don't neglect to notice when he's capable of accepting stricter training. If you encourage bird chasing too long, he may get the notion that there's nothing better in life. When you're satisfied that birds are his first love, it's time to get on with his education. It may happen well before his first birthday; it may take longer.

No doubt you'll enjoy these trips to the field. They're lots of fun and little work when the dog doesn't have to be corrected for what he's doing wrong—things that will be considered very wrong later on. But not everyone has the time to start his dog.

What then? The obvious answer is a professional trainer. Ask him at what age he prefers to begin working with your dog.

Another solution is less obvious and more risky, but it certainly brings out the best (or worst) in a dog in the shortest time. If you have a farmer friend who lives away from highways and will keep your dog for a couple of months, the youngster can start himself. Just running free in the country will teach him how to handle creeks, fences and cover, as well as where to find the birds. If he has hunting desire, it shows in a hurry. If he's five or six months old and lays around the farm yard for another two months without showing interest, get a new prospect.

C. L. Owens, head trainer at Gunsmoke Kennels, says the time the dog runs free is rather critical. While it has to be long enough for the dog to learn something, it can't be too long or the dog will become a self-hunter, paying no attention whatever to where his master is when in the field. Owens believes that sixty days is about the right length of time for a dog to run free.

This system can be a real headstart in training but it can also be a disaster if the dog is hit by a car, gets

A little competition is good incentive for the young dog.

hung in a fence, falls in an abandoned well, etc. It has to be a calculated risk. And although the farmer couldn't be held responsible if something happened, he'd feel a responsibility to watch over the dog and couldn't be expected to do it for nothing. He'd also have to feed your dog, so he'd have to be a real friend or be well paid to accept your proposal. If you have such a friend in a relatively safe area, however, those sixty days can be a big help in the education of a pointing dog. Spaniels and retrievers will not benefit from running free. The main purpose of this practice with pointing dogs is to acquire independence and enhance questing desire in the process. We could use the desire but not the independence in Spaniels and retrievers. They must work closely under tight control in order to flush game within shotgun range. Even though they are allowed to chase birds during early trips afield, they're not doing it while independent of us.

Retrievers—and Spaniels too, if they're expected to retrieve from water, and most are—should spend part of their early fun-in-the-field time swimming. Although Retrievers seldom require encouragement to enter water, the best way in the world to get them started is to go swimming yourself. Or just wade into shallow water. They'll be in right behind you.

Begin play-training by teasing the pup with a dummy at the water's edge. Splash it in the water. Drop it perhaps a foot from shore. Talk an exciting story. If the youngster has any instincts, he'll be after it. Praise his prowess excitedly as you accept the dummy from him, probably against his will. Tease again, and drop the dummy perhaps a foot farther out. If the pup is hesitant, splash the dummy around in the water just under his nose, then let it drift off slowly with a very gentle push. It's moving away and encouraging chase, but too slowly to be gone before the pup can muster courage to wade into the water.

After a few times of wading progressively farther after the dummy, you'll have the puppy swimming and retrieving. Spaniels and Retrievers of good stock will be playing your game in minutes.

If you own one of the versatile breeds, he needs the water training just described as well as trips afield to build bird interest.

The fire is lit. Now we'll bring it under control.

Obedience

Until now, we haven't been very demanding of the dog. We've corrected him sharply for breach of manners a number of times, but, for the most part it has been play. We've wanted our dog to acquire a lively interest in birds *before* obedience training. In fact, if you turned to this section immediately, thinking obedience is the first thing to teach your dog, stop right here. Go back and read the sections on puppy play and fun in the field before proceeding further. Above all else, a bird dog needs desire. If it isn't acquired before strict discipline, the dog will never reach his genetic potential.

If your dog is ready, we can bring out his best with the obedience training methods of professional gun-dog trainer Jack Godsil, of Galesburg, Illinois. Jack's philosophy is summed up by an experience he had in an all-night diner on the way home from obedience competition in Minnesota. He stopped for coffee in the wee hours of the morning and found three obviously undisciplined young men showing-off and smart-mouthing the elderly woman who ran the place. Jack listened quietly until one fellow decided not to pay all he owed and was giving the old lady guff about it. Godsil came off of his stool with a catsup bottle in his hand, and the bill was paid before Jack could get across the room.

In saner times, our society applied whatever pressure was necessary to exact acceptable behavior from its citizens. It worked rather well, can work again, and certainly does when Godsil trains dogs.

Mrs. Godsil echoes Jack's philosophy. Jeri helps take care of the kennels and entertains the wife and children when a family brings a dog to be trained. "If the children behave badly," she says, "I know Jack is out there accepting another spoiled dog that's going to give him a rough time."

The bleeding hearts might have been delighted with the light-handed way we recommended handling dogs to achieve bird interest in the previous section, but here's where we part company. Once the dog is birdy, we'll have to bring him under control. We don't advise cruelty, just lean on him with whatever pressure is necessary to control him. But control is absolutely essential.

Jack Godsil believes gun-dog obedience is more important today than it ever was. "The average dog owner is a different person than he used to be," Jack said. "Many are city people whose only contact with a dog has been in a book. Years ago, people knew dogs. They wouldn't fool around with a poor hunting prospect. When they brought in a dog for training, they'd say, 'try the dog a month and either send me a bill or the collar.'

"In the past twenty years it has changed to where I'd guess 80 percent of the dogs a trainer gets are house pets first and hunters second. If the dog's a poor

This is half of Godsil's kennels. New dogs quickly learn that one sharp whistle blast means stop barking or stop whatever you're doing. A regular farm-type fence charger is attached to the gates to teach new dogs to stand back respectfully while the attendant brings their food or cleans their pens.

Trainer Jack Godsil teaches obedience with a properly positioned choke chain and a leather leash. This is the beginning position for teaching "sit."

Jab the rear down and jerk up sharply on the choke chain at the same time.

hunting prospect, they won't get rid of him anyway. For that reason, control becomes more important than stylish point. The dog spends more time going along on camping trips, picnics and vacations than he does hunting. And he probably lives in the house with the family. This kind of close association with the family demands a better behaved animal than the hunting dog of years back."

What Jack means by "better behaved animal" is obvious the minute you drive up to Jack's house. A newly arrived trainee begins barking in the kennels, as is to be expected, and a few others add to the clamor. But whoever comes out to greet you—Jack, Jeri, their sons, or a kennel boy—will hit the barkers with one or two sharp whistle blasts. They shut up. The new dog may need an additional voice command, but in a few days he'll learn to be quiet with the others.

Anyone who has spent time around a training kennel knows what a din these dogs can set up. It was refreshing to stand in Jack's yard and talk in a normal tone of voice. After a time I noticed the wind was coming from the kennels toward the house. I'm not fussy about dog odor—what puzzled me was why I didn't smell any. That's usually a serious problem where numbers of dogs are confined. About that time,

the boys began feeding, and I learned why things are so orderly.

No dogs jumped anxiously against the gates when the boys approached with food. The dogs stood back respectfully and waited until told to eat. Contrast that with a dog running through his mess on a wet day and splattering dirt all over you by jumping against the gate or fence while you're trying to get in. Jack has his pens wired with a fence charger. The new trainee only requires a harmless jolt or two to cure him of unruly jumping.

Dogs relieve themselves soon after being fed. About thirty minutes after feeding, cleanup begins at Godsil's. The concrete runs are hosed down daily and scrubbed with street brooms. Soon after dogs are up and moving the next morning, they'll relieve themselves again. A second major pickup is attended to at that time, but any time anyone notices an occasional stool during the day, they stop what they're doing and pick it up.

Regularity and consistency are key words to the cleanest and quietest kennels I've seen. They are also the key words that form the basis of any training program. A dog must be taught what is expected of him and what will happen each and every time he does

Follow the rear to the ground.

It's important to praise the dog *every* time he does something right.

or doesn't behave in the prescribed manner. The owner who doesn't bother to praise the dog's successes *every* time is as bad off as the fellow who punishes a misdeed one time but lets it pass another. Neither can get first-class performance from his dog.

"The hangdog look we sometimes see in an obedience ring," Jack said, "is usually on a dog that lacks confidence because he's not sure what's expected of him. When they're sure of right and wrong, they're confident. Make the training always black and white, always right or always wrong. Punish sternly when they're wrong. Praise as intensely when they're right."

Besides emphasizing obedience in gun dogs, Godsil travels 40,000 miles a year enjoying a busman's holiday. He calls obedience his hobby and travels widely to handle dogs in shows and obedience competition. And, of course, he obedience-trains all breeds for the public.

Jack's greatest success in obedience competition was Milo of Ben's Major, U.D., owned by Frank Holmay. Milo was the highest-scoring Golden Retriever in the United States for the years 1968, '69, '70 and '71. He was retired in the fall of '71. In the 1969–70 season, Milo was also the highest-scoring sporting dog in the U.S. He was the only dog that placed in the National Utility Dog Tournament both in 1970 (the first year it was held) and again in 1971. Out of 46 times in the ring, Milo failed to place three times. Milo's crowning achievement was election to the Golden Hall of Fame for obedience work.

Godsil travels over the country giving seminars to kennel club trainers who later hold classes for dogs and their owners. These obedience classes are worthwhile for about 90 percent of the dogs, especially Retrievers or Spaniels. Pointing breeds are not particularly suited because they should be taught to whoa and stand while dogs in classes are taught to sit and stay. Pointers taught to sit may sit on point. You can take the chance if you like. The advantage of belonging to a class lies in its discipline. You are committed to a progressive series of lessons with homework in between. Not everyone is a self-starter who can continue a program of dog training without external pressure.

Jack begins by selecting the right equipment and using it in the correct manner. A simple leather leash and a choke chain are all that's needed. Notice we said choke chain. We did not say choke collar. It is *not* a collar. It's a training instrument and should not be left on the dog after training. A choke chain is a chain-link hangman's noose, and too many dogs have lost their lives wearing it as a collar. Buy a proper collar with a nameplate. You may insist on a metal collar. They are practical, especially on retrievers that are frequently wet. Leather dries slowly, is uncomfortable and deteriorates quickly. A strong chain-link collar with a nameplate is available from The Slip Check Company, Centralia, Missouri 65240.

You may be surprised to learn that a choke chain can be put on a dog backwards. With the dog at your left side, slip on the chain, and look carefully. If the chain comes up through the sliding ring, it's wrong. When you jerk, the chain will draw tight and continue choking the dog. That's not its purpose. We'll use it as a "jerk chain." Jack says that short, sharp jerks of the leash apply a quick pressure to the nerves in the back of the neck. We jerk for correction. A steady pull or choke could not be applied quickly nor instantly released when the dog makes a favorable correction.

If the chain goes down through the sliding ring, it's on correctly. Try it to be sure. If it releases after a jerk, it's correct; if it remains tight, it's backwards.

The dog will be worked on the left side unless you're left-handed and don't want your dog on the same side as your gun. I really think it makes little difference, but it's less confusing, perhaps, if all dogs are trained the same. I have an idea the custom began when men commonly rode horseback. Horses are mounted from the left to this day because swords were worn on the left and would get in the way when mounting from the right. The dog at heel, whether war dog, coursing hound or whatever, would be on the same side as the sword and out of the way for a left-hand mount. A dog heeling on the right would also be in jeopardy when a right-handed man drew his sword. Anyway, we'll train on the left.

All commands will be simple and preceded by the dog's name. It's "Duke, sit!" Dogs can learn a few one-syllable words. But they have trouble with conversation, so don't say, "Come on, Duke, sit down now, old boy. Hurry up." And you're not asking the dog. Order him. You use his name for attention and follow with the sharply spoken command. But please don't yell. It's undignified for both of you and damages your

The "stay" command is reinforced by the hand in front of the muzzle.

Godsil's dogs are taught to sit and stay before going through a gate or door of any kind.

man-dog rapport to suddenly go from permissive puppy play to screaming angry signals. Simply let the dog know you mean what you're telling him to do.

The instant "Duke, sit" is out of your mouth, jerk the leash up sharply with your right hand and hit the dog's back in the region of the hindquarters with the thumb and middle finger of the left hand. *Do not pull* up on the leash and push down on the back. Jerk sharply and jab quickly. Praise profusely when the dog is seated. After a very few times an intelligent dog will avoid the jerk and jab by being on his rump almost before the command is out of your mouth. That's what you want. Praise him *every* time.

Practice this a few minutes every day. Don't put it off for days and then decide to practice a whole hour on Saturday. The dog's attention span is short. Long sessions will sicken him of obedience while short ones can be enjoyable if he's praised profusely for the wonderful things he does. If you've missed a few days, so be it. Continue where you left off. Don't try to make it up.

Keep in mind that every order is followed by a sharp jerk in the direction you want the dog to move. The order was "sit," so his head was jerked up and back. After the dog has learned sit, the next lesson is "stay."

Order "sit." Praise him. With the leash in the left hand, bring the palm of the right hand toward his face and command, "Duke, stay!" Immediately step out with your right foot. (Later, during heeling practice, you'll lead off with the left foot.) He'll probably start to follow. Jerk up sharply to stop him. Praise him.

After Duke learns he must stay, stand in front of him, then step to one side and the other to test him. Praise profusely, but keep the leash high in case a quick correction is needed. When you can walk back and forth in front of the dog and all the way around him, he's ready for the next lesson.

When Duke was a pup, you squatted to make him *want* to come. Now he has to learn that he *must* come. Give him a sit-stay command, and step back to the end of the leash. Say "Duke, come!" and jerk sharply. Stop him in front of you with a sit command. Later on this will be the position for delivering a bird. Praise extravagantly.

After the dog learns whoa by hand and voice, introduce the whistle. One sharp loud blast is best for whoa.

The important command for Spaniels is "hup." Godsil is reinforcing the whistle blast with a jerk on the choke chain.

Sit, stay and come are usually learned in just a few sessions. Now practice until Duke is quite good, giving a sharp jerk on the leash when he responds too slowly and praising highly every correct move he makes. We can't overemphasize the praise. If the dog gets stubborn and it requires considerable effort to make him sit, for example, don't follow the accomplishment with, "There, now, damn it. That's what you're supposed to do!" As much as you'd like to lay a two-by-four across his skull, when he finally gets it right, you've got to be all smiles and compliments. That's the incentive he'll work for.

If you're training one of the pointing breeds, it would be wise to substitute whoa for the sit and stay. Stand that dog, instead of sitting him and simply substitute whoa for stay. Move out as with the stay command, but say "whoa" when you jerk the leash to make the dog stay put. If you didn't stop him with the leash, and he has moved, pick up the dog and carry him to where he was told to remain. If the dog decides to sit down while patiently awaiting your next command, stand him. We don't want him associating whoa with sitting because later on we'll whoa him often on point.

I think it's best to refrain from praising the dog during a stay or whoa command, especially when you're too far off to make an immediate correction. Dogs often interpret praise at this time to mean they're no longer required to stay put. So wait until the dog is released with the come command. Then reward him with praise. With pointing breeds, come can be taught from the whoa position.

Godsil may teach whoa as we've just said, or he may loop the check cord around a post. In this way the dog can be stopped from behind while he's facing you. You can call him, let him come a few feet, then order "whoa" and enforce it.

Jack may also teach whoa while the dog is heeling. Retrievers and Spaniels, especially, are taught this way. While walking, order "Duke, whoa!" Stop and jerk back on the leash. Duke will soon learn to stop before the jerk. Most dogs sit. If he's pointing dog, stand him back up.

Those who are training Spaniels will probably want to use the word "hup" instead of sit. It's the custom among Spaniel trainers and handlers, and the command is a little sharper and demanding. Since the Spaniel has to be stopped at a distance, sometimes while in the act of chasing game, the sharper the command, the more useful it is.

Heel is taught by ordering "Duke, heel!" and striding forth with the left foot. We leave the dog with the right foot, remember, and have him join us by leading off with the left. These two separate actions help reinforce two separate commands.

Duke will probably follow without further encouragement. If he was left behind, a sharp jerk on the leash will urge him in your direction. Get his head next to your left leg as you walk and keep him there if he wanders by sharp jerks on the leash. Sweet talk him while he's doing it right.

Trainers used to swing the leash end or use a whip to rap the dog's nose when he got out of position. This is quite unnecessary with the choke chain and leash method.

You may want to repeat the command when the dog gets too far out of line, but don't nag at him with a constant repetition of heel, heel, heel. Dogs, children and adults react alike to nagging. We all tune it out. After the first few times, the demands are just sounds, not orders.

Retrievers must be taught "down." It's often necessary for them to lie down in a boat or blind. During jump shooting it's even more important to keep the dog down. In fact, while sneaking up on a pothole full of ducks, it's essential to be able to drop the dog and leave him without saying a word.

A dog's rear end can be pushed to the ground easily as we learned with the sit command. But the front legs stand straight under the shoulders and won't buckle even under considerable weight. So the old method was to give a command and pull the dog's front legs forward and out from under him. That brings him to the ground and after enough repetition, he learns what's being demanded of him.

That's still a good method, but Jack uses two that are better. The first is a straight-arm maneuver. The dog is walked at heel, but Jack has a grip on the leash very close to the dog's choke chain. While moving, the command is given and Jack drops with his arm very straight and rigid, essentially driving the dog to the ground. This would be very difficult with a standing dog, but while walking, the dog's front legs are off balance and lose their rigidity. Down he goes, on command. Praise him highly.

The "end of leash" method is best for training a jump-shooter's retriever. Walk the dog with the left hand close to the choke chain as in the straight-arm procedure. Hold the long end of the leash in the right hand. This time, after the "Duke, down" command, come down with the dog, but swing the long end of the leash across the animal's shoulders. A light slap across the shoulders may be all that's necessary. Apply whatever degree of slap necessary to get the message across.

This method of training has the added advantage of the dog being able to see your hand on its way with the leash. After a little practice the dog will drop to the hand without leash or spoken command. The dog dropping and staying down to a slight and silent hand motion is invaluable when stalking ducks.

Jack adds a couple of niceties just to make the dog a better citizen. The first is kenneling, or getting into anything, on command. If they're reluctant or unwilling, he grabs an ear and helps them along. Obviously, with an ear hold, you don't heave a dog into

A buggy whip is great for reinforcing the whoa. It takes a slap across the front legs at first, but after that the swish of the whip is a whoa command. Later on, if the whip is used to flush birds in field training, the dog is hearing "whoa" all the time and quickly learns to be steady to flush.

This is another method of teaching whoa. The dog is ordered to come, then whoa. The rope restrains him from behind, and the dog does not readily associate it with the one in your hand. He learns he must also whoa when he's farther away than the length of a leash.

...x as you could with a grip on the collar. The ear
...d only encourages or pressures the dog into obe-
...ience. It also creates a more lasting memory.

Godsil also makes them sit and stay in front of the
automobile, kennel or gate before ordering them to
kennel. "That way they don't come out of the field
dirty," Jack said, "and jump past the hunter into the
car the moment he opens the door."

Jack advises his clients to reinforce obedience training by making the dog sit and stay before receiving its
food. "If there's no control around home for ten
months," he says, "the dog certainly won't obey
during the two-month hunting season in situations
that are far more difficult to control."

The final touch on basic obedience training for Jack
Godsil is a relaxation of the rules when a session has
ended. "I let my dogs jump up on me a lot, especially if
I had to discipline them during the training," he said.
"It compares to a spanked kid crawling into your lap.
It's their way of making up."

Field Training Pointing Breeds

By now the young dog is accustomed to the ways of
the wild and can be depended upon to obey basic
commands. He has chased birds to his heart's content
and should realize they can't be caught. Maybe he's
already holding his points. If so, give thanks. If not,
he'll need help. But keep one thing in mind. You and I
didn't drive through downtown Chicago the first time
we got behind the wheel. Your dog may not be
staunch on point before he's a year old. Work with
him. Bring him along at his own rate. An enthusiastic,
inspired student learns to solve his own problems; a
disinterested, harassed, frightened student makes
them.

George Vuillemot, gun-dog trainer from Beecher,
Illinois, uses an assistant with two or three pigeons
stuffed in coat pockets to start steadying a dog on
point. A bird is planted in light cover, and George
brings the dog up from down wind. The assistant
stands behind the planted bird, hands on the other
pigeons in his pockets. If the dog breaks point, the
assistant instantly tosses a bird into the air.

At the same time, George is controlling the dog with
a check rope. He brings the dog back to where the
point was broken and stacks him up again. If the dog
breaks point again, out goes another pigeon. The
pigeons, of course, fly back to their pen and can be
used over and over.

It doesn't take long for the dog to recognize that his
action is causing the bird to fly. Pointing is hesitation
before pouncing on prey. Obviously, the dog does not
want the prey to escape and will learn to modify his
action so it doesn't happen.

Once the dog is doing a fair job of holding point, this
training should be discontinued. If kept up too long

The straight-arm method can be used to teach the down
command, but it must be done while walking. The front legs
are too rigid when standing.

the dog learns the planted bird is always in front of the
assistant. He begins to point the assistant.

The "bird pin" method can be used both to build
enthusiasm and staunch the dog on point. Dr. McCue
first made this practice public in *Hunting Dog Magazine.* The pin is now marketed by Dogs Unlimited,
Jackson, Ohio.

The pin is a small stake to be driven into the ground.
The above-ground part is slotted with a hole drilled to
hold a cotter key. A rubber washer can be inserted into
the slot and held in place by the key. A rubber band is
fastened to the washer, and a pigeon is tied to the
other end of the rubber band by a length of soft yarn.

The pigeon tries to escape and is encouraged by
feeling the "give" of the rubber band. It keeps jerking
and trying to get away. This is great to interest a
twelve-week-old puppy in birds. But he can't be
allowed to catch the pigeon. When he nears the bird,
the cotter key is jerked free by means of a string, and
the pigeon flies off.

This same method can be used to start older pups
that haven't been introduced to birds. After a time,
the youngsters begin to realize they can't catch the

A voice command reinforced by a slap across the shoulders is a little harsher but better in the long run for teaching down. After a few times, the dog drops at just the sound of the leash as shown here. It no longer has to touch the dog.

birds and that the attempt only causes them to fly. The young dogs point or flash point. A check cord can be used to encourage steadiness.

At this time, the bird will be tied directly to the washer without benefit of a rubber band. We no longer want the pigeon to think he can fly. In fact, the bird should be planted in heavier cover where the dog can smell it but not see it. Make him hunt for it. Not being sure of the bird's whereabouts and not wanting to make a wrong move that will flush it is what staunchness is all about.

If the pigeon moves or flutters, and the dog can see it, he may assume the bird has begun to fly. He may break point and run at the pigeon to prevent its escape. We stop him from catching it, of course, by jerking the cotter-key string. You are then free to handle the dog on a check cord. He can be slowed down to prevent a catch and/or somersaulted when he hits the end of the rope as punishment for chasing.

Pigeons can also be dizzied before they're planted. They'll lie quietly without being seen. This works with the bird pin or without. Tuck the head under one wing, hold it in position with your hand, then swing your arm around and around like a windmill. Lay the bird gently on the wing that covers its head. Place the pigeon in cover in such a way that the grass or weeds help prevent the bird from rolling over. The bird may stay in this position ten minutes or more while you bring the dog hunting into the vicinity. If you want the bird to "wake up" quicker, don't swing it. Just tuck its head under the wing, hold it there a moment, then gently lay the bird in the weeds.

Assuming that the dog has already demonstrated adequate bird interest as discussed in the section on fun in the field and he is pointing, we can begin to bear down on making him staunch. Hunt him on a check cord. When he points, try to be close to the rope. If he's so quick to break that you have to approach him from behind with your hands on the rope, croon your coming with a soft, low whoa-a-a-a. If the dog is already fairly staunch, approach slowly from the side so he can see you coming and be less nervous about it. Never approach on the run or excitedly.

The dog may break before you reach him. Dive for the check cord and rear back on it when he hits the end. Dump him hard. You can yell "whoa" if you like, but don't do it until your hands are on the rope, and you're sure you can enforce the command. Actually, I don't think "whoa" is necessary. The unceremonious somersault he gets for chasing is enough. Then he knows it happened because he chased birds, not because you yelled "whoa" and he didn't stop.

If you get to the dog before he breaks, gently grasp his collar with your left hand (for insurance) and stroke him from head to tail while you croon whoa-a-a. As the dog becomes more staunch, pick him up by the tail and turn him. Stroke upward on the underside of his tail to style him. Pull his tail gently. He'll lean forward intensely. Push down on his front shoulders. He'll stand high and rigidly. Push forward on his haunches gently. No predator wants to be shoved into the prey; *he* wants to pick the movement. And so the dog will resist steadily. Dogs love to be handled on point. Learning to expect and anticipate it helps make them staunch. Handling also improves style.

Jack Godsil uses a long buggy whip while teaching whoa during obedience lessons. When the dog begins standing fairly well without restraint, Jack walks around in front of the dog much like a hunter will later to flush the birds. If the dog begins to break command, Jack orders "whoa" and slaps him across the front legs with the whip. Actually the "swishing" sound of the whip frightens the dog more than the slap. Later, when teaching staunchness on birds, Jack can caution a creeping dog with just the sound of the whip. Later still, when teaching steadiness to wing, Jack uses the whip to flush birds. Every time the whip swishes, the dog regards it as a whoa command. His steadiness is greatly reinforced.

Godsil gets control established while working in a small enclosure. This includes basic obedience and working birds while on a check cord. The dog will advance to a larger enclosure for greater running area to test his behavior before going to the open field. This practice has several advantages. The trainer is more relaxed because the dog can't run off before he's under control. The dog can be caught quickly for correction when necessary. The dog understands what's expected of him before he goes to the field. The handler doesn't have the fight a dog creates in the field when he has to try to put it all together at once.

(Perhaps we'd better reiterate that this is not the very beginning of training. As we've stated before, pointing dogs should be taken to the field to gain birdiness before they're taught formal obedience. Godsil tests his trainees in the field and gives them all the early bird chasing he thinks they need. He even runs with them to encourage chase in timid dogs or those that lack desire. We are now at the point where birdiness is already established, and the dog is to be brought under control.)

A large enclosure is also helpful in shortening range. If you want the dog to hunt at his full natural range, there's no need for this. But if you want a 60- or 70-yard dog, and your new Pointer runs twice that range, work him in an enclosure. If that's not possible, try to find parallel fences about as far apart as you want the dog to range. They'll act as barriers of sorts. Start the dog quartering in the direction of one of the fences. Just as he nears the fence, blow the whistle for attention. When he looks, point in the direction of the opposite fence as a hand signal and walk toward it. A dog is easier to turn just as he approaches an obstacle.

Jack uses one sharp blast on the whistle for whoa, twitters or trills for come, and turns the dog with two blasts. I differ only in preferring a long whistle to turn the dog. Let me point out, however, that Jack is the one earning his living by training dogs. And, come to think of it, I don't carry a whistle for a short-range dog, and then I turn him with two sharp notes between my teeth. But there is one thing about whistles we're in

To develop steadiness, Vuillemot has an assistant bring up the dog. He stands behind the planted bird and has extra pigeons stuffed in his shirt or coat pockets.

absolute accord on. Jack doesn't hack on a dog or keep nagging him with a whistle. And I think there's nothing more intolerable to man or dog than someone coming through a field whistling like a traffic cop in downtown St. Louis.

Whistles have their uses and can be abused, of course. They're essential with wide dogs, and get attention quicker than the voice does with any dogs. Godsil introduces whistle signals when the dog begins to come under control during obedience lessons.

Most trainers introduce the new whistle command immediately after giving the command. "Whoa!" One sharp blast. I've noticed that the whistle can also be given before the voice command, and before long the dog anticipates the spoken order and reacts to the whistle. Either way works.

Although the dog was introduced to gunfire long ago, I haven't yet mentioned shooting birds for him. Actually, we can do that any time we'd like to reward the dog for work well done no matter what stage of

If the dog creeps, George flips out a bird. The dog comes to recognize that his movements cause the birds to flush. He learns to point staunchly and to remain steady to wing in the bargain.

training, but a bird should be shot only when the dog has handled it correctly. *Never kill a bird the dog has flushed.* From then on he won't want to point.

Another thing I'd better emphasize is *never let your dog catch a bird.* That can happen easily when working with pigeons or young game birds that aren't properly conditioned to fly. It sometimes happens when old birds are released in an unfamiliar area. And then there are days when pen-raised birds, even old ones that have flown before in training, just won't cooperate. They sit like idiots instead of flushing at the sensible time. But if your dog catches a bird once, he'll think he can do it every time. And he'll try every time. If it does happen, it's back to severe discipline to stop the dog from chasing. It may help to discontinue bird training for several weeks while the memory fades.

The last "never" comes from C. L. Owens, head trainer of Gunsmoke Kennels. *"Never shoot the first bird your dog points,"* Owens said, "or I'll guarantee he'll flush the next one." Practice this throughout the early training.

Owens advises letting the dog point a couple of pheasants, but make him stay steady to flush and shot. Then kill one for the dog. That brings up the eternal argument: to be, or not to be, steady.

Dogs entered in field trials must be steady to wing and shot, moving only when sent on. Trainers involved with field trials insist that they want to flush the birds while the dog watches. If a bird is shot, the dog is paying attention and can mark the fall better. If there are other birds in the area, they aren't being chased out of the country by a wild-running dog while the gunner reloads. This is considered good dog manners.

The average argument against requiring the dog to be steady to shot is based on the notion that the sooner the dog gets into motion, the less chance there is of a bird getting away crippled.

The fact is, the hunter is too wrapped up in gunning at that moment to pay attention to restraining his dog. It's hard to do, so why bother with field trial niceties when the hunter sees no real advantage in it? The field trialer did bother, is proud of his dog's training and manners, and regards the custom highly.

Two old hands at the game offer some entirely different arguments, however. My father, William Mueller, now in his seventies, always trained his Pointers to hold staunchly until he arrived and got in a ready position. On command, the dogs went in and flushed the birds. "Why the hell should I get in the brush or briars or timber and get all tangled up so I can't shoot when the birds get up?"

Dad expected his experienced dogs to pay attention to which birds were shot and where they fell, but he didn't expect them to stop to shot and stand until sent. If the dogs couldn't mark the fall properly, Dad didn't get excited because he wasn't that dependent

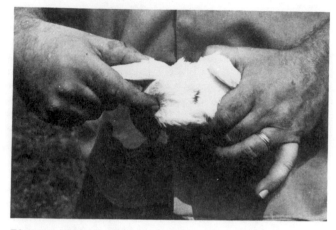

Pigeons can be planted with or without cages. To plant without, tuck head under one wing.

Then lay bird in weeds so wing with head under it is on the bottom. If you want the bird to "wake up" quicker don't swing it for the extra dizzying.

on the dogs. He did the shooting and also marked the fall. He could get a dog to the vicinity in a hurry. His way might not suit anyone else, but I will say he lost few birds.

Veteran of more than forty years, Roy Speece says that he used to go so far as to use blanks in a pistol to train his dogs to break with the shot. The shot was the command to fetch.

"You see I am a hunter and, I like to think, also a conservationist," Roy says. "No dog alive can retrieve as large a percentage of wild birds if steady to shot as it would retrieve if allowed to break with the shot. The argument that we may miss a shot at a straggler if we do not hold our dogs is rationalizing the anti-conservation of cripples in favor of getting one more shot. And I have been accused of being a meat hunter! I do not retrieve 100 percent of my birds and anybody who claims that they do just hasn't hunted much. I do retrieve every single bird possible within the abilities of my dog and myself. I am sure that holding a dog for even seconds would lessen my percentage of retrieves.

"If you drop a running pheasant where other pheasants have been loafing, there seems to develop a maze of scents that the best of dogs cannot untangle. In this case it's often a sight retrieve or none at all—and no field trial man with his 'steady-to-shot' dog is going to talk me out of this. Another example of saving birds that would be lost with the added seconds from a steady-to-shot dog is where a bird can get under large brush piles or even go to ground . . . "

If Roy's bird is missed, he stops the dog with a whoa and continues on the hunt. More of Roy's methods will be found in the section on versatile dog training.

Of all of these practices, which one is right? Very obviously, they are all right for someone. Pick out what works for you, your dog, the birds you hunt, the area you hunt and the customs you prefer. But don't consider the other fellow's practice as completely wrong just because you didn't happen to do it that way.

However you want your dog to handle birds, the important thing is to make up your mind, be consistent in the training and get the dog into lots of birds. Birds! Birds! Birds! Lots of birds! That's what makes a bird dog.

There are rarely enough wild birds available for a man to train a dog today in a reasonable amount of time. Pigeons are the cheapest birds for training, and they can be used over and over if you keep a pen of homers. Plant them, let the dog point, but shoot few. The rest will fly home again. A homer pen should have a "trap" that allows birds in but not out. If you train at a distance from home, train the birds by first releasing them a few blocks from home, then a mile in the direction of the training grounds. Keep extending their flights until they know the route and you won't have any lost birds.

Jack Godsil likes to start dogs on a single quail because they hold well and have a strong, attractive scent. But it requires more concentration on the part of the dog than a covey does. Young quail will stay in one spot if tossed tail first into grass or weeds with an underhand motion while you move on. Small release cages are available that allow you to be sure where the birds will be.

After a while, some dogs get wise to the man scent on these birds and don't quite take the game seriously. They may not point as intensely. Tails drop or wag. A far better method for continued training is a quail recall pen.

You've probably heard quail giving their recall whistles after you've flushed and split a covey. If left alone, they'll regroup quickly. Quail regard a pen as home. If you release half of a covey, the ones in the pen will call them back. A funnel-shaped entrance lets birds in easily, but they almost never manage to get out. In an hour or two all the birds will be back in the pen if you didn't drive any of them out of the quarter-mile recall range.

A fairly large pen can be built in the training area, or a smaller portable unit can be carried any place you go. Either way, the birds are fed and watered and housed continually in their pen. If you use Purina game-bird feed, grit isn't necessary for digestion. If you use a grain mixture, keep a container of sand in the pen.

Dogs like to be handled on point. Style them by stroking up the underside of the tail.

With a fairly steady dog, Godsil flushes the bird himself, ready to shoot the blank pistol, and also ready to blast "whoa" with the whistle if the dog is overcome by temptation.

When dogs are ready for steadying to wing and shot, Godsil has an assistant toss birds after the point.

At first, only allow a couple of birds out at a time. Place them just outside of the pen carefully. Try to avoid making them fly. They'll run around the pen until they find their way back in. After a couple of weeks and all of the birds are experienced, half can be released and flown. The other half will call them back. Let females out one day, males another. If let out together, they might build a nest somewhere.

These birds become strong fliers and are not contaminated with man scent. If a dozen or two are housed in the recall pen, that means six to twelve possible bird experiences for the dog every time out. And that's what it takes to make a finished dog.

Single quail can be planted and flown with a bright ribbon tied to one leg to tire the bird and make it easy to find again. The bird may fly two or three times before tiring out enough to be caught. Pheasants are planted (head under wing and dizzied) and flown in the same manner, but a stick is usually tied to one leg. It's always tied to one leg to unbalance the bird in flight.

Young pheasants will recall to a pen, especially if they were raised in it. They also hold well for dogs and are big and easy for the young dog to hunt. When older, they run ahead of the dogs and often quit returning to the pen.

After the dog has worked birds for a few months, and before he hunts with another dog, he should learn to honor or back another dog's point. Keep your young dog on a check cord until the old dog points. Unless the youngster instinctively honors from a distance, bring him within several feet of the old dog and stack

him up. Use the methods described earlier to staunch the dog. Have an assistant flush and shoot the bird. Grip the collar to ensure steadiness to wing and shot. Practice this until the youngster backs as soon as he sees another dog on point.

If you're training the young dog to be steady to wing and shot, retrieving shouldn't be allowed until he's under perfect control. Substitute that reward with praise and letting the dog smell the bird after you fetched it. When your dog is ready for it, use the methods described in the Retriever training section.

You may prefer to strengthen steadiness by only allowing the dog to point dead birds instead of retrieving them. Some dogs do this naturally.

If your plan is a perfectly mannered dog, steady to wing and shot, don't get overly hurried. He may be a two-year-old before you can achieve it. Even then he may make mistakes. It may take a full three years to achieve absolute steadiness. But that doesn't mean the dog can't be gunned over during that time. In fact, hunt him as hard and often as you can and keep administering correction as needed.

It's a splendid thing to train and hunt a dog—next, perhaps, to teaching a boy and watching him enjoy the happiness of hunting. Don't miss it.

Retriever Training

Retrievers benefit greatly from puppy play and early guidance, so if you haven't read the first three sections on training, do so now. On that basis, we'll add some special Retriever puppy play and build onto obedience lessons those things which are essential to fetching. If you own a Pointer or Setter, you may not want to study water work. If you have one of the versatile breeds, you probably will. Retrieving lessons are essentially the same for all breeds, but taking hand signals isn't so important for pointing dogs. You'll probably be hunting the dead bird right there with the dog, anyway, if it's a hard one to find.

If played with enough, Retriever puppies will fetch before they're weaned. They can even be introduced to birds at that tender age. Tie the wings of a pigeon together, and let it walk the puppy pen. Before long the pup will be following, then sniffing, then carrying. Make sure the wings are securely tied. Getting rapped on the nose with the leading edge of a pigeon wing may cure a pup of birds for months.

Tommy Sorenson, professional Retriever trainer and field-trial handler of Wentzville, Missouri, and winner of the 1973 National Championship with Baird's Centerville Sam, starts pups with dead birds to make sure there's nothing frightening about the in-

troduction of feathers. The bite of a duck applied to the end of a nose can cause a severe setback to a pup or to an older but timid dog.

To interest a puppy in retrieving, just roll something in front of him. Try a sock stuffed with rags. He'll pounce on it in play, shake it a bit and perhaps carry it—maybe even to you. If he does, act like Isabella greeting Columbus arriving with a boatload of gold. If he doesn't, clap your hands, and call his name. He may not deliver it at all, but don't worry. This is building interest, not obedience. Don't force him.

At this point, Tommy advises letting children play with the pup for socialization, but don't allow them to attempt training at any time. Children are usually too soft and lack the judgment needed to make the right training decision.

As the pup grows older, play will come nearer to the real thing. Begin sending him after the dummy with "fetch" or whatever command you'll use later. Probably most trainers send with the word "back." Some field trialers send with the dog's name on the theory

This is a pheasant recall pen at Gunsmoke Kennels. Young birds hold well for dogs and return readily; old birds do neither. Funnel-shaped "throats," like throats in fish traps, are installed around the pen at eye level for pheasants. That allows them to get in, but not out.

Trainer George Vuillemot approaches a young dog on point by coming up the check cord — otherwise the beginning dog may jump for the planted bird as you approach.

that no one else's command can possibly set the dog in motion at the wrong time. The dog doesn't care what word you use as long as it's used consistently.

Not being consistent and sufficiently repetitious is what Sorenson regards as the amateur trainer's worst problem. It's also possible to overtrain a dog—that is, drive him so hard in such long sessions that he becomes stale. Fortunately, undertraining is less harmful, and that is the amateur's more common failing.

Never let the pup or young dog chew the dummy. He may become hard-mouthed. He'll want you to play tug of war with the dummy, of course, but don't allow that either.

Very likely, the pup will think up the game of touch football just as soon as his legs are long enough to run. He'll carry the ball, and you're supposed to see if you're fast enough to lay a hand on him. Don't fall for it. Begin lessons inside a garage or basement away

from distractions and where you can easily catch him when necessary. This is also a good place to teach obedience later on.

After the pup is fairly reliable about bringing you the dummy, work him outside with a check cord. But try not to use the cord any more than necessary. If the youngster still wants to run and play with the dummy or circle you instead of making a direct delivery, run backwards, calling and clapping your hands. He'll chase you. As he catches up, drop to his level and accept the dummy. Praise him as though it was all his idea.

Remember, this is fun and preliminary training. Don't get demanding on anything, like sitting until sent or other formal manners. It's just chase and fetch. Encourage delivery to hand by moving back if he's inclined to drop it, but never demand it. *Never* run or even walk toward a dog to accept the dummy. He'll tend to stop short or even run away. Later on the dog will be inclined to drop the dummy or bird several feet before he gets to you.

Further bird interest can be developed by letting the youngster chase pigeons after he's perhaps five months old. Clip most of the wing primaries and let the dog smell the bird. Tease him just a bit. Make him want it. Then toss the bird. It will fly only several yards. But it will make considerable commotion in the process and give the dog sufficient encouragement to chase.

As the young dog demonstrates that he is interested and will retrieve birds, begin tossing pigeons with fewer and fewer primaries clipped. The birds will be flying farther and farther, and the pup's range will begin to stretch.

To improve marking, have an assistant carry a dead bird (or one that won't flutter far) to a distance in an open field. Have him call for attention. ("Mark" is a good command for this.) Then he tosses the bird. If the dog has been introduced to gunfire (as he should have been by now) have the assistant fire a .22 blank as he throws the bird. Send your dog for the retrieve.

Young, inexperienced retrievers have difficulty with distant falls. They want to run out several yards and begin the search. Have the assistant move farther and farther out to increase the young dog's range and improve his marking.

To begin water work, Tommy Sorenson recommends swimming with the dog. He'll catch on quicker, be less fearful and love water all the more. Swimming with the dog is how this all started for Tommy. When only a youngster himself, he bought a Lab pup named Rick for $35. "I'd take him in swimming with me," Tommy said, "and if I'd dive, he'd go underwater after me. Sometimes he'd wait and grab my hand as it came up."

When Rick was a year old, Sorenson entered him in a Minnesota field trial and got talked into an all-age entry. Rick took second behind a four-year-old Lab, and Tommy was offered $1,000 for his dog right after the trial.

Rick wasn't sold, but it was a turning point. "I thought about being offered $1,000 for having all that fun training a dog," Tommy said, "and right then I decided that's what I want to do." He has been doing just that ever since. He started with Tony Berger while in college, and trained privately for Mr. and Mrs. Mahlon Wallace, Jr., for six years, but he has been a professional for the past fifteen years.

If you're not a swimmer, wade in and encourage the pup to follow. If he already loves the dummy, roll it into the water a foot from shore. Keep increasing the distance, and he'll soon be fetching as far as you can throw.

When the youngster shows water love, introduce decoys. Tommy starts by tossing a dummy or shackled duck fairly close to shore so the dog has a nearby incentive. Then he sends the dog on a line that takes

him through decoys placed on land. If the dog indicates he's going to investigate a decoy, growl "leave it," or simply "no," in a gruff voice. He probably will. Or he will after hearing your disapproval several times. If he persists, disapprove with a slingshot.

Taking a line through floating decoys follows after the dog ignores those on land.

Some waterfowlers never want their Retrievers to touch a decoy, period. I prefer the dog to bring back whatever I send him for and leave everything else alone. I've been in too many situations where I needed my dog to retrieve the decoys. That doesn't happen on the river when the spread consists of blocks tied in tandem, but it's common in pothole situations. The best place for decoys may be in water over your boots or waders. I feel it's the dog's job to do the swimming. Tommy agrees. You can make up your own mind according to your hunting circumstances. If you elect to have a decoy retriever, wait until he's doing well at taking a line through temptations, then send him for a single decoy. Practice that, then increase the number.

Early water work is also a good time to teach the dog he must deliver to you directly. If he's still trying to run around you on land, start emphasizing water

Experienced dogs can handle live birds, but the bite of an irate duck on the end of a tender nose can make a pup bird-shy for some time.

Restrain the dog before sending him to fetch the dummy to see if the retriever is ready for serious obedience training.

work. He'll see you waiting on shore, and he'll try to avoid swimming directly to you. He can't change direction very fast in the water. Wherever he goes, move down the shoreline with him and be right there as he leaves the water. He'll finally get the idea that there's no use trying to avoid the inevitable. If practiced enough, the conditioning often carries over to land work.

Having mentioned practicing enough, it might be well to point out that we can progress from one thing to another quite rapidly in a book. The dog needs a great amount of repetition in all phases of training, despite how good he looks one day. When you think he has one thing down pat, keep practicing it another month or two.

Tommy suggests you also observe the young dog's degree of ambition. All the young dogs look forward to their play period at Sorenson's kennels, but he notices some are sluggish at work. Such dogs should get out

only when working. Then working becomes the diversion they look forward to.

Sometime between five and eight months of age, the dog may be ready for obedience. Time depends on the amount of inborn enthusiasm as well as preliminary conditioning up to this point. Don't start strict obedience too early or it will dull his interest. You'll have a mediocre mechanical mutt instead of a guided missile with brains.

One easy way to tell is to begin demanding that the dog remain steady until sent. If that slows the dog to a jog when he goes to fetch the dummy, forget obedience for now. Go back to teasing with the dummy, throwing excitedly and letting the dog chase it at will. Preserving enthusiasm is more important than saving time.

To steady the dog before being sent, make him sit before you toss the dummy. Restrain him by the collar. Make a short throw. Switch hands on the collar so your left arm is free to swing out before his nose to guide him on the line. That takes a few seconds and teaches the dog he must wait until you say it's time to go. Send him with enthusiasm in your voice command.

If the dog doesn't show evidence of dampened spirits, make throws and waits progressively longer.

Now put him through obedience as outlined in a previous section. Ease up if he gets dull. Keep it fun by making the sessions brief. Ten or fifteen minutes daily for two or three weeks will make an amazingly well-behaved animal. You'll have to continue less-frequent reinforcements, of course, but the groundwork can be established in a very short time.

With obedience under way, it's now easy to make the dog sit before you when he delivers the dummy or bird. That might be an unnecessary nicety. A great many hunters are satisfied if the dog brings a bird and drops it anywhere near them. I much prefer the delivery to hand because a dropped cripple might fly away. I have a strong conscience about letting cripples escape.

If the dog comes to think he must sit before dropping the bird, there are no premature drops. To establish this, the dog has to come all the way in to you. Trot backwards if necessary at first. Don't advance toward him. When he arrives, bring your hand under his chin to hold his mouth shut and order him to sit. Then say "give" or "out" and accept the delivery.

A dog that gives trouble in this respect should be worked in the water exclusively until the problem is cured. Rarely will the dog drop a dummy or bird while still in the water. And you can always be right at water's edge to prevent a premature drop.

Maybe your dog behaves exactly opposite. He doesn't care to give up the bird. With the thumb and middle finger of your left hand forming a U under the dog's jaw, press his lips against the rear molars on both sides of his mouth. Say "give," and take the bird with your other hand.

Professional trainer Jack "Robby" Robinson, of Chillicothe, Illinois, gives an example of another method. He tells about a hardheaded Retriever that was owned by a fellow who kept up a constant stream of chatter. The dog, of course, tuned him out and did as he pleased, keeping the duck until he was good and ready to drop it or eat it, whichever whim suited his preference at the moment. One day, however, a veteran Illinois River waterfowler joined them in a hunt and offered his help with the dog. The first thing he did was take the knothead behind a building when the owner wasn't around.

When it was fairly well understood who was boss, they went hunting. The riverman accompanied the dog away from the blind on its first retrieve. The knothead brought it to him but was reluctant to give it up. The riverman grabbed an ear, jerked it up, blew in it hard and the duck came right out of the dog's mouth.

Tommy demonstrates the ear-pinch method of force training. The dog automatically opens its mouth and receives the dummy. The dog learns that the sooner he grabs the dummy, the quicker the mild pain is relieved.

Retrievers should sit before giving up the bird. A crippled duck dropped on the ground could get up and fly off.

The owner was ecstatic. "What in the world did you say to the dog to make him release that duck?" he wanted to know.

If you have a knothead that keeps testing your authority, don't forget there were *two* very useful corrections in Robby's story.

We haven't mentioned a thing about force training. Although we are already forcing the dog to do things our way, the accepted definition of force training includes the use of pain. The dog opens his mouth and accepts the dummy or he feels the pain of his ear being pinched between his collar and the trainer's thumb. He learns to reach out a few inches, then a few feet, to grab the dummy to avoid the pain.

It really isn't all that much pain, but as Tommy Sorenson says, it's the most distasteful part of dog training. He once refused a good job offer with another trainer because force training was going to be his task. I used the method on my first Retriever and haven't since. The pain didn't hurt him to amount to anything. What hurt him—and me—was who was administering the pain. He looked to me with complete trust

and I was violating that trust by hurting him for no reason he could understand.

The first time my present dog had to break ice, he tried valiantly. He'd reach out and lunge, trying to get on top of it. I could see that the footing collapsing underneath him was shaking his confidence, so I shouted encouragement. But he came back. Twice more I sent him and he finally got to within six feet of the duck, then he quit entirely and would not take the line a fourth time. I had a long walk through deep muck to get around that marsh, and I had to get him within a yard of the bird before his confidence was restored enough to make the retrieve. We had a quick fun game of chase and fetch right then to restore his mental attitude. Had I force-trained that dog, he may have completed the retrieve the first time I sent him. But I don't mind occasionally having to go with a dog in a hunting siutuation. I think most hunters aren't fussy about that. You have to make the choice.

Field trial dogs must be absolutely reliable, of course, and I think if a professional recommended force training on a bold dog he was training for me, I'd let him do it. But I wouldn't.

If a dog of a retriever breed has to be force trained to make him fetch at all, replace him. There are too many good prospects around. A Pointer or Setter frequently won't have these retrieving instincts and may require force training if you insist they fetch your birds. The continental or versatile breeds usually have more retrieving instincts, and some are quite good. You may want to force train to make the dog a more dependable retriever. I'm not criticizing the method. I just don't like to do it.

As the dog becomes proficient in obedience, add whistle signals. Command "sit," then blow one sharp blast. After practice, the dog will respond to the whistle alone. Begin sending the dog with two rapid notes. While it isn't necessary to send a dog with the whistle in a hunting siutuation, and you probably won't do it, it will be useful later in handling the dog at a distance. Twitter or trill the whistle to recall the dog.

I told Tommy Sorenson that I think nothing mystifies the beginner more than casting a dog to right or left. It's easy to send the dog out or call it in, but the fellow with his first dog starts waving his arm in an "over" command, and nothing happens. Tommy uses two good methods. (Incidently, I've blurred my own ideas with Tommy's in much of this. I've tried to put it together in a way I think a new hunter and a new dog might be able to train each other. If the methods or sequence don't seem right to other pro field-trial trainers, please give me the blame, not Tommy.)

Tommy's first method of starting the dog on handling is probably the one an amateur will choose because it requires no special facilities. A dummy can be used, but a live, shackled bird will provide more incentive. Set the dog in front of you. Carry the bird several yards to your left while the dog watches.

Trainer Tommy Sorenson starts his dogs on dead birds. Later, shackled live birds are used . . .

but bills are taped to prevent young dogs from being nipped.

Return and face the dog. Now send the dog from that position with your left arm pointing and your body moving in the direction of the bird. Do the same on your right. Send the dog each time with the two-note whistle. Practice and praise.

When the dog gets used to being sent from this new position back away a step and repeat the practice. Back off progressively farther as the dog catches on. Also place the bird progressively farther away.

While this is going on, make the dog sit to the whistle occasionally while bringing in a dummy. Get him used to stopping and sitting to the one sharp blast of the whistle no matter where he is. After considerable practice, this can all be put together. The dog can be sent, stopped, then moved right or left. Always make it a 90-degree change in direction; never try varying angles.

Tommy also uses a baseball diamond mowed in a field of fairly low cover. A crossroad also joins the four bases with the pitcher's mound in the center. The dog tends to run down the mowed aisle, so direction comes easy and veering off the line is minimized. Standing at home plate, for example, the dog can be sent after retrieves from three different directions. Tommy uses the pitcher's mound crossroad to teach hand signals.

The dog and Tommy stand at the crossroad. The bird or dummy may be placed to the right or left or down the leg behind the dog. Again, the dog has seen them placed. I already explained the right or left hand signals. To send the dog for the bird placed behind him, Tommy raises his arm straight up, then blows the two-note whistle. Now the dog can be sent back, right or left with hand signals and brought in with the "come" whistle.

To increase distance, Tommy moves back while the dog continues working from the crossroad.

By placing birds to right and left, then adding back, we can introduce doubles then triples. The same thing can be done without the diamond and earlier, too, if desired, with dummies and birds on both land and water. During the first multiple retrieves, send the dog first to the dummy thrown last. He'll remember that one best and be inclined to head for it anyway. As the dog comes under better control, you'll be able to send him in any sequence desired.

Tommy starts blind retrieves after the dog marks well, has been through obedience, and can do doubles and triples on land and water. However, the basis for blind retrieves can be laid earlier if you like. After the dog is taking a line easily, drop a dummy a few feet behind you—not far—but don't let the dog see or hear you do it. Now turn the dog and face him in the direction of the dummy. Send him. He'll run a few steps out of habit before he remembers he didn't see a

Dogs should be trained to go through decoys early. If you wait until opening day, your dog may retrieve several decoys before he ever gets to the duck.

Tommy uses a mowed "baseball diamond" to teach taking a straight line, handling singles, doubles and triples, and learning hand signals.

dummy thrown. But by the time he's inclined to stop, there's the dummy right under his nose. He'll get used to trusting you. When you send him, there's something to retrieve. The distance can be gradually increased. This confidence is essential before beginning long retrieves controlled by hand signals.

One of the most annoying things a retriever does is climb out of water onto an island or point of land and begin searching for the fall when he knows good and well, or should, that the bird is in the water and farther on. Even to a well-controlled dog, islands and points are magnets. Hide an accomplice with a slingshot on the island or point. If the dog is stung a few times for getting out on islands and points, they'll lose their attraction.

A real problem retrieve is on the opposite shore of a lake, creek or ditch. If the dog starts from well back from the water, he thinks the bird should be on his side. He doesn't swim across. If he starts with a water entry, he thinks the bird should be on the edge of the shore or bank. He will rarely work back far enough. During training, be sure to set up this situation because it's going to happen on the hunt.

Start with a simple retrieve from the edge of the opposite shore. Gradually move the starting point back from shore, but keep the dummy at the same

place. After the dog is entering water from a fairly long land run, begin moving the dummy farther from the water's edge.

How old is the dog before he achieves all of this? Two, perhaps? There's no rule. It depends on the dog. Tommy points out, however, that while much can be taught at a very early age, judgment and proficiency come with age. "One of the Wallaces' dogs was doing double blind retrieves at six months. He compared to a hunting dog of three years. But it still took six years before the dog became a field champion."

Obviously, no one waits for perfection before taking a dog hunting. Teach the youngster what you can and after introduction to gunfire, take him hunting at your first opportunity. It's amazing how quickly these water dogs catch on.

Flushing Dog Training

As "whoa" is the single most important command for pointing breeds, so is "hup" for flushing dogs. It doesn't matter if it's "sit" or "hup," but the dog must understand the order in four languages: English, shotgun, bird flush and whistle. The single most important objective for the flushing dog trainer is to

The dog has seen which leg of the "crossroad" Tommy has chosen to plant the dummy, but he sits until sent.

Tommy tips off the direction with his hand and by turning . . . then sends by extending his arm and moving in that direction.

bring the dog under exacting controls without diminishing its desire to hunt.

As advisor, counselor and demonstrator in these matters, I am privileged to have had the help of Clifford Wallace, of Wadsworth, Illinois. During his active years, he was one of the world's all-time great dog trainers. I'll begin with some of the things that made Cliff outstanding because the more an amateur trainer can emulate him, the better his chances of success.

My father was making conversation with an assistant trainer one day and said, "You really have to love dogs to train them for a living, don't you?" The reply was, "I don't think so. Sometimes I don't care anything about them *at all!*" With that viewpoint, I doubt if he'll ever train a great dog.

I also recall Jack Godsil saying, "I don't think anybody can properly train an animal he doesn't like."

Cliff says simply, "I like them." The behavior of Cliff's dogs reveals how much, and maybe more important, exactly how. It's the how that can give us guidance.

Cliff's handling of John Olin's Saighton's Sizzler in the 1970 English Springer Spaniel National Champi-

onship made an indelible impression on my mind. The official guns had an unexplained run of bad luck and missed five out of six birds. Sizzler had to push out pheasant after pheasant before they managed to drop the dog's second bird to complete his retrieving test. Every new bird was another chance to make a mistake, and I'm sure Cliff felt the pressure. But it didn't show, and he didn't complain. He and Sizzler pushed on with relentless determination and turned misfortune into a most spectacular win.

That wasn't Cliff's most spectacular achievement, however. Shortly after the championship, he suffered a stroke that made speech almost impossible. With the same relentless determination, Cliff set out to beat his handicap by persistent self-training. He won the biggest part of the battle in time to bring Sizzler back for another try at the National Championship in 1971. Incredibly, he won it again.

But winning was nothing new for Cliff Wallace. There was a time when easterners didn't even recognize the midwestern field-trial circuit. Cliff and Solo Event, owned by James Simpson, Jr., were largely responsible for changing that by being almost impossible to beat wherever they went.

The arm straight up means back. The dog remembers the dummy is behind him, and spins around to make the retrieve.

As the dog becomes accustomed to being sent right, left and back, Tommy moves farther and farther back from the crossroad where the dog is working. It then becomes easy for the dog to accept hand signals from a distance.

Wallace was also highly successful in Retriever trials. But it wasn't his illustrious field-trial record that impressed me most. *How* he did it was what interested me.

During the 1970 stake, Cliff walked Sizzler up to the gallery with the dog on leash and waited his turn to compete. Compared to other Springers that walked in at heel and sat patiently without restraint, Sizzler didn't put on much of a show. And then Cliff cast the dog in front of the judges.

Talk about control! Most handlers yell voice commands or blast whistles. Sizzler never looked directly at Cliff—he was hunting pheasants—but out of the corner of his eye he was constantly aware of Cliff's every movement. Cliff would turn his body in a very subdued version of the "body English" a bowler might use when unconsciously trying to turn his ball into the pocket for a strike. Sizzler turned with him and quartered the field, literally sizzling across the ground. If Sizzler reached out too far, Cliff stepped back and the dog drew in.

Cliff used only a small, inoffensive-sounding whistle when it was necessary to stop the dog. I deeply admire anyone who can control a dog quietly. It means the

dog knows what is expected and wants to do it. It means the trainer has confidence in the dog because they have worked together endlessly. Most of all, it means there's a man-dog rapport on a far more satisfying level than the master-servant relationship with which too many of us are content.

I learned later that Cliff places little emphasis on teaching heel, sometimes not bothering with it, because a Springer Spaniel should never get the notion that his place in life is at his master's side. His place is up front and hunting. All of Cliff's training emphasizes bringing the dog under exacting control while not at all dulling the edge of its bird-hunting desire.

Cliff's attractive, perceptive wife Polly, told me she believes he was able to get his dogs so revved up in the field because they catch his own tense feeling of urgency, especially in field trials.

Chances are you've already noticed several things about Cliff's manner of training that an aspiring Spaniel trainer can do well to imitate. Patience, determination, working at it frequently, but never long enough to let the dog go stale; these are beginnings. Quiet control comes from adding the same **things that make a good parent: sharp and adequate**

Of dogs, trainer Cliff Wallace simply says, "I like them."
Their behavior reveals how much.

When Cliff pets a dog, it is seated before him. With both hands, he lightly strokes or sort of smooths the hair back on both sides of the dog's muzzle and face. Dogs do that to each other with tongues from puppyhood on. The puppy licks the dam's or sire's muzzle to beg for regurgitated food. Later the expression modifies to respect and affection in a solicitous way of saying, "You're superior to me." Later still, mates will build each other's egos with the same licking way of expressing love, for love is certainly the act of an individual regarding a mate as more important to himself than he is. Don't think for a moment that dogs don't recognize humans as having superior intelligence. Imagine, then, what emotions are evoked in a dog when this respected superior being gives him this message of love—and does it in a muzzle-encompassing, two-handed manner that no poor dog with a single tongue could ever hope to match.

If this seems a little far out, try it. I immediately tried it on my own dogs. Every one reacted with the tentative lick that barely passes the lips. Look at the eye expression when a dog licks like that. There's no mistaking it for anything but adoration.

These were my dogs, however, and they already love me. So I tried it on my son-in-law's English Setter. Peggy has a perpetual and rather aloof willful expression in her eyes. It says she is watching for a chance to escape her pen and go hunting. Maybe she has other expressions for Ron, but that's the only one she ever gave me. While I always thought highly of her, I did regard Peggy as unaffectionate. When I petted her as Cliff does a Springer, her tongue came immediately to her lips, and her eyes fairly glazed over with emotion.

Springers also have a little willful streak. They're sensitive, demonstrative and ingratiating, but they'll sometimes use it as a wile to get their own way and you'll hardly realize it happened. Follow Cliff's example in getting the dog's affection, but don't get the notion that it's the whole key to training. Cliff is as tough with discipline as he is generous with affection.

Spaniel training begins with puppy play and fun in the field just as it does for other breeds. If you haven't read the sections on those subjects, do so now. Cliff always started puppies at retrieving before they were weaned. Until eight or nine months old, pups are taken out regularly to run, play and chase birds to their heart's content.

During this play time, groundwork can be laid for quartering and handling. Just don't get strict about it before formal obedience is taught.

The puppy is probably already retrieving socks or dummies. And you may have learned that it's easy to send the dog away from you with a wave of the arm to make the retrieve. Even tossing the dummy with an underhand pitch is conditioning to sending with hand signals. He has reason to want to go. In the field, modify that slightly. When you put him down, start him with an arm motion, but now to right or left. Add

discipline for bad behavior, praise and evident pride for good behavior, and the good sense to be consistent in both.

It may be hard to imitate Cliff's mental attitude so that feelings of urgency, excitement and affection are transmitted to the dog, but try. If you're bored, the dog will be, too.

Cliff pinpoints another feature of dog training that is hard to imitate. It comes with experience to those who have innate good judgment. He says the real secret is not so much what the trainer does but when. He has to recognize when the dog needs just a little more as well as when just a little more would be too much.

I've also noticed that some people seem to have natural mannerisms that evoke deep affection from dogs while others can only get a polite wag of the tail. Dog talk is a language of body movement and facial expression. They're experts in understanding us even when we aren't aware we're saying something. Whether Cliff is aware of what he does or if it's a trait that came naturally, I didn't get to ask. It took a while before I realized I had seen something important. But when Cliff shows a dog affection, he is appealing to all of its natural responses.

a little body movement in that direction, and he'll catch on. Before long, he'll associate arm or hand signals with the direction to take even when he's running in front of you.

Introduce the whistle. A beep-beep gets the dog's attention. Signal and move in the direction of your arm. You can zigzag in the field to a smaller extent to show direction while the dog makes wider casts.

Don't try to turn the dog just as he's about to reach a bush, clump of cover or other objective he wants to investigate. That's asking for and encouraging later disobedience. Whistle and signal when he's starting to turn of his own accord or when no greater attraction is holding his attention.

Spaniels are usually natural quarterers or learn it easily. If you're working with a retriever, it may take a year longer to achieve good control. But a flushing dog should be quartered no more than 25 yards out front and 30 yards to either side of center. That way the diagonal line from you to the dog is always under 40 yards, and game is within gun range. To accustom yourself to that range, it isn't a bad idea to stake off a 60-yard swath down a field of low cover. Walk down the center and try to keep the dog within boundaries. You'll be learning how the dog looks when within proper range.

This is sort of advanced puppy play. We're teaching the dog his job, but we're not insisting that he does it right every time.

If we want the dog to run with his afterburners fired, we'll have to make certain he finds enough of what it takes to build enthusiasm. At first, that can be the dummies he's already accustomed to retrieving in play. Scatter them strategically, and guide him to them. But switch to birds soon. That can be pigeons. Dizzy some and plant them, but don't send the dog until they're awake and ready to fly. Work into the wind so the dog can scent, flush and chase them. If gunfire hasn't been introduced, as outlined in previous sections, wait no longer. While he's chasing and having a ball, introduce the .22 blank and work up to the shotgun.

Spaniels are ideal pheasant dogs. And, of course, pheasants are used in field trials. So that's the bird Cliff dizzies and plants in training. If they're young and not too great a distance from their pen, many will recall. (More details on this in the section on training pointing dogs.) Pigeons will home to their pens easily. Quail recall easily, but Spaniels are rarely used on this bird, although they certainly could be. Whatever birds you plant, don't place them too closely. At this point, he shouldn't be chasing one and flushing others in the process.

When the dog is wildly enthusiastic about finding birds it's time to put him through obedience training as outlined in another section. Make sure that you're not diminishing bird interest by the pressures of obedience. Check him now and then. Ease up if

The most important command to a Spaniel is "hup" or sit. He hups while waiting to get in the vehicle . . .

while waiting to load . . . and while waiting to hunt.

Cliff reinforces the whistle command for hup with a hand signal.

necessary. Keep the pace moving according to your dog's temperament.

After the dog has become obedient to voice commands, add the whistle. He already knows its use in quartering. After the "Hup!" blow one sharp blast. When the dog has heard both commands a number of times, blow the whistle alone, and see if he responds. If not, continue both for a time. Do the same with a twittering whistle for "come."

Teach hup to gunfire in the same way. Whistle hup, then shoot. After a time, he'll hup to shot. This will reinforce steadiness in later hunting situations.

When the dog hups on command every time, even while running, he's all ready to be steadied on birds. This is the most touchy time of the entire training period, Cliff points out. Now the dog has to sit at the flush of the birds he dearly loves to chase. There's always the danger of the dog thinking he's being stopped because he's not supposed to bother those birds. But hit the whistle hard when the bird flies.

Shoot birds for him, but don't allow the dog to retrieve the first one of any day. If he gets the first one, he assumes he's to retrieve them all and will break to shot. That's not too bad, really, but if you want a finished dog, he'll have to be steadied. Don't let him

retrieve every bird after the first one, either, if he's to be steady to wing and shot. Just let him retrieve part of the time so he understands he doesn't go unless commanded. At last, he'll hup to voice, whistle, shot and flush.

There is a definite advantage in having a steady flush dog. He won't be chasing the missed bird down through unhunted cover, flushing all the pheasants along the way.

Work hardest to hup the dog to the whistle. Then flush and shot (if you can concentrate on the dog at that time) can be reinforced by the whistle. When the dog is driving a runner, you can also stop and hold him until you catch up. Then you can urge him onto the track again. There's no use in flushing a bird out of gun range. But get there in a hurry. Pheasants have to be driven hard, or they'll run off and fly out of range anyway.

Retrieving should be taught the Springer or Cocker from a very early age, as we mentioned earlier. They're usually naturals at this, so it takes little effort. If the dog will be used in water work, however, follow instructions in the Retriever training section.

Cliff points out that other breeds of dogs are trained by enhancing what comes naturally. The Spaniel

The whistle and hand tells this Springer to hup before giving up the bird. Cliff's dogs bring him birds as though they're bearing gifts.

hears "no, no" to everything he wants to do most. For that reason, and because of the nature of the dogs, they must be brought along wisely in their training. Rough treatment results in a dog that's more worried about his handler than he is about birds.

Versatile Training

This, I believe, is one of the most fascinating subjects in the book. While the versatile concept is not new in North America, its application in the field has been minimal. And while the extravagant claims for versatile, or so-called all-purpose, dogs have been widely published, few people know and understand the really exciting truth. If you think you've heard it all, what is the meaning of "stöbern"? Have you ever trained a dog on robins? Do you know when a Pointer should become a Springer? Would you start a versatile dog on quail, grouse or pheasants?

Versatile, in North America, means able to handle all types of birds successfully. It means pointing, retrieving from land or water and having the ability to switch from birds like ruffed grouse that spook if crowded to birds like pheasants that won't hold unless they are. Versatile, in North America, does not mean

handling fur, except for a few dogs that point rabbits and trail and retrieve cripples.

In fact, it was the highly touted claims of European dogs being able to work fur and feather alike that destroyed the "all-purpose" or "Alle Gebrauchshund" image on this side of the Atlantic. Impatient and inexperienced trainers were led to believe that these wonder dogs could do everything except sign the hunting license. When confronted with the fact that only expertly and highly trained individual dogs were truly all-purpose, most Americans chose to believe there was no truth in any of it.

The versatile concept is back again, but for an entirely different reason. The idea was promoted after World War II by organized and unorganized efforts to make money. Today the concept is being promoted by organized and unorganized efforts to improve and preserve hunting dogs as opposed to dogs bred for competition. For more on the sponsoring organization, the North American Versatile Hunting Dog Association, and its manner of testing rather than competing dogs, be sure to read the section on versatile trials. The tests also illustrate methods of starting versatile dogs that aren't duplicated in this section.

At any rate, fur is largely ignored by today's versatile trainers. Jerome J. Knap, of Guelph, Ontario, used a German Shorthaired Pointer for trailing a wounded moose, and has a German Wirehaired Pointer doing non-slip retriever duty on rabbits that are brought around by Beagles, but these uses are exceptions. Most versatile breeds do their best work on birds, while hounds excel by far on fur. More of today's hunters also make that division when choosing dogs.

The people who choose versatile breeds are nearly all themselves versatile hunters. Most specialists do better with other dogs. A southern quail hunter, for example, would penalize himself if he bought a close-working Griffon to hunt bobwhites exclusively.

A great many of these versatile hunters are surprised when asked how their dogs make the switch from pheasants to ruffed grouse. They never thought about it. Their dogs made the transition without problems, so there was no reason to study how they managed it. But it is a fact that all birds handle differently. Bobwhite quail hold beautifully if not crowded. Western quail run and Hungarian partridge like to flush ahead of hunters. A dog that slams into pheasants silently, swiftly and suddenly can hold them. They run ahead of a slow, cautious dog. But a slower dog can learn to handle pheasants by crowding the birds every time they run. The ruffed grouse is unpredictable and easily spooked if the least bit crowded. Sharptail grouse, prairie chickens and sage hens hold well if encountered suddenly. Chukar coveys like to run uphill to escape, but singles hold well.

It's easy to start quartering from a hup position off to the side . . .

. . . just whistle and walk in the direction you want the dog to run.

Obviously, the dog has to make adjustments. Can this ability be trained into a dog or must it be native, inherent intelligence or a combination of both?

Dr. Fred Z. White, whose Brittany Spaniel Saxon successfully hunted ruffed grouse, pheasants, quail, prairie chickens, chukar and woodcock, believes versatility can be enhanced by starting the dog on the right game.

"The dog that cat-walks, trying to get closer, bumps his birds," Dr. White said. "Saxon was started on quail that he didn't dare crowd. That education stuck although he learned to road pheasants later. When we switched to grouse, the dog had no trouble at all."

Trainer Bill Kepler, of Oneida, Wisconsin, solves the problem by adhering to field-trial practices. "I want to flush the bird," Bill says. His dogs are to hold point until tapped on the head or told to move up on a running pheasant. Then his dogs don't crowd the birds when Bill wants to switch to grouse.

"The dog tells you when the pheasant has moved," Bill added. "He'll slacken his point, slowly wag his tail, or give some indication that the bird is gone."

The most unusual versatile training method comes from a most unusual hunter. If you've encountered him before in these pages you know that Roy Speece, of York, Nebraska, does his own thinking. The fact that someone else or even the majority does it differently in no way prejudices Roy's mind. His conclusions are drawn from active investigation and wide experience. He has hunted all of North America's gallinaceous species except three. He keeps one dog at a time and expects it to "adapt to any of the 20 or so species of upland birds plus adverse water work." Of the dogs available to do this, Roy regards the Spinoni and Griffon as two of the few that haven't "had running blood bred or bootlegged into them."

How does Roy start a versatile pup? "My puppy and I hunt every evening—robins in the park are about the best—and cheapest. I do not like pigeons because they will not run; wing-clipped pigeons seem to give off a wounded-bird smell. Of course, I don't shoot robins or even carry a gun but we stalk them. If they stop, we stop, and compliment each other for it. The commands are 's-t-e-a-d-y,' drawn out, for the stopped point and 'OK' for the moving or walking point. 'Whoa' means stop for sure! If a puppy breaks, it is 'whoa,' and no compliments are exchanged. If the bird flies and the puppy doesn't break, we again compliment each other. We have done the best possible, you see.

"The puppy learns to work the bird if the bird moves and it learns to point (in this case, sight point) the bird if it stops. We must then very carefully transfer this sight puppy work to adult dog scenting conditions, but we do not punish for birds that bump unless the puppy breaks. Do you see that in this training we push birds that move and we point birds that stop?"

If you're very, very perceptive, you may have caught a hint that Roy is striving for something beyond just roading pheasants, but we'll return to that in a moment. Roy likes his dogs steady to wing, but on their way to retrieve at the sound of the shot. He points out that the practice is conservation oriented in that it saves seconds in getting to a wounded bird. And it isn't difficult to teach:

"With a retrieving dummy, the first step is to make the dog hold steady on the throw unless you fire the pistol. If you throw and fire the pistol, the dog can retrieve. No pistol, no retrieve—not even later. These lessons come after the puppy is trained to retrieve to hand.

"Now you see the puppy is ready for the transition in the field. When a bird flushes that is not shot at, the puppy is not supposed to break. We can't shoot hen pheasants in Nebraska and so our dogs get lots of this no-shoot work. If a shot is taken, the pup has been schooled to go for the retrieve.

"Fine, OK, but what if I miss the bird? Back at the robin stage of hunting my puppy learned to 'whoa.' Now this whoa must be used forcefully enough to stop an excited pup after a missed shot at a live bird."

Roy Speece, of York, Nebraska, trains versatile dogs on robins! He also has the courage to talk about versatile pointing dogs being used as Springers in certain circumstances.

The Wirehaired Pointing Griffon, and the German Wirehaired Pointer probably have the most versatile coats. The two are hard to tell apart, but as a rule the Griffon has a little more of a "woolly bear" look. The dense undercoat protects them in extremely cold water. The wiry outer coat sheds water fast and protects the dog in the most punishing cover.

Now back to that hint of something more in "pushing birds that run and pointing birds that stop." Obviously, this is ideal training for pheasants whether holding or running and perfect for chicken and bobwhite, but what if the birds are western quail or another species that will not hold? Should a pointing dog flush them?

Roy places much emphasis on control. He wants the dog to hunt where he says and most of the time that's at close range. Pointer and Setter men will scoff. "Yeah, he wants to shoot over his dog's mistakes as well as his points." Roy realizes that Pointer purists may swear his dog is bumping, but he has the courage to talk about a facet of versatile work that is seldom mentioned even by others who practice it. "Our dogs are versatile to us partly because they become Springers when they can't be Pointers," he says.

Roy hastens to add that flushing bobwhite quail in an open field would be bumping to him, too. Flushing game is acceptable only in certain circumstances and/or on certain species. And Roy is convinced that

the right dog with the proper training and enough experience (it may take hundreds of birds) can tell just what circumstance confronts it by its powers of "scent discernment."

"Long ago I associated the versatile dog's willingness to put its head down and track (hound blood was fused into our versatiles, you know) with the ability of some of those dogs to sort out the attitudes of the birds," Roy said. "Crazy? I don't think so. I'll bet you that my Spina can tell the difference in foot scent between a pheasant that has crept into cover to hide and foot scent of one that will not hold. I will also add that she can tell foot scent of a wounded bird as different from the other two.

"The scents that a dog experiences are as distinct and varied as the many colors, shades and hues that our eyes see. or the noises, notes and chords that our ears hear. I think that the proper dog with the proper training and the proper experience can sort out these scents for its master.

"A high-headed dog simply cannot do it and I'm not

knocking the specialists—I'd want one myself if I ran dogs in the trials.

"But my dog is a pointer, a land or water retriever, a Springer and a trail hound with the ability to discern attitudes."

I wouldn't argue with Roy's theory because I've also noticed scent discernment in hounds. Two coon hounds I've known have treed every track they started for as many as thirty nights in a row. The reason isn't simply superior ability. Other hounds in the pack would start a track. If these two didn't give voice, it was almost guaranteed that the raccoon would never be treed. They knew from scent discernment whether the track could be finished. If they opened on the track themselves or joined the pack, it was almost guaranteed that the coon would be treed.

When Roy's dog recognizes a runner, he follows and the rest is control just as in hunting with a Springer Spaniel.

"My dog points the stopped bird, stalks the moving bird and pushes the moving bird to flight," Roy says. "Control of the dog is necessary so that the hunter can stay with the dog, so it's 'whoa'—'OK'—'whoa'—'OK,' etc. The dog must stay in range. My old Britt would look back over her shoulder to see how close I was. The good ones eventually learn to keep the hunter close to them without nagging.

"If you have a reasonably smart dog, bred to do what you are trying to do and trained in a sensible manner—trust your dog. It may be a while but it will pay off for you as a hunter. Remember your puppy wasn't allowed to chase flying birds that were not shot at—your puppy was scolded if it didn't stop with a stopped bird and your puppy will 'whoa'."

Mrs. Edward D. (Joan) Bailey, secretary of the Wirehaired Pointing Griffon Club of America, adds an interesting variation of this advanced versatile work:

"The German word for this ability to turn into a flusher is 'stöbern.' A literal translation would be 'get in there and root around 'til you find everything.'

"Mostly the way it's used in Germany is to have the dog sit at one corner of a small woods or brush patch of a couple acres. The hunters go around to the opposite end and take up stands. Then the dog is given the command to go. The dog windshield-wipes his way toward the hunters, pushing the game ahead past the gun. Mostly it's used for rabbits and for boar.

"We, ourselves, have one dog that is particularly good at this work. But we do it differently and use it for birds rather than rabbits. Hunting grouse here we let her have her head while we walk slowly around a cedar swamp or a pine plantation. Our bitch works in and circles back out, then repeats the circle in. We never can see her because it's too thick. But birds come swinging out. She always stays about even with us. She also spots likely thickets and takes off to the far side and drives back toward us. At these places we just stop and wait 'til she comes back through. We work wood lots and shelter belts for pheasants in Nebraska the same way. Yet she points solidly when field hunting or if we go into the cover with her.

"We think the versatile breeds don't have the one-track brain of the Pointers. Probably the pointing instinct is not as rigidly or as highly developed in the

Pointing is essential in a versatile dog, of course, but the instinct shouldn't be so highly developed that . . .

. . . the dog won't lower his head and follow the track of wounded or running game.

versatiles. This is what permits 'stöbern,' tracking, retrieving, and cooperation with the handler in a dog that also points."

The versatile dog is not the super animal that promoters of two decades ago asked us to believe. But now that the ballyhoo and the bandwagons have passed and the air is cleared, something very fine is emerging: a hunting dog, one that will find his place in our shrinking coverts more and more as the years pass. To understand more about his training, be sure to also read the section on versatile hunting-dog trials.

Correcting Bad Habits

The best way to cure any bad habit is to never let it start. Be aware that it may happen, and take steps to prevent it. As a rule, it takes minimal effort to prevent a problem, but a monumental labor to cure it. Remember, too, that dogs are individuals, and all have faults. Sometimes an amateur trainer can correct them; sometimes it takes a pro. Sometimes we have to live with it or get rid of the dog.

GUNSHYNESS—I'll start with the worst first. Timidness and noise shyness can be an inborn trait, but far more often the dog is gunshy because someone foolishly blasted near the dog or pup without preparation and frightened it out of its wits. I gave instructions on how to safely introduce gunfire in the section on fun in the field. If the sin has already been committed, I wish you luck.

The usual first try at a cure begins with banging the feed pan or water bucket while feeding the dog to associate noise with something pleasant. Begin mildly and increase the din as the dog becomes accustomed to it. Introduce .22 blanks if allowed where you live or, better yet, take the dog afield and fire when it's having fun in the distance. The one truly noise-shy bitch I've owned had to be conditioned this way every year before opening day. She was not a serious case, however.

A Retriever belonging to my son-in-law was less afraid of noise than she was the sight of the gun. We started her cure by chaining my Retriever next to her pen. He can hardly contain his enthusiasm for the sight and sound of the gun. When we began target practicing with .22 shorts, he lunged against the chain and ran the length of it endlessly. He gave the bitch a good sales talk with his infectious enthusiasm. My son-in-law finished the cure by continuing target

Dogs other than the generally accepted versatile breeds can be taught versatility. This English Setter bringing in a squirrel also fetches rabbits (but does not chase them) although her primary duties are pointing and retrieving quail and pheasants.

practice near the pen and insisting that she sit outside her house and watch.

This method works even better if a gunshy dog can be staked out with several gun-loving dogs. Space them closely.

If the dog's enthusiasm for birds has been adequately developed, it might help to stake him on a long chain where it's possible to shoot birds that will drop within his reach. Such a situation might be outside a barn where pigeons enter. Or you might throw pigeons in his direction and shoot those that fly over him. Let him eat the first bird. Stop the lesson and lay the dog up for a couple days. Shoot another in the same manner, and let him eat it. After that feed him the heads. Hopefully, you'll now be able to shoot more than one bird at a time.

Some trainers have fed their dogs salty food and then shot .22 blanks over them when they came for water. If they ran for the doghouse, the water was removed and brought back later for another attempt. I can excuse the ignorant for doing this. But you and I know that lack of water can be seriously damaging to a dog, especially in warm weather. Anyone who would carry out this method for any length of time is too unfeeling to own a dog.

The same type of thing is also done with food. The dogs eats while being fired over or the food is removed until the next day. This isn't quite as cruel because dogs can go without food for long periods without damage or even the serious suffering they would experience from lack of water. If you must be harsh, try the starvation method. Don't deny them water.

In another harsh method, the trainer attaches the dog's leash to his belt and wades into the water until the dog must swim. The dog can't escape when the trainer shoots. He can't even lunge against a chain in terror. He swims frantically, but supposedly finds it futile and in the process realizes at last that gunfire is not hurting him. It must be a terrifying experience for a gunshy dog. I haven't tried it and seriously doubt I ever will. I much prefer the methods that take longer but which build on a dog's enthusiasm.

NATURAL SHYNESS—I spent a lot of time gradually working the dog into bird enthusiasm in earlier sections. That plus a lot of human association greatly helps natural shyness. If the pup isn't socialized before 14 weeks, 16 at the most, it may never completely trust humans. Restore the dog's confidence to whatever degree possible by setting up situations where he wins, and avoid failures like being rapped by a pigeon's wing or pinched by a duck, etc.

RANGE—While gunshyness is the most serious dog fault, range—either too little or too much—is probably the most aggravating to the average hunter. Why the slow, easy-going, old or fat get the fast, wide-ranger while the swift, lean athlete gets the plodder is a mystery on a level with why it rains on weekends. I've discussed using a whistle in early training to turn the dog when he reaches the range you desire. If you don't want a wide dog, be sure to make a friend of him and encourage him to return to you frequently. If friendship and whistles fail, slow him down with a length of garden hose attached to his collar or heavy chains of whatever weight is necessary. Thorough discipline will bring the dog under better control, but when he's far out he may know you can't reach him. Using a slingshot for earlier wrongdoing when not too far away can help build a myth that you can reach him no matter where. Dogs often shorten their range naturally as they mature, so if the dog doesn't run much beyond your preferred limits, don't get excited.

It's a lot harder to make the plodder range than to hack in the ranger. Running with a fast, wide dog will often draw the slower dog out. And always run the slower dog only as long as he is enthusiastic. Put him up if bored. Don't give him play time. Make running his play. If he potters where birds were sitting hours before, order him on. If he persists, a marble off his rump from a sling shot will move him on. Do the same if he insists on stopping to inspect and cock his leg on every bush along the way.

BUMPING—If thoroughly grounded in obedience and brought along in the manner prescribed earlier, it's

Handling corrects some dogs if they slacken on point. This often happens when dogs notice man smell on planted birds and recognize a phony situation.

unlikely that the dog will start bumping birds unless he happens to catch one. In that case, you may have to lay him up for weeks while the memory fades. Then work him under controlled conditions with a check cord and one of the methods to ensure that the birds do fly. In any case, use a check cord and dump him hard if he chases.

Some pointing dogs slam right into the birds seemingly for the sheer joy of seeing them scatter. Get rough. Others creep as if they're uncertain of the bird's location. Dogs may also begin creeping when man scent tips them off that it's a phony set up. Dogs that see the birds may also creep in and try to pounce on one. Avoid much of this in the first place by never letting a dog catch a bird. If too late, return the creeper to an obedience refresher and come back to birds with a check cord, choke chain or pinch collar, if necessary, and intentions to see that the dog does it your way. If you haven't used a buggy whip to enforce whoa, introduce it now.

BLINKING—This is often the result of a soft dog getting harsh treatment on point. Perhaps in the early stages he caught much hell for not being staunch or steady enough and enjoyed little praise to balance it. He gets the idea that birds are the cause of all his trouble. So when he smells them he leaves.

Ease up on the blinker. Help him regain his bird interest. Plant birds, bring him in on a check cord, don't fuss over his point, but stack him up with a great deal of praise. Shoot the bird and let him retrieve. Feed him the head.

If this is tried repeatedly and fails, it's back to the beginning. Encourage him to chase if you have to run along yourself. Once his bird interest is revived, bring him back to pointing slowly.

FALSE POINTING—Young dogs that lack confidence may become too cautious and point birds that are not there. Or they may point everything they see that looks like a bird. When you know it's a false point, just walk on and ignore him. This seldom continues as a serious problem.

SLACKENING—Slackening or softening on point is sometimes the result of too much work on planted birds. The dog doesn't get excited because he smells man scent and knows it's a game. He stands, but not stiff and tense as he should be. His tail flags slowly. Work the dog on more wild birds or quail from a recall pen. They don't have to be handled and are air washed when flown.

If the dog is steady to wing, he can be brought back to an excited, tense point even on planted game by stomping around in front of him as if to flush the bird. Do flush it finally (from the release cage or whatever) and shoot it. Let the dog retrieve and make a great fuss over his achievement.

Handling on point also helps some dogs. Stroke the dog his full length. Pick up his tail and turn him. Push forward against his rump to stiffen him.

BOLTING—A dog usually bolts or runs off because he can't enjoy being around his master. Discipline is too severe and demanding, so the dog takes off at the first opportunity and indulges in a spree of running, self-hunting and having fun by doing whatever he likes.

Ease up on the dog. Make friends, really pals. Take him along (on leash) wherever you go whenever possible. I've seen show-type Irish Setters, however, that couldn't care less about their masters. Get rid of the dog if it lacks master orientation to that degree.

When his confidence in you has returned, hunt some planted birds with the dog dragging weight for insurance. Shoot some birds to intensify his enjoyment. And refrain from raising hell because he isn't perfect.

HARD-MOUTH—Many dogs get hard-mouthed with age. After getting rapped about the head with strong wings a number of times, they learn to avoid it with a sharp crunch. I had a dog that got pretty bad, but I couldn't get excited over it. Every puncture on a bird I clean, whether tooth or shot, is slit open and the blood, dirt and feathers removed. I don't fool myself that soaking in salt water will remove these things. And I like my birds well done. So a few well-cleaned, sterilized teeth marks accompany the shot punctures; I'm not that squeamish.

If you are or if the dog is trying to eat birds, there

Picking the rear end up by the tail and moving its position helps staunch the dog on point.

are a number of cures. Dad tried the old "nails through a bird" method and had several hair-raising minutes until he got one of the nails extracted from the roof of the Pointer's mouth. It cured the dog. But if old Sam hadn't been such a hardhead, it would have cured him of retrieving.

Spiked quail harnesses are superior substitutes. They're as effective as the nails, but no spikes continue to stick the dog's mouth. The spikes can also be filed to a blunt point. Live birds are retrieved gingerly, nevertheless.

Or wrap a bird in hardware cloth. The rough wire usually encourages a softly handled delivery. If it isn't enough, run some sticks in and out of the mesh to add discomfort to a hard-mouthed grip.

CHASING LIVESTOCK, CHICKENS—As difficult as it is to find hunting territory these days, we don't want our dog repaying the kindness of a farmer by chasing or killing his livestock or fowl. The best way to avoid this is by letting the pup get acquainted with these creatures while you visit with your farmer friend during the early fun trips afield. If he gets aggressive, correct him. It's easy when he's little, and he grows up knowing that these are the "friendlies."

If the dog does kill a chicken, you can beat him with the dead bird, your flushing whip, hand, limb or whatever, but get on him instantly. Make the dog think he's about to die for his deed, or make him wish he could.

You can wire the chicken to the dog's neck and let it hang until it rots, if you like. It may further discourage him. But I wouldn't wait and hope for results. I'd get on him while he knows why I'm doing it. Then I'd give him chance after chance at other chickens and use the flushing whip every time a bad thought crossed his mind.

Chasing cattle can result in being chased right out of the pasture. But farmers don't appreciate that kind of ruckus even if the dog isn't likely to hurt the animals.

Sheep chasing is extremely serious. These animals are not very bright and are easily injured or killed. Dad had a sheep killer when I was a boy. The dog was outstanding on quail, but unpredictable on sheep. He'd behave for long periods, then suddenly decide he wanted a sheep. He never got one because Dad sprayed him with bird shot every time. Bird shot at sixty yards will not injure the dog. One time the sheep were too close and Dad had no choice but to cut down even if he killed the dog. It was during the depression years, and he couldn't afford to pay for the sheep. The dog lived, but his hide felt like a washboard. I see no other choice in that kind of emergency.

If you have a valuable hunting dog these days,

Eager students often jump for the dummy.

A knee at the correct moment soon puts a stop to jumping.

These young dogs are in training quarters at Gunsmoke Kennels. The barrels are facing the field where they watch other dogs work birds. The enthusiasm of the working dogs is infectious. And they learn to love the sound of gunfire for the same reason. Gunshyness is easy to prevent, almost impossible to cure permanently.

however, there's a more practical solution. Read the section on electronic trainers.

KENNEL BARKING—Barking around the home for no reason is aggravating to you and more so to the neighbors. I've heard it can be stopped by tying a bell in the pen and ringing it with a string every time they bark. Jack Godsil uses one sharp blast on the whistle to stop barking.

I douse a persistent barker with a bucket of water while repeating "shut up" in no uncertain terms. Even when it's hot, and they'd love to be wet down, dogs hate water when thrown in anger. I tried Godsil's whistle method on these dogs that were voice- and water-trained, and they seemed to respond immediately. I imagine it gets their attention and distracts them from whatever reason they're barking. Since they know I blow the whistle, they also know it's a good idea to shut up.

EATING FECES—Stool-eating dogs apparently aren't suffering from a lack in their diet as was once thought. It's more likely they're suffering from boredom. Take them out more often. Give them something to chew on and play with in their pen. Provide a self-feeder so they spread their eating out over a long period and have something to do by nibbling whenever they get nervous. If none of this works, a veterinarian can give you a low-level parasite killer to add daily to the dog's food. Parasites have nothing to do with it, but the stools will smell so bad, the dog won't pick them up. And he'll surely be free of worms in the process. Unfortunately, if the dog is incurably hooked on stools, he may still eat those from another dog.

FIGHTING AND BITING—Some aggressiveness can be avoided by never teasing the pup, never playing tug of war with a rag, and never wrestling the pup on his back while he tries in frustration to bite your hand.

An incorrigible fighter may behave around other dogs while hunting and yet attack when around the vehicle or kennel. Your presence and jealousy often triggers it. Once a fight has started, hitting these dogs has no effect. They either don't feel it when the adrenalin is flowing or they credit it to the dog they're fighting. Twisting an ear sometimes will stop it, but be sure you have the other hand in the dog's collar in such a way that he can't swing back and bite you. Be prepared to choke off the dog's air by twisting his collar or using a belt as a noose. A large, determined dog can be next to impossible to pry off another.

I doubt if any form of correction besides electricity ever permanently cools an aggressive dog.

Training with Electricity

How effective is training with electricity? A guard-dog trainer I know has succeeded in making his male dogs turn away and leave females in heat. The purpose is to eliminate any possibility of the dog's being lured away from its post. He did it with electricity, and the conditioning of dogs for any other reason should be much easier. In an experiment involving electricity, a dog that was shocked by a feed pan just didn't eat anymore. He had to be moved and fed from another container to prevent starvation.

How dangerous is training with electricity? Perhaps more than you think and not for the reasons you might guess. I'm told that the higher salt content in dogs' blood makes them more sensitive to electric shock than humans. Nevertheless, a very brief shock from an electronic trainer is only a jolt and cannot physically injure the dog. Even if the shock collar should "stick" and continue to jolt, there is no injury unless the dog hurts himself in some way through panic. The danger to the dog's personality is considerable, however, if the trainer doesn't know what he's doing.

A fellow I know has two things that mix like alcohol and driving: a short temper and a electronic trainer. Instead of using the trainer for correction as intended, he uses it to vent his anger when his dogs aren't behaving to suit him. The jolt is seldom timed with the dog's mistake; the button is pushed for revenge. His dogs know only that life is full of torture and they had better fear their master. Instead of gaining knowledge from their training experiences, they get more hang-ups. If you're an individual with a short fuse, save yourself the price of an electronic trainer. It will do you and your dog more harm than good.

John Ingram demonstrates how stepping forward to accept a retrieve will cause a premature drop while . . .

. . . stepping back or squatting will encourage delivery to hand.

The whole electronics training kit: transmitter with dummy collar on left and shock collar on right, battery meter and battery charger on the lid of the case.

Professional trainers are generally in agreement that while they seldom have to use electronic trainers, these instruments are extremely effective when needed and properly used. Cliff Wallace, for example, says there is a place for the electronic trainer, but it is not the cure for all ills. It must be used judiciously.

Jack Godsil expands Cliff's capsule advice by pointing out that electricity should be used for enforcement; it is not a teaching method. Jack uses a shock collar infrequently for control of a problem when the dog is at a distance. And then he's careful to use electricity only after he's sure the dog understands what the command means. "Trying to do the job fast is the most use electronic trainers are put to today," Jack said. "And that makes trouble."

I think it would be a good idea to understand at least a little of how a shock collar functions before using one on a dog. It compares in theory, although not mechanically, to the ignition system of an au-

tomobile. You may know that battery current through the spark coil is interrupted by points making and breaking in the distributor. When current through the coil starts or stops, a magnetic field expands or collapses around a great many more turns of wire in the secondary winding of that coil. The moving lines of force in the magnetic field induces a very high voltage by cutting across those many turns of wires in the secondary. If you've touched a spark plug when the engine was running, you have an idea how much voltage is being induced. Do-it-yourself television repairmen sometimes get a similar experience when touching the high-voltage connector that goes to the picture tube. Although the jolt may range from 20,000 to 30,000 volts, no one has died from the shock because all of these devices have little current-carrying capacity. In other words, when the high voltage is touched and amperage begins to flow, the voltage falls off rapidly and harmlessly.

In contrast, people or dogs can be and have been electrocuted by only the 110 volts present in any plug in the home. The conditions usually include touching 110 volts while wet or standing in water, but the important thing is that the 110 volts will not fall off, but will continue to force high amperage through whatever it touches. Obviously, NEVER try to use house wiring as a cheap substitute for an electronic trainer.

The collar mechanism that supplies the shock to the dog's neck does not have a distributor, of course, but a small solenoid or buzzer-type vibrator does the same job of making and breaking contacts. The transmitter that the trainer holds in his hand does not supply the shock. It is a tiny radio transmitter that sends a signal when the button is pushed and notifies the receiver in the collar that now is the time to shock.

Not many people are left who remember the old TRF (tuned radio frequency) radios. Those who do will also remember how difficult it was to tune them to separate stations. One station interfering with another was an aggravation. Early shock collars also utilized TRF receivers. But imagine another "station" or signal of some sort interfering on a shock collar! All kinds of extraneous signals would trigger the receiver and shock the dog at the wrong time. If you owned a TV with remote control and had the station change automatically when someone dropped a ring of keys or the phone rang, you have some understanding of extraneous signals.

Superheterodyne circuitry replaced the old TRF radios. All modern radios use it, and manufacturers of electronic trainers also recently went to this design. It features narrow selectivity that tunes out unwanted signals. Don't criticize manufacturers for not using it sooner. Size is of great importance for the collar receiver. Can you imagine an old table-model radio hanging around your dog's neck? It wasn't until tiny transistorized circuits were developed that trainer

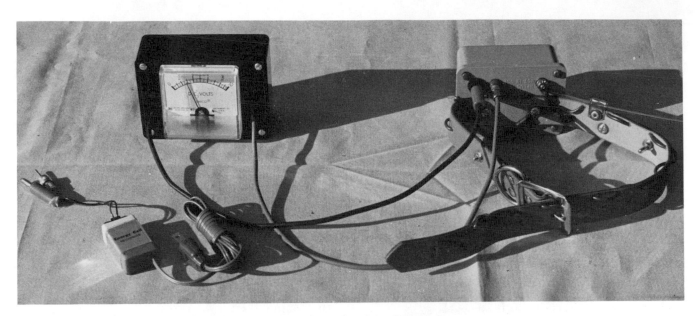

An essential part of the equipment is a meter to test the batteries. One of the main problems amateur trainers have with shock collars is forgetting to charge the batteries. The meter connected to the collar shows the batteries are fully charged. When they are not, they can be recharged by the energy cell shown at the lower left.

Space-age electronics has made it possible to build interference-free electronic trainers. In front of the collar and transmitter are the same miniaturized circuits that are inside the units. Between the two circuit boards are the rechargeable batteries used in the collar.

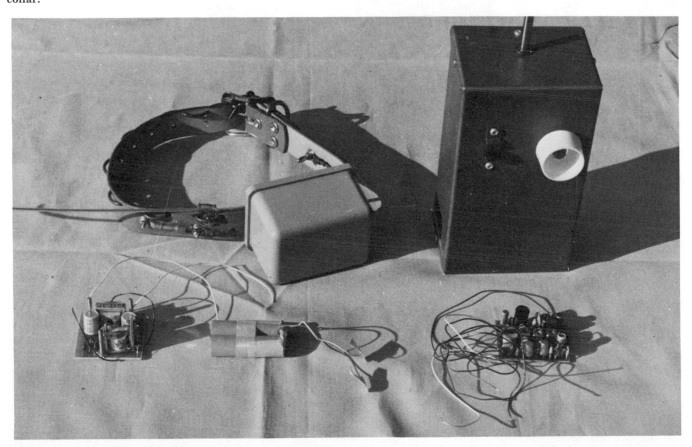

The dog begins by wearing a dummy collar for at least two days. If the shock collar were fastened on the dog and immediately used, the dog would learn he must obey when the collar is on, but not necessarily otherwise.

The shock collar installed with the antenna in a position to receive signals from the transmitter.

makers could modify the superheterodyne design for their own use.

Electricity was used in dog training before remote-controlled shock collars were marketed, however. The earlier "livestock prod" was, and still is, quite handy. It uses a buzzer/induction-coil shocker similar to that in a shock collar. The difference is that there is no radio transmitter and receiver to trigger the shock. The prod is turned on by pushing a button on the handle. Two electrodes stick out of the end of the prod. When they're shoved beneath the dog's hair and touch the skin, they shock the dog when the button is pushed.

Inventive trainers realized they could also connect the two wires of a fairly heavy, strong cable to those electrodes. The other end of the wires could be connected to electrodes stuck in opposite sides of a dog's collar. Now the dog could be shocked from a distance limited only by the length of the cable. If taped or otherwise securely fastened to prod handle and collar, the cable could also be used as a check cord of sorts.

At an earlier time, the cable was connected to a magneto salvaged from an old-style hand-cranked telephone.

Electricity, then, is not at all an innovation in dog training, but its use is not widespread because of the expense and its somewhat limited range. And its effective use is even less widespread because many people don't understand how to use electronic equipment and don't bother to read the instructions carefully. A service manager for one manufacturer told me that 70 percent of the units sent in for repair simply needed batteries, had been abused by careless treatment or had no trouble at all. Since these units should not have been mailed to the factory for repair, it's safe to assume their owners couldn't comprehend the instruction manual or didn't bother to read it. *If you're going to use one of these instruments on an animal, please learn the how, why and what for.*

One of the important things that new owners of electronic trainers like to short-cut is putting the dummy collar on the dog at least two days in advance of using the real item. This accustoms the dog to the feel of the collar. If the shock collar is suddenly fastened around his neck and moments later he's shocked for disobedience, he knows exactly what caused it. You've taught him to obey when the heavy shock collar is hanging on his neck and to do what he wants at other times.

After proper precautions are taken and it's well understood how to use the trainer, be certain to choose the right moment for correction. The dog must be in the act of doing something he knows to be wrong. And you must be positive he's doing it. Don't guess. *Never push the button on an electronic trainer when the dog is out of sight.*

Electricity is a great corrective measure for fighting dogs, probably the only really effective cure. One aggressive dog of mine was warned repeatedly and whipped soundly the one time he managed to attack another dog. He was as aggressive as ever, so I took a prod and led him near an enemy. One treatment at the first sign of fight stopped him cold. I even hunted him and his enemy together on pheasants. Every time he'd cross the enemy's path, he'd look the other way so he wouldn't have bad thoughts.

Like all other forms of dog training, however, don't consider the cure complete just because it was done with electricity. Dogs need refresher courses. I failed to continue his lessons, and months later another fight started in a moment of carelessness.

Killing poultry and chasing livestock are two more problems that are hard to cure by any other means, but electricity works wonders.

A friend of mine in a suburb had Pointers that barked every time a train went past on a nearby track. He tried to leave the collar unit in operation all day long, however, and had trouble with batteries going dead at the crucial moment. Try to time these periods of annoyance, and turn the collar unit off during the balance of the day. If the dog is simply a barker, I'd keep the collar working during the evening. You can oversee it at that time, and that's when he's probably most annoying to the neighbors. The jolt must come immediately after the bark, however, or the dog will not understand why he got shocked.

Tri-Tronics, of Tucson, Arizona, makes a collar specifically for barkers. It's actuated by sound. When the dog barks, the collar bites.

An editor friend couldn't keep his Pointer from dashing out of the house for a run whenever anyone opened the door. He was fast and clever, and ordinary discipline was not working. One jolt with a unit made by Sensitronix, of Houston, Texas, put an invisible barrier across the doorway. I haven't heard since, but I'm sure the lesson had to be repeated after the memory faded a bit.

While we're on the subject of memory fading, C.L. Owens of Gunsmoke Kennels, Springfield, Illinois, said they had a shock collar stick, which is something all trainers seem to fear with these things. Owens said the dog nearly ate up the man who got the collar off, but the dog wasn't ruined as many would expect. They just put the dog back in his pen and left him alone. Owens didn't try to hunt the dog until he thought the memory had faded, and the dog got over it without problems.

"We use shockers a lot," Owens said, "and haven't ruined a dog yet."

Don't use a shock collar during field training until the young dog has a firmly established bird interest. Some suggest not using a collar before the dog is a year old, but I think it depends on the individual dog. A bold, aggressive dog that's pure hell on birds can take a shock in stride and come out the better for it, if it's properly timed. The soft dog, even over a year old, may have his hunting instincts permanently arrested. He needs encouragement at that point, not correction.

Another friend of mine uses an electronic trainer to establish range. He doesn't care for big-running dogs, so he takes the youngsters afield and whistles and turns when they quarter beyond his liking. While they're young and lack self-confidence, it's fairly easy to keep them near. They gradually learn his preferred range. But when they get older and bolder, they don't feel they need him, so wider they go. That's when my friend jolts them back where he wants to hunt. He says in no time at all, they know his range almost to the inch.

I hope I've made it clear, the shock collar does not teach anything *to* a dog. It stops the dog *from* doing something he already knows or should know to be wrong.

Just suppose we have a dog that holds his points beautifully while on a check cord, then bursts into a covey of quail with wild abandon when he's too far away to catch. If he does this consistently (not just accidentally on a day of poor scenting conditions), he can be corrected with a shock if jolted just as the birds flush. On the other hand, suppose we have a youngster that never pointed in his life. He doesn't know he's doing wrong if he doesn't know what's right. We can't get angry and jolt him for not pointing when he doesn't know he's supposed to point. He'll probably just think it's wise not to fool with birds at all.

One of the difficulties in using electricity, I believe, stems from the name we give the device. If we could forget it's called an electronic trainer and always consider it as an electronic corrector, I think we would never be tempted to use it at the wrong time.

The dog is now remote controlled in that he can be shocked from a distance whenever he breaks the rules.

7/Field Trials

Bird Dog Trials

It would surprise me very much if one out of ten dyed-in-the-wool hunters ever got around to reading this opening sentence, much less the whole section. It's rather popular for hunters to dismiss field-trial dogs as borderline bolters, racehorses and next-county runners. There are all kinds of field trials, however, and all kinds of field-trial dogs. If dog-loving hunters were to ride a few braces in the right kind of trials, I don't think they could help but enjoy themselves.

Dog men thrill to good dog work, and some of the very best is seen in the field trials. I sincerely believe a man who is genuinely interested can appreciate an exceptionally attractive blonde despite a lifelong preference for brunettes. And perhaps a foot hunter can enjoy the performance of a lithe, fast, wide-moving, intense Pointer dog of championship caliber despite the fact that he wouldn't want his bitch mated to one.

I don't insist, however, that the average hunter would enjoy entering his dog in a trial. Competition destroys good fellowship for some of us and enhances it for others. Know which you are. Try watching a local trial first. When stakes are small, people are friendlier and more helpful. While dogs are great levelers, and bank presidents and janitors are treated alike at field trials, you may enounter clanishness among the contestants and people involved in major events.

Smaller trials are also more interesting to a hunter because the dogs entered are more like his own. After riding for a day in one of the national championships and seeing no bird work at all, it's easy to think old Duke could show these speed merchants some of the birds they ran past. Maybe Duke could. Duke is probably a close-working dog that handles single birds beautifully after a covey flush. These major circuit contestants are covey dogs. They run the edges of fields, timbers or fence rows, covering ground as fast as legs and nose will allow, trying to locate as many widely spotted coveys as they can in the shortest possible time. After a day or two of field trialing, the local quail may have considered it prudent to move back from the edges and borders along the course. They aren't to be found where the dogs are trained to search. If you don't know about this, all of the intelligent running patterns, speed, pace and style in the world will still leave you thinking the dogs are idiots.

Many of these wide-running dogs are capable of completely changing their manner of search when taken on an actual hunt. As Gunsmoke Kennels trainer C. L. Owens said of Smokepole, "If you left your whistle and horse at home, you could foot hunt him on the square in downtown Springfield." W. C.

Kirk said National Champion Johnny Crockett could be hunted on foot all day, but if you got on a horse in prairie country, he'd range from half to three-quarters of a mile away.

I happened to be at a Spring Championship for Red Setters when I was giving a lot of thought about what to put in this section. A veteran hunter of many seasons rode the morning course to find out what field trials are all about. He hadn't ridden a horse very much in twenty years and he was thoroughly sore, but he was back that afternoon to handle his dog. Rusty had never been to a field trial, either. Nor had he ever seen his master on a horse.

Rusty was braced with a wide-running Irish that knew its way around field trials. At the breakaway Rusty decided he wasn't going hunting without his master, but couldn't find him anywhere. "I'm up here, Rusty," the man finally called. Rusty ran around with renewed vigor but never thought of looking up. After another couple of calls, Rusty got close enough and realized the sounds were coming from above.

Rusty stood against the horse and smelled his master to be absolutely certain, then went hunting. But he couldn't believe it. His master on top of a big animal. He came back to check that out once more. But he stood against the judge's horse by mistake,

Anyone who enjoys dogs, horses and the outdoors in big chunks can't help but enjoy riding in a field trial.

then the other judge's and at last his master's. Reassured, he went hunting, but every once and a while Rusty was back just to be sure.

When the dog was satisfied that his master really was going to follow along behind on that big animal, he began hunting at shoe-leather range. He loafed just once by starting to trot down a field road. "Rusty," his master called with a swing of his arm, "get over in those weeds and hunt." He did. It was obvious he and his master had seen lots of quail together.

Near the end of the half-hour run, a change was already taking place. The wide-running Irish had covered a tremendous amount of ground. Its casts were beginning to shorten and its pace was slowed. Rusty, on the other hand, was just getting used to horseback hunting. He was speeding up and reaching farther and farther until it disturbed his master. The gentleman began hacking Rusty in.

I thought that was significant. I'm not saying Rusty could become a great field-trial competitor, but I am saying that the average field-trial dog is different from the average good hunting dog more in training than in natural inclination. So why not accept the other fellow's way of training his dog and enjoy watching it work?

The great ones in field trialing, of course, do have more fire than average. Most of them would have been greats in hunting, also. Many are and have been. But great ones are rare. Herb Holmes, owner of Gunsmoke Kennels and one of today's top amateur handlers, says that out of the very best of breeding only five percent range wide enough to make top field-trial dogs. He should know. He has owned a thousand Pointers at one time. Offhand, I can't recall anyone back to Gaston de Foix in the late 1300's who had that many at once. But Gaston was a nobleman. I figure Herb was a little more careful how he bred and selected. Taxpayers weren't buying and feeding his dogs. Herb may still have over 300 at once, so he obviously has ample opportunity to evaluate ability in percentages.

Field trialers have always said that their aim was to breed better bird dogs by comparing ability in public and maintaining breeding records of winners and their offspring. Some have made mistakes and still do. Breeding for more run has produced bolters. A pair of young fellows were watching the antics of a German Shorthair pup that obviously didn't give a hoot where its master was. "That's the way to breed 'em," one young man said. "When they don't pay any attention at all to where you are, they'll really range."

Hunters wouldn't appreciate that kind of breeding, especially in Shorthairs that originated as close to medium-working dogs. But despite the exaggerated fervor of some breeders, comparison under the judges still turns up winners that are bird dogs.

The winner of the Red Setter Championship I mentioned earlier was Pat Ryan's Clancy O'Ryan. Col. Ed Schnettler handled him. Clancy glides across

Readying the dogs for the breakaway in a National Amateur Shooting Dog Championship.

the ground with the reach and drive of an animal with perfectly matched fore-and-aft running gear. He flows. There's none of this rocking-horse bounce. At the breakaway the average foot hunter would feel sure Clancy was bolting. But Clancy reaches his objective—a fence row, timber edge or whatever—and hunts it out. He's a speck out there, and sometimes he can't be seen. Then he's out front, following another edge and swinging wide to the other side. The foot hunter would begin to realize that this is quartering but on a grand scale. Suddenly time is up and the hunter would wonder how they'll ever catch that dog. Schnettler or Ryan signals, and a moment later the biddable Clancy is at their feet.

For a century, field-trial breeding has molded Pointers and Setters. If we like these breeds, we can't fault the system that spawned them. If we're not quail hunters in open country and don't appreciate these dogs for our style of hunting, there are other breeds to gun over and other trials to watch. But we can still ride in the gallery and thrill to the optimum performance of big-going, class bird dogs.

We focused on Clancy because he was there and doing it right when I was looking for an example, but I don't want to give the impression that he is the crowned king of field trials. He is one of the very best Red Setters. But as a breed, and despite great improvements within the past two decades, Irish Setters only rarely hold their own with top Pointers and English Setters.

The big circuit field-trial season starts on prairie chicken, Hungarian partridge and pheasants on the Canadian prairies in September and ends with quail in the National Bird Dog Championship which begins the third Monday of February at Grand Junction, Tennessee. Other trials of varying importance continue into May. A few scattered events are held in the summer. My own home state of Illinois ranks among the top in field-trial interest with around 300 events held every year.

The majority of trials are held by clubs belonging to the Amateur Field Trial Clubs of America. *The American Field,* 222 West Adams St., Chicago, Ill. 60606 publishes notices of trial dates and results of the runnings. The American Kennel Club also sanctions a number of trials sponsored by specialty clubs. Trials vary considerably, so there are some to interest everyone. The person who loves horses and dogs and big doses of the outdoors picks Pointer-Setter trials. By way of contrast, the New Brunswick Woodcock Championship is conducted with all handlers and judges moving on foot at a sedate pace. Specialty trials for certain breeds are held with handlers on foot but judges and gallery riding. In these trials handlers push their dogs by walking at a pace much faster than that of a normal hunt. Weimaraner and Vizsla trials are examples. German pointing breeds are now shot over in field trials to prove retrieving ability before a winner is named. Dogs that have a chance to place in the trial are called back for a shoot-to-kill test. Wirehairs must also prove they will back another dog's point. A test on water retrieving is not a part of

Breakaway at the Spring Red Setter Championship.

competition but Wirehairs are required to demonstrate this ability before becoming field champions.

Despite the great variety of field trials and their varying rules, judges are looking basically for the same thing during the running. Judges are not bound by hard, fast rules, however. A point system, tried in the early days, was found unsatisfactory. Judges are chosen from men known to be impartial to breed or man, honest, capable of quick and accurate decisions, fearless in upholding these decisions, and of considerable and successful bird-dog experience. When such men are found, and they are, they're asked to work without pay, and they do.

Back in 1946 the Amateur Field Trial Clubs of America appointed a committee to collect the best judicial opinion available on situations that occur most frequently. Their findings were published privately, and the booklet is now being made available as a contribution to the sport by Gaines Dog Research Center, 250 North Street, White Plains, N.Y. 10625. The booklet, *Standards of Judicial Practice and Field Trial Procedure,* is not to be considered a rule book, but it is probably the best source of opinion available on what is sought in the field-trial bird dog. Much of it is the same things hunters expect of good Pointers and Setters.

If a dog is trailing, chasing or just running with his bracemate and interfering with the other dog's work, his handler is warned to stop it.

Derby dogs are not required to back, but All-Age dogs are penalized if they don't. Dogs that won't back in All-Age Championship Stakes are disqualified.

A dog that stops to flush may be credited for good manners. But if he carelessly or deliberately caused the flush, he'd be penalized.

In Junior Stakes, puppies would not be required to point, only to show natural ability in searching. Fall derbies are expected to flash point. Spring derbies should be staunch, but not necessarily steady to wing and shot.

Some hunters think style is held in too much esteem by field trialers, but merriness in search, faultless motion and intense points are marks of dogs that love their work and do a good job because of it. Most hunters and field trialers alike are thrilled by the sight of a stylish dog.

Range is important. Too many non-field trialers are inclined to think of wide dogs as aimless runners. Judges are looking for dogs that hunt, not straightline, their way out. Distance from handler is not the criterion; intelligent search of cover and objectives are.

Coming up from behind is sometimes unavoidable when the dog has been hunting certain objectives, but back casting and hunting already-covered territory are severely penalized by judges just as they are by hunters.

Unproductive points are excused unless it happens two or more times and appears to be habitual.

The best bird dog may not win the trial. The chances of the draw are involved. Influence of bracemates and time of running are factors. Handler mistakes or cleverness can alter situations. But these things make field trialing a sport that men and dogs can return to time after time.

Field trialing is a separate sport from hunting, in a way. And yet it isn't. We think of the Marilyn Monroe type as girl, only a little more so, and that about says it for field-trial dogs: bird dogs, only a little more so.

Retriever Trials

While bird dogs are judged principally on what they themselves do in the field, Retriever trials are very much contests between man-dog teams. The world's best handler can't win with a poorly trained dog; neither can the world's best dog win with a poor trainer.

And while the pros and cons of bird dog trials are argued over favoring and selecting for exaggerated characteristics such as running, range or style, Retriever trial critics center their attacks on the handling that team work implies. "Does the field-trial Retriever have natural ability or is he a mechanical circus performer?" "By selecting for easy handling, aren't we breeding naturally dependent dogs that no longer have hunting instincts?"

The perennial question about field trials generally has always been, "Aren't they too artificial to simulate real hunting conditions?" And in that respect Retriever trials are artificial. I've never seen a day's hunting where any two retrieving situations were identical. But no two dogs can be compared fairly unless the situations are as identical as possible. And it would be extremely difficult to set up a situation in a field trial that would be absolutely impossible to encounter on a hunt.

I'm reminded of a fellow who said of something I wrote, "I didn't read either one, but just looking through them I believe so-and-so's article has an edge on yours." No one, including field trialers, objects to well-informed, studied, constructive criticism. Everyone, including field trialers, is angered by the fool who looks at a few pictures, reads half of the captions and a headline or two, then fancies himself qualified to issue a blanket condemnation. So let's not condemn the Retriever trial "article" until we've read some of the facts.

Unlike bird-dog trials that have been around for a century, Retriever trials are comparatively new. The Labrador Retriever Club held its first trial in 1931. The American Chesapeake Club followed in 1932. By 1935, the Midwest Field Trial Club brought competition to the Midwest. A Chesapeake, Skipper Bob, became the first field champion in 1935. A Lab, F.T.C. Blind of Arden took the *Field & Stream* trophy in 1935. National Championships immediately followed. Dilwyne Montauk Pilot, a Chessie, was named best Retriever in 1936. Most of the competition was won by

Lew Simon, of Antioch, Illinois, stomps cover to flush bird so his winning Vizsla, the late Jodi of Czuki Baret, can be tested on being steady to wing and shot.

Judges are expected to be impartial to breed or man, honest, capable of quick and accurate decisions, fearless, and knowledgeable. When such impeccable men are found, they're asked to work without pay.

Coming up from behind is sometimes unavoidable if the dog has been hunting certain objectives, but back casting is severely penalized.

Well-trained field-trial dogs stand on command and wait for the breakaway. The Shorthair on the left has turned his head back, watching for a signal from George Vuillemot. The Pointer is watching that his bracemate doesn't get to leave without him.

While not yet under judgment, it's likely that the dog's manners will be noticed on the way to the line.

pro handlers, but in 1951 the A.K.C. established Amateur Field Trial Championships, followed in 1957 by the National Amateur Retriever Championship and at last the numerous aspiring amateurs had a realistic goal. Amateur participation has tripled as a result.

Increased participation also created pressures. More dogs entered in a trial means one of two things: spend more time or move the dogs through faster. Judges are nonprofessionals who must return to earning a living. It's a weekend sport for amateurs who must also return to work. Professionals can't ignore training duties back home while trials drag on and on. Even the annual Nationals have to be limited in time so participants can travel across country, compete dogs and return home after a week's absence at the most. More time cannot be spent evaluating dogs.

The burden of moving numbers of dogs through the trials has fallen on the judges. Theirs is the thankless task of dropping many dogs for minor infractions early in the trial so there is time to properly evaluate the superior animals in the remaining series. It's quite possible that those dropped early would have won had they not committed an impulsive mistake. It's also possible that faults which caused dogs to be dropped in early series will be ignored after the field is narrowed.

It might not seem at all fair to those whose dogs are dropped, but until entry numbers are reduced or more judges can be appointed to evaluate dogs simultaneously in various tests with final results averaged or some other means is found to speed up the process, some dogs will not be able to demonstrate ability in all of the series of tests. Judges are forced to plan tests that will probably wash out considerable numbers while not losing over half of the dogs. Talk about tightrope walking! Can you imagine being a judge and losing all the dogs in one series?

A side effect of the numbers pressure gives rise to the complaint that trainers are being tested for training ability instead of dogs for hunting ability. In the marking tests, dogs are expected to show ability by finding their own birds. But if they curve off the line and pass upwind, they may go right on out of the vicinity of the fall. Judges may urge trainers to handle quickly in these situations. Time is saved. But the more a handler uses his whistle during a marking test, the more likely his dog will be dropped.

Handling quickly to save time also saves the dog the trouble of hunting. And this is the basis of the complaint that natural hunting ability is being ignored in favor of handling trainability. Handling when the dog is about to leave the area of the fall, however, may just stop a time-consuming miscalcula-

Dog is alert to mark fall as judge signals for bird during a National Championship.

It's essential that the guns drop the birds neither too far nor too close, and in the right direction.

tion that would cause a dog to be dropped anyway. On the other hand, a dog that stumbles into a bird accidentally at full speed should receive no more credit for marking than a dog that knows the area of the fall and hunts it out until he finds the bird. Intelligent hunting is favored by judges who, I'm sure, are also anxious to drop dogs that show evidence of poor marking ability.

As I said earlier, competition is between teams. So judges are looking for both natural ability and training. Even before the dog gets to the line and before he's under official judgment, his training may be noticeable. If the dog is allowed to be leashed, but pulls like an Alaskan sled dog, it probably won't go unnoticed. Neither will an All-Age dog that should be at heel but drifts all around the handler searching for places to leave his card.

At the line, teamwork may fail if the seated dog's eyes aren't next to his handler's legs. If the handler stands back, it could become a case of "out of sight, out of mind." The dog could break and start for a fall before being sent. While the judges aren't anxious to drop a dog (they do want to see the good ones work) the dog that breaks won't be seen in the next series.

Marking the fall is essential to both members of the team. While dogs' ability to mark may seem uncanny at times, they are rarely consistent. There are times when they don't see it right and need handling. Of course, this becomes absolutely essential on doubles and triples. If the handler also forgets, the team is in trouble.

Teamwork is probably at its best when the man is handling his dog by whistle and hand signals to a blind retrieve (planted bird the dog didn't see fall). It's up to the handler to send his dog near the bird on the downwind side. Once the dog has the scent, he has the bird. But a dog may habitually drift off the line. The handler must compensate. He could probably guide the dog into running geometric patterns out there all day, but the less whistling and waving he does to get the bird to hand, the more it will impress the judges.

You may notice handlers wear white jackets while on the line. When the dog stops to the whistle and looks back for instructions, all is lost if the handler blends in with the gallery or other background. Handlers may also move their bodies in the directions of the hand signal so their dogs are sure to see the commands.

Handling and training are put to the extreme test when the dog must enter or leave water at an angle. It's natural for the dog to prefer running down the bank to enter water as close as possible to the bird. That's what they'll learn to do in hunting situations, and for that reason old hunters sometimes become

Handlers wear white jackets so their dogs can see the hand signals.

Dogs wait their turn in a blind.

"too smart" for field trials. But trials give control the acid test, and the dog must handle. In important stakes, the dog might have to take a line that crosses a winding creek perhaps three times at various angles before reaching the bird. That could also happen during a hunt. If the dog ran down the bank before entering and refused to handle, the birds would be lost.

Sometimes a test takes dogs to a distant fall in water close to shore. The most direct approach would be a long swim near and parallel to the shore. And more than likely this dog would get out and walk. Teamwork overcomes this natural urge. The handler sends the dog on a line farther from shore, then turns the dog into the bird.

Tempting the dog to switch birds is a test that drops its share of dogs out of the trial early. When the dog is approaching, bird in mouth, the guns drop a pheasant nearby. If the dog drops his bird in favor of the fresh one, he's had it. In a hunting situation, it would be thoroughly frustrating to have the dog drop a cripple to fetch a dead duck. Again, training and control win out.

So far, the teamwork seems one-sided. It all boils down to firm control by a handler who can anticipate problems and avoid them by manipulation. Is it true, then, that field trials are mechanical exhibitions?

To begin with, a German Shepherd could be taught every "trick" a field-trial Retriever knows and proba-

bly more. But without hunting desire or bird interest, it would be a mechanical performance. A dog can't be mechanical and full of desire at the same time.

When a dog leaves the line, he not only must have a keen desire to get that bird in his mouth, he must be equally determined to return it to his handler post-haste.

Sometime during the trial the judges will learn how well the dog uses his nose. He might stumble onto a bird once or twice, or even find birds through superior marking (and certainly that's natural ability) but there's no way to win a retriever trial without a good nose.

Without a high degree of desire, a dog does not have the determination to stick it out until he finds the bird. Quitters don't win field trials.

Style is noticed by judges and appreciated by hunters as well. A dog that enjoys his work and shows it is preferred by all. A Retriever must handle birds with a soft mouth and that can seldom be taught.

All of that control I talked about earlier can only be developed if you have a dog that is naturally trainable. While outstanding trainers can do marvelous things with dogs, dregs don't often rise to the top. Train-ability has to mix with style, drive, determination, soft mouth, marking ability and desire in order to make a champion.

I asked Tommy Sorenson what difference, if any, he sees between hunting and field-trial dogs and their

Dog awaiting his turn must remain steady while opponent fetches his bird.

training. Tommy handles and trains both. He sees no difference in dog requirements. It takes a superior dog to be a winner or outstanding hunter. The only difference he sees in training is that the field-trial dog gets more of it—more birds, more practice, more endless hours of training.

Most of the Retriever trials in the United States are sanctioned by the American Kennel Club. A copy of field-trial rules for Retrievers can be gotten free by writing to 51 Madison Avenue, New York, N.Y. 10010.

The Retriever Field Trial News, 1836 E. St. Francis Ave., Milwaukee, Wisconsin 53207, publishes news, articles and trial dates. It's a good way to find a trial in your area if you're interested. It's also a good place to locate pups out of working stock. When you see your first Retriever trial, I think you'll be amazed how well trained these dogs are. And many of the amateur dogs rival those trained by pros.

Another thing that may not amaze you at first, but will in time, is the performance of the bird throwers and guns. If you've done some of that in training your Retriever, you'll appreciate how difficult it can be to throw birds so they go in the right direction and so their elevation is proper for good marking and safe shooting. Ater the bird is perfectly thrown, the guns must drop the bird just right. It can't be too close and so mutilated as to encourage hardmouth. It can't be too far because they may drop crippled and running. In fact, the throwers and guns must perform consis-

tently, dropping every bird like the others so all tests are equal.

When attending your first trial, be sure to stand in the area designated for the gallery. Do nothing to distract the dogs. Leave your dog at home or in the car and don't play with the dogs that are entered. Just be courteous and quietly ask questions. If you're a hunter, you may not believe that this degree of training is necessary. But I wager you'll go home with a revised opinion of what old Feather-Mouth is going to be doing by next duck season.

Spaniel Field Trials

Field trials for Spaniels, now almost exclusively for English Springer Spaniels, more closely duplicate hunting conditions than do any other trials for gun dogs. "Luck of the draw" does not inject the element of sporting gamble nearly as much as it does in pointing-dog trials. Nor are all dogs' tests quite as equal as they are in Retriever trials.

Great care is taken in selecting appropriate running grounds. Adequate cover is desired to test each dog's willingness to breast it, but judges must be able to see the dogs. And they don't want some dogs to be slowed by rooting through heavy brush while others glide across bare stubble to flush pheasants that scarcely have a place to hide.

The running grounds are staked out in two side-by-side, 50- or 60-yard courses. Two dogs will run at the same time, each staying within the boundaries of his own course. The handler walks down the middle of the course, and the dog quarters a windshield-wiper pattern ahead of him. An official gun walks to the outside of each handler. Judges stay near the handlers.

Next in line is probably the bird bearer. As likely as not it will be a young lady. And every man seeing his first Spaniel trial will want to offer to carry her burden. It seems unmannerly for so many men to be walking behind in the gallery while a woman carries the retrieved pheasants in a trapper's pack basket. But try to get it away from her! Men and women alike consider it a privilege to carry birds because it allows them to walk ahead of the gallery and be closer to the action.

Pheasants are constantly being released so every dog can have two birds in each series. While dogs are running one course, birds are planted in another. If only one course is available, birds are planted while everyone walks back to the starting line.

Dogs wait their turn either at heel or on leash. When Springers are called upon to run, they're expected to cover ground not only briskly and quietly but efficiently. Probably most will quarter in the mechanical zigzag pattern they've learned. The more intelligent ones may compensate for wind, trying to work into it as much as possible. For instance, if the wind is coming from the side and angling into the handler's face, his dog might gain ground while facing the breeze, and return almost straight downwind to the other side of the course. Spaniels should never cast behind their handlers or cover the same ground twice. Dogs are severely penalized for not covering all of the ground and passing game as a result.

When the dog flushes a bird, he must "hup" or sit instantly to mark the fall. In fact, the dog must even hup to flush or shot on his bracemate's course. It's difficult enough to sit and watch the bracemate getting the retrieve, but it can be downright nerve-racking to the dog that happened to be making game at the time.

This happened to Saighton's Stag on the second day of the 1970 National Championship. Stag, owned by Dr. C. A. and Janet Christensen, of Cornelius, Oregon, and handled by Janet at the time, was forced to honor just as he was boring down on his own bird. While his bracemate went for the retrieve, Stag sat bursting at the seams, struggling for self-control. At last he couldn't stand it and made a quick three-foot leap, almost on top of the pheasant that had been filling his nose with maddening scent.

That's the breaks. Stag was out of the trial. Control in Springer Spaniel trials is precise and exacting.

The Christensens also own F.T.C. Misty Muffet, winner of the 8th National Amateur Championship. (Spaniels, like the other breeds, have both open and amateur competition. This gives the amateur a realistic goal.) Whether she's running, making game, marking or just waiting her turn to run, Misty Muffet shows a great deal of energy and bird desire. She requires very little obvious control from her handler, which is important in trials. When handlers must blast whistles and yell at the top of their lungs, judges consider the dogs to be nearly out of control.

After the hup at flush and shot, Misty Muffet likes to stand on her hind legs to mark the fall better. This is helpful in a hunting situation and isn't detrimental in a trial unless the dog dances or moves about. But since it's easier to move from a standing than a sitting position, it emphasizes the tight control necessary in field trials.

Cliff Wallace, the pro trainer/handler who led Saighton's Sizzler to the National Championship in both 1970 and 1971, regards exacting control as the way all dogs should be trained. "Big-going bird dogs

Good guns are vital to a successful trial.

could be better trained to handle," Cliff offered as an example, "but they've never been asked to do it." Wallace grew up in Texas where they needed big-going Pointers, and his father always had about twenty of them, so his knowledge came first hand. What stops many trainers, especially amateurs, from achieving the kind of control so necessary in Spaniel trials is the time involved. "It takes four years to train a dog for top-level field-trial competition," Cliff told me. And Cliff never finishes training a dog. It goes on and on to maintain this exacting control.

The field-trial Spaniel does not break shot, of course, but remains seated until sent for the retrieve. Judges take note of the dog's aptitude in marking and ability to find the bird quickly. Guns are asked not to drop the pheasant too close because each dog should have a chance to demonstrate its skill. Nevertheless, the falls can't be nearly alike as they are in well-run Retriever trials. Where the pheasant gets out is a

matter of luck. Judges take this into consideration, however, when comparing the dog work they've seen.

Retrieving is important in Spaniel trials because fetching game is a primary purpose for owning these dogs. If the situation calls for taking whistle and hand signals, the field-trial Spaniel must be capable of doing it with energetic willingness. Delivery must be prompt and stylish, not forced and sluggish.

Sizzler was a good example of delivery. He handed pheasants to Cliff Wallace as though he was bearing gifts. It goes without saying that judges are always watching for proof that the dog has a tender mouth.

Land work is the primary function of a Spaniel, so field-trial emphasis is on terra firma. In the National Championship, at least five land series are required compared to two in water. Many series are necessary to narrow the field in a relatively gradual manner so dogs aren't judged on a brief burst of behavior, whether good or bad. Of course, only the best are

Handlers, judges and guns precede the gallery of onlookers while the brace of dogs hunt in parallel marked-off courses.

The final test is the second water series. Pheasants are simply thrown and shot down to prove the Springer can and will retrieve from water.

called back for the second series, and so on through the fifth, but a dog can't win with a flash of brilliance. The final winner may not have performed perfectly (at least none have to date) but consistent excellence is demanded before a champion is named.

Only the finalists make it to the second and last water test. Hunting Spaniels spend less time in water situations, and field trialers follow suit. The tests are ultra simple. Pheasants are thrown out over water and shot down. The dog must be steady to wing and shot, of course. Otherwise, the short retrieve proves no more than the dog is willing and able to swim.

The "Standard Procedure for Spaniel Field Trials" specifies that water-test requirements should not exceed "the conditions met in an ordinary day's rough shoot adjoining water." Rough does not mean difficult. It's an English term that means taking what comes, whether it's pheasants, ducks or whatever. The tests certainly do not exceed these conditions and probably should be more difficult to be meaningful. Nevertheless, trainers can't ignore water training for

their dogs just because the tests may be easy. In fact, it makes sense that the dogs be quite good in water. It would be ridiculous to train a Spaniel to stay in the competition through five land series only to let it fail in the water.

Sometimes contenders make it to the water series neck and neck. The trial, then, is won or lost in the water. Because this is a possibility, some trainers—Cliff Wallace is one—believe water tests should be dropped altogether or be conducted more nearly like those for Retrievers. Then trials couldn't be won by brief spurts of water excellence or lost by a once-in-a-million mistake. The water series, like the land series, would then be based on seeing the dogs in enough situations to judge their training and ability properly.

Spaniel trials are much older than Retriever trials and younger than the bird-dog trials which began in 1866. England's first Spaniel trial was held in 1899 with Springers and Cockers competing together. Cockers won, but the larger Springers soon afterward showed themselves to be in a separate class.

Springer Spaniel field trials are sometimes won or lost in the water.

Cliff Wallace and Saighton's Sizzler, winner of both the 1970 and 1971 English Springer Spaniel National Championship.

The first championship Spaniel trials in the United States were held in 1924. The English Springer Spaniel Club of America held its event at Fisher's Island, N.Y. The Cocker Spaniel Field Trial Club of America held its championship at Verbank, N.Y. Soon thereafter, trials spread to the Midwest and Pacific coast.

Spaniel field trials have not enjoyed the widespread acceptance of bird dog and Retriever trials. The trials are not at fault, however. There just aren't that many people in North America who prefer the Spaniel hunting style. The trial standards call for a performance that should not be different from an ordinary hunt, except the dogs should do their work in a more perfect way. And this is essentially the way trials are held.

A good example of difference by perfection is the dog that's taking the line of a running pheasant. On a hunt, most men would hustle to be within gunshot when the pheasant flew. Only the very best trained dogs could be stopped and hupped while the hunter caught up so the chase could be resumed within gun range. In a field trial, handlers may run a bit, but not far. The dogs can not only be stopped, they can be called off of a line and put back on if desired.

The emphasis is on control because, as Cliff Wallace says, so much of what a Springer learns is "no" to what he wants to do. While training enhances natural instincts in other breeds, it restrains the urges of Spaniels.

Springer Spaniel fanciers who are interested in field trials or anything else about their favorite dogs are fortunate to have a good breed magazine: *The Springer Bark,* P.O. Box 2115, San Leandro, California 94577.

Versatile Hunting Dog Trials

Versatile hunting-dog trials are so different from field trials that they might not even belong in the same section of this book. Field trials are grand sporting events, and in many ways hunters have

Since all parts of a dog contribute to his hunting ability, versatile trials begin by inspecting and rating conformation.

benefited from the subsequent breeding of great animals that first came to light in national competition. But I also recognize that dogs are bred first for field trialing. That hunters benefit from an upgrading of the breeds is a secondary effect. In general, I'd say hunters have gained much and lost little from field trials. But now there is an organized trial that's aimed at improving breeds strictly for foot hunters.

Versatile hunting-dog trials are not trials as we know them. They're tests. Individual dogs are evaluated against a standard. Dogs are scored, but they do not compete. Competition may develop among people who want high-scoring dogs, of course, and it's an achievement to win a I prize classification, but dogs are not placed as in field trials. The idea is to evaluate young dogs in terms of natural ability. Class awards are given accordingly, and future breeders know exactly what the dog was capable of when young. As training continues, the dog may be entered again to demonstrate improvement. Records are accumulated, never changed. When mature and fully trained, the dog can enter a utility field trial to test its degree of usefulness.

While the primary purpose is to evaluate dogs and encourage better breeding in future hunting dogs, a secondary benefit to those who enter is learning how to train their dogs. The natural ability tests demonstrate sound methods for starting young dogs. Obedience is taught in training clinics before the trials.

The North American Versatile Hunting Dog Association is the organization responsible for this new approach to excellence in dogs. We should say, "new approach in America." Some very old European practices were modified to suit North American conditions. But don't let the word "versatile" get you to thinking that this is another promotion to sell a new European breed that outhunts the specialists on all species, then cleans the game while you settle back with a hot toddy. NAVHDA does work with the recognized versatile breeds; it also recognizes any purebred dogs as possible versatile bird dog breeds. Their aim, as indicated by the word versatile, is to encourage development of hunting dogs that boast as many talents as possible to the highest degree possible.

NAVHDA held its first utility trial in 1969. The first natural ability trial drew 10 dogs in 1970. Three more in 1971 drew 35, and 70 dogs were entered in four 1972 trials. Spring trials are currently being held in at least a dozen states, plus Canada. Although growth has not been explosive, the movement is experiencing widespread interest. Once limited to a few northern states and Ontario, NAVHDA now has members in almost every region of North America.

The breeds most often regarded as versatile are German Shorthaired and Wirehaired Pointers, Pudelpointers, Griffons, Vizslas, Weimaraners and Brittany Spaniels.

All breeds are eligible, however. When we say versatile in North America, at this point in time we're talking about handling several species of birds before and after the gun. Few of North America's bird dogs are taught to handle fur in any way.

NAVHDA is in very capable hands. Several very dedicated people have consistently served as officers. Dr. Edward D. Bailey, of Puslinch, Ontario, is a professor of animal behavior and is currently the director of judging as well as secretary of the association. Dr. Bailey's wife Joan is secretary-treasurer of the Wirehaired Pointing Griffon Club of America and the gifted editor of *The Gun Dog Supreme,* the Griffon Club's news bulletin which the Dog Writer's Association of America voted best of its kind. Donald Smith, of West Simsbury, Connecticut, is a German Wirehair authority. Jerome J. Knap, of Guelph, Ontario, is the author of many excellent magazine articles on sporting dogs. Sigbot "Bodo" Winterhelt is a Pudelpointer breeder of Orono, Ontario, who had been a trainer and breeder of versatile dogs in Germany for 30 years.

There are many things an inexperienced hunter or even breeder may not know about dogs in general and his in particular. There are few things he won't know, however, if he enters a young dog in a natural ability trial and pays close attention. Any dog born in the year before the trial is eligible. And it's during this period in life that hereditary flaws become apparent. If the hunter is aware of them early, he can save years of wasted effort by promptly getting a new prospect. The breeder will know whether a young dog is suitable to be part of his future program.

Let's take a look at a typical natural-ability trial that was held at Hugo, Minnesota. The trial was conducted on Sunday at the Maple Island Hunt Club, so a training clinic was held there on Saturday. The significantly different approach to teaching obedience, particularly the all-important "whoa" and mild-force retrieving, was instituted by Bodo Winterhelt. He believes a dog is less sure of himself when off the ground on a bench and is, therefore, more cooperative. This speeds the early obedience training.

Every part of a dog contributes to his capability, or lack of it, as a hunter. And NAVHDA judges consider all of it. The trial begins by coat and conformation judging. This is not a show. Dogs are not compared, and no winners are declared. This is an examination. Are the dog's shoulders sloped at the proper angle to give it adequate reach? Are the stifles correctly bent to provide drive? Are front and rear balanced to allow

Dogs are checked and rated for coat, jaw alignment, shoulders, legs, chest cavity—everything that enables a dog to do his job.

Stu Mandelkow tempts the dog with a live pheasant—the first step in either tracking tests or training.

the dog to flow across the ground? Or will poor structure cause a tiring rocking-horse gallop? Are the pasterns so straight that they'll fail to absorb the jolt when the running dog lands on his front feet? Does the rib cage give adequate lung room? All of these points and more greatly affect a dog's performance and endurance in the field.

Coat is especially important to the versatile breeder because these dogs are expected to retrieve from water, sometimes in low temperatures. Good wire coats are difficult to breed, so extra attention is required. Short-haired dogs may not retrieve in very cold water, but they need a dense coat to protect them from briars and brush. It takes a trained eye to recognize all the desirable and undesirable physical traits of dogs. But you could enter a dog in shows a half dozen times before you even found out it wasn't capable of winning. And never would a judge give you a detailed appraisal as is done at NAVHDA trials.

When field tests began at Hugo, it was immediately obvious that some dogs had been started on game while others were pure innocents. Since natural ability is so important to breeders, I began to wonder if these trials might not end up like puppy events in

other types of field trials. Precocious puppies sometimes come on strong when rigorously trained. They look good at first, then fail to continue in development because the pressure finally destroys the young dog's interest. Won't handlers learn to train dogs before ability trials? Won't these trials be self-defeating if trainers put too much effort into this?

After watching a trial and considering the eventualities, I'm hopeful—even confident—that this won't happen. In the first place, a good early score will not help a dog become a well-known stud if he can't show outstanding ability when he's of stud age. Secondly, there's no fame and fortune or prestige and purse to tempt a trainer into risking his dog's future. And finally NAVHDA judges are looking for *natural* ability, and they're quite capable of recognizing the difference.

As a matter of fact, NAVHDA recommends starting young dogs to bring out latent abilities before entering a trial. Seven hereditary characteristics are judged: nose, search, water love, pointing, tracking, desire to work and cooperation. The latter is a good example of judges' ability to discern natural from trained ability. "We're looking for cooperation as opposed to obe-

The track is begun by pulling a few body feathers—then releasing the bird.

dience," Don Smith said. "When the handler turns, will the dog come with him, or will it decide to go on hunting where it likes?"

"Dogs often make long, straight-out runs when we're walking downwind," Joan Bailey said. "We always hope they'll quarter on the way back. If handlers will quarter, they'll lead their dogs into doing it, and we can judge cooperation."

When one dog follows his handler's movements without a signal, and the other responds only when ordered by whistle or voice, it's easy to recognize the difference between natural cooperation and obedience.

Judging is conducted in three separate events: water, tracking and hunting. Cooperation is evident in all three, but most of all in hunting. Desire to work shows itself everywhere. Sluggish or mechanical workers get poor scores.

Tracking is an interesting test as well as a way to start a dog in this work. "Handlers are often amazed by what their untrained dogs do in this test," Don Smith said. "One Weimaraner ran a pheasant track for 250 yards. Young dogs have trailed as far as 400 yards in these trials."

The dogs start where the feathers were pulled.

The dog is encouraged to smell and develop a desire for the bird.

The bird is thrown a few feet out.

The dog is shown and allowed to smell a wing-clipped pheasant. Then the dog's vision is obscured by natural cover (a group of handlers or a blind) while judges pull a few breast feathers and drop them where the track will start. The pheasant is released and men run along on either side to keep the bird moving and going in the desired direction. The dog is led to the feathers and released to start the track.

Judges look for both eagerness and determination. Some dogs will forget nose and brains, and dash about in the vague hope of accidentally stumbling into their bird. Hopefully, they'll realize the mistake and resort to using their noses. Willingness to drop their heads and trail is an important trait in versatile gun dogs. It becomes even more important as game coverts shrink in numbers and size, and men become too conservation-minded to allow cripples to escape.

Equally important to a versatile dog is water love. The dog that unhesitatingly enters water of any temperature usually has a strong retrieving instinct motivating him. And a dog must be determined to retrieve under any circumstances if he is to be versatile.

Each dog is given two retrieves. The first bird is rolled out near shore so the young dog has nearby incentive that can't be easily forgotten. He can walk out and fetch that one. The next bird is thrown about

The object in this part of the natural ability trial is to see if the dog will enter water and swim.

twenty feet to make sure the dog will swim.

Search and pointing are judged in the field with planted birds. The bird dog should show system in his search. It would be called running an intelligent pattern in field trials, but on a smaller scale for hunters. I hesitate to use terms that may carry field-trial connotations into natural-ability trials, however. NAVHDA encounters enough problems along that line. "A.K.C. judges have a hard time switching to NAVHDA rules," Bill Jensen, of Minnesota, told me. "They keep thinking in terms of placing dogs."

I also noticed that some handlers with obvious experience in A.K.C. foot trials would start out at a brisk pace to push their dogs into faster work. Judges immediately cautioned them to slow down to a normal walk. No one can maintain a pace like that on an all-day hunt, and these dogs are being tested strictly for hunting.

Besides system in search, the dog must also be eager to find game and have the endurance to sustain that eagerness. Hopefully, the dog will hunt with a high head to catch body scents. Dogs that run a straight line out and follow the same one back are severely penalized. They can't smell much going out and only themselves coming back.

A gun follows the judges into the field and waits for a signal. When the dog is happily engrossed in his work, the judge raises his arm and the shotgun is fired. If the tail drops, there is suspicion of gunshyness. If the dog goes merrily on his way, the test is repeated to be absolutely certain.

At this stage of the young dog's life, he's not required to be steady, but he must demonstrate ability to point. Style doesn't count, but the point should be intense, and it should produce a bird.

Nose is being tested throughout the trial. Scent may not be utilized during the simple water tests, but it's very much involved in tracking, search and pointing. Judges will note how far from game the dog catches scent. Much searching and few birds indicates a poor nose if other dogs are finding them. False pointing, if habitual, may also indicate a poor nose. During the time I followed dogs in the Minnesota trial, we had one Griffon that never missed a planted quail or failed to act birdy in a spot where other dogs had found birds earlier. Most dogs trotted right on past. The difference had to be nose.

Dogs are scored from 0 to 4 in all tests. Multipliers are then used to place emphasis on the more important characteristics. Nose is highest with a multiplier of 6 because without it, the dog's ability isn't worth mentioning. And it's judged carefully throughout the test. As Don Smith said, "You can't give a 4 nose to a dog that got a 0 in tracking."

Utility trials for fully trained dogs include all the natural-ability tests plus steadiness to wing and shot, retrieving shot birds, handling and obedience.

When the multipliers are applied to scores in each natural ability test and the figures are totaled, a dog might get a perfect score of 104. One ten-month-old Griffon in Connecticut actually did that. Any dog that gets 93 or more is credited with a I prize. And the owner of that dog leaves with the confidence that his dog is highly trainable and in possession of genes worthy of passing to another generation.

These are trials that will make hunting dogs. If you're further interested, contact Edward D. Bailey, R.R. No. 1, Puslinch, Ontario, Canada. Dr. Bailey and Sigbot Winterhelt also prepared a book on versatile dog training which is available from Don Smith, Box 188, West Simsbury, Connecticut 06092.

Walking in with the dog gives him more courage if it's his first time in the water.

The *really* versatile dog makes an impression by delivering the bird right to a judge.

8/Dog Care

Quartering

Where the dog will live and how is not necessarily the simple decision it seems when we bring home that quiet, inoffensive little seven-week-old pup. Will we be happier with it in the house or outside in a kennel? Will it be happier inside or out?

That's only the first decision, but it's an important one. A pup is such a delightful creature that we may want it near us inside. It will be worth the trouble of toilet training and avoiding chewed shoes and furniture. And there's no longer any doubt that close relationships with humans improves our hunting dogs. Bird dogs have good coats and won't catch cold when taken afield in the winter provided they're not tied outside to chill after a hunt. If we have children, so much the better. A few nips and slaps, and they'll teach each other marvelous things about respect and citizenship.

One thing for sure, there's nothing lonelier than a dog kenneled outside by himself to make his own amusements for 23 hours and 50 minutes of each day while waiting for food, fresh water and a pat on the head.

On the other hand, if some of the family will regard the dog as a nuisance, he may be better off outside. A hated dog can get some pretty warped behavior patterns. If the whole family works, the dog will probably find life more interesting outside where he can see things happening during the daytime.

The best thing to do for an outside kennel dog is get him a buddy. Two or more dogs are quite happy in adjacent pens. It isn't wise to keep two males or two females together in the same run. Sooner or later there'll be a fight. Even if your dogs are well disciplined, there's always a chance of a fight while everyone is gone. Males and females rarely fight and can be kept in the same run except for three weeks twice a year while the bitch is in heat. From any viewpoint adjacent runs are most satisfactory.

The eternal question about runs is what kind of floor material shall be used? Concrete is easy to hose and keep clean after the stools are picked up. In a large kennel there is hardly any other choice. For the average hunter with one to three dogs, however, I think it's seldom the best choice. Concrete is too cold in the winter and too hot in the summer. Remember the hot concrete streets when you were a barefoot boy? Imagine lying on that in the summer. Or imagine trying to warm up a spot to lie outside in the sun during the winter.

Jack Godsil, who must use concrete because of the size of his kennels, says a pretty fair solution to discomfort is a bench at the rear of the run. The dog can lie on it or under it, depending on whether it wants sun or shade.

Concrete runs are cold in the winter and hot in the summer, but may be necessary for cleanliness where many dogs are kept.

Tommy Sorenson keeps his field-trial Labs on runs of "chat," or pebble-sized crushed limestone.

Tommy Sorenson uses concrete runs for some dogs, but keeps his top field-trial Retrievers on "chat," which is pebble-size crushed limestone. "It's more natural on their feet," Sorenson says, "and more comfortable in any temperature."

I've used chat in my own pens and find it satisfactory for most dogs. I dug a ditch around the perimeter of my pens and laid concrete blocks to prevent dogs from digging out. Then a good grade of wire fencing was laid on the bottom of the run and covered with chat. The wire will stop the dogs from digging holes in the runs. However, if the wire rusts, and the dog digs through, you've got a real mess with soil (probably urine-saturated and smelly when wet) mixed with the chat. Use good, heavy wire.

A friend of mine built his pen of two-by-four framing, then covered it—sides, top and bottom—with heavy hog-wire fencing. The pen could even be moved since no posts were sunk in the ground. He put about four inches of sand in the bottom for cleanliness. Stools come up easily from the sand, instead of sticking to the wire bottom. Urine soaks through sand easily, which reduces smell.

Sand or chat sticks to the stools, of course, so some is lost daily and must eventually be replaced. This is not a great problem. In fact, when new chat is added the limestone reduces smells further and helps kill germs and parasites.

These military-type dog houses at Gunsmoke Kennels allow the dog a full 360-degree run.
The sweeping chain makes the run self-cleaning.

The main problem is maintaining the bottom wire to prevent dirt from being dug into the sand or chat and turning the pen into a muddy mess during wet weather. If you own calm dogs, there are no other problems with chat or sand that I know of. Nervous pen runners are troublesome on these materials, however. Their running, scooting to a stop and turning soon has the chat, pebbles or sand piled up all around the outside of the pen. Unless constantly raked back, the pen floor becomes a bare dish to hold water and smells. A concrete floor is the only thing that will save your sanity with a nervous dog.

Gunsmoke Kennels has experimented with about every kind of dog housing there is. Their facilities vary from the common to a house raised off of the ground on a short, thick post. The dog is chained to a loose ring around the post, so it has the run of a complete circle around the dog house. C. L. Owens said the system is self-cleaning. The chain sweeps everything outside of the perimeter of the dog's run. The idea was first developed by the military.

The first dog house I built was almost big enough for a Shetland pony. That seems to be a common mistake. But mistake it is. A dog warms his house during the winter with nothing but body heat. If the house is too big, it can't be kept warm.

A house should be tall enough for the dog to sit up and wide enough for comfort when curled up to sleep.

It's most important that the construction be tight so there are no drafts. I've seen many scrap-lumber dog houses that showed light between every board. Imagine how the wind sweeps through on a cold winter night. Build the dog house of plywood, masonite or cover it with tarpaper roofing or siding.

Excellent dog houses can be bought by those who don't care to build them. Canine Pal, of Gary, Indiana, makes an insulated metal house. Custoglass, of New Strawn, Kansas, makes Fiberglas houses. Fiberglas is a very sanitary material and is easy to keep clean. Choose a home with a flat, sloping roof. Dogs enjoy using them as sun decks.

I see lots of dog houses without door coverings during extremely cold weather. Healthy dogs won't die from exposure, but I see no reason why dogs should be miserable all winter just because they can survive it. A burlap sack, old rug or what have you nailed over the doorway is very little effort for the comfort it provides. Of course, young dogs will regard such coverings as new tug-of-war toys. Correct them at every opportunity and nail the sacks back in place. They are not capable of reasoning that the sacks they tore down would have kept them warm that night.

Manure is always a problem with owners of several dogs. The offal of a single dog might be included in the garbage where no ordinance prevents the practice. Doggie Dooley is a portable stool dissolver that uses

A permanent barrel-type house at Gunsmoke Kennels
features a feeder in the rear.

This dog house is off of the ground to
avoid dampness. The roof is hinged for cleaning.

chemicals and water to break down the feces and
destroy odors. Another model is sunk into the ground
over a pit where dissolved stools seep into the ground.
One friend of mine built a septic tank just for his dogs.
He hoses the stools into a gutter and hence to the tank
daily. Stools of inside dogs can be flushed down the
toilet if the dogs are taught to defecate on paper. It
wouldn't make sense to scoop feces out of the dirt and
carry them inside to the toilet. Too much dirt, sand,
rocks and other debris would settle in the plumbing
and eventually clog the pipes.

If you've never quartered a dog in the house, a few
tips will ease the burden of training. First, get yourself
a collapsible dog crate. That is by far the most simple
method of house breaking. Pups are very particular
about keeping their nests clean, so put the crate in the
kitchen or wherever an eye can be kept on the pup and
make the crate his nest.

Keep the pup in the crate at all times, except when
playing with him or when he's eating or drinking.
When he whines and shows signs of nervousness, take
him outside or wherever you want his duty done.

Make sure the crate isn't too large, or he'll defecate
in one end and live in the other. If you've purchased a
large crate to be used in traveling when the dog
matures, partition it in some way to reduce the size.

Since the pup won't dirty his nest except in an
extreme emergency, he can be left for a few hours

without fear of consequences. If he sleeps in the crate at night, there'll not be a pile waiting to be cleaned up in the morning. But when you do get up in the morning, don't dawdle in getting to the pup. Get him out quickly while he can still hold it.

The crate method has two more advantages. If the pup whines or yaps at night, an old blanket can be draped over the crate. Most pups quiet down in complete darkness. Probably every bit as important as the other advantages is the fact that using a crate only burdens the pup with learning one thing at a time. Right now, it's "don't potty in the house." Learning to stay off furniture, not to chew valuables, to stay out from under foot and other lessons of citizenship need not bear down on him all at once.

If you've ever watched a pup getting nature's urge, you've noticed how he seems to be prancing around nervously vacuuming the ground with both ends. When one end detects just the right place, gates open at the other. You can use that trait to teach the dog to relieve itself wherever you choose.

Dogs prefer to relieve themselves where they or others have before. National Scent Company has developed a housebreaking scent that takes advantage of this instinct. Put a couple of drops in a strategic spot, and make sure the pup smells it at the crucial moment. Keep in mind that the pup's nose will be on the scent and that the mess will be a body length away.

I tried housebreaking scent on a Lab pup, and she was unfailing about defecating on the paper. It did not give 100 percent control over her urination, however. We gave her a bed instead of a cage and short-coupled her to it at night to prevent accidents. During the day, she was kept within a few feet of her bed on paper by means of a leash. Like the cage method, this prevented her from having to learn everything about citizenship all at once. It will not stop the pup from relieving itself at will, however, as the cage method does.

The dog's own urine smell on a scrap of soiled paper can be used in place of breaking scent. I experimented by letting the Lab pup have a choice, and she invari-

Nelson Nungesser, of Highland, Illinois, demonstrates the best way to housebreak a pup. Get him a cage. He won't dirty his nest, so the pup learns to get attention so he's taken outside when duty calls.

ably chose the commercial scent. It's also less offensive to humans and can be placed accurately on large paper that will stay in place. The scrap of paper usually migrates to exactly the wrong place by the time it's needed.

The whole breaking process can also be minimized by keeping in mind that a pup—or older dog as well—will defecate soon after eating. Learn how long it takes and watch for it. Don't forget that pups should be fed three to five times a day. But don't make food available all day long or defecation can't be timed.

Much the same thing applies to water. Allow the pup to have all it wants with its food. But don't give it free access to water or the pup will be at it continually. You'll be running for the pup every few minutes.

This is even more important at night. Cut off all water about 6 p.m., and the pup will be fairly well dried out before you go to bed. There's no point in losing sleep just because you bought a pup.

When the pup is housebroken and learns to enjoy more freedom, he'll be on the furniture. Chase him off with a rolled-up newspaper. He'll learn to stay off, until you leave, at least. If you begin to notice dog hairs on the sofa, lay newspapers over the pillows. Set some mouse traps underneath. The traps snapping under the delinquent pup will remind him of the rules.

If he chews furniture, wet the spot and smear with pepper. It's a better idea to visit a pet shop and buy a can of aerosol spray made to stop chewing. It can be used on strategic chair legs, etc., to stop the practice before it starts. But give the pup something he is allowed to chew. There will be less conflict.

And that, I think, is one of the most important concerns in quartering dogs—fewer conflicts, the fewer the better. Think ahead and anticipate what might cause conflicts for household and dog. Everyone will be happier, including the dog that will develop into a much more confident companion afield.

Feeding

Dogs need 43 nutrients in proper proportions to

Kept in its bed by means of a short coupler there's little fear of the pup relieving itself during the night. Pups do not mess their own nests if they can avoid it.

Author's daughter Ann places a couple of drops of breaking scent on paper. The paper toweling will be used to help soak up urine later. Newspaper is not completely effective.

Pepper always looked for the scented spot.

maintain good health and fine spirits. Dogs can get these nutrients in several ways. How they do is a matter of convenience, cost and palatability.

Wild canines get most of what they need by consuming the entire kill. Vitamin-rich innards are eaten first. Muscle provides protein. There's calcium in bone, and no bones are left behind except those too big to crack. Feathers add trace minerals when the whole bird is gulped. Canines will lick salt from the earth when they find it and feel the need. Whatever is still lacking will be gotten from small quantities of greens, berries, fruits and vegetables.

A rabbit a day would probably keep the vet away for most of our dogs, but most dogs would starve while waiting around to get their requirements in that manner. The next-most-likely dog to starve or half starve while waiting for its requirements is the animal whose owner is a do-it-yourself dog dietician. This fellow goes to great trouble and expense to bring together a balanced diet of misinformation, old wives' tales and ignorance. Hamburger for protein, eggs for coat, milk for calcium, and so on, will add up to a very palatable, unhealthy diet. We forgot vitamins. The dietician is sure to add vitamins. Even if he feeds a complete commercial ration that already contains vitamins and minerals in the correct amounts and proportions, he'll add more.

Actually, getting some nutrients in the wrong proportions can be as bad as having none. Calcium and phosphorus must be fed in a 1.2 to 1 ratio. An imbalance can cause rickets.

Raw egg white contains avidin which can tie up the vitamin biotin. An occasional egg won't hurt a dog, but if fed on a constant basis the dog may lose hair instead of acquiring the intended slick coat.

Unsaturated fats are also fed for coat conditioning. If that's overdone, the need for vitamin E increases. A bitch may abort or a male go sterile from insufficient vitamin E.

Many people have the notion—sometimes aided and abetted by advertisers—that since dogs are carnivorous, their perfect diet would be 100 percent muscle meat. I've already mentioned the need for calcium. A bird dog of average size requires about 6000 milligrams daily. There are 50 milligrams of calcium in a pound of muscle. It would take 120 pounds of meat daily to supply the minimum requirement.

People have fed the all-meat diet, of course. Teeth came loose, puppy teeth didn't form properly, and dogs became lame, maybe losing weight in addition. By an all-meat diet, I mean meat only. Canned meat with vitamins and minerals added is a complete diet if its manufacturer has complied with government standards for dog foods.

What about the cereal-based dog foods? Isn't it wrong to feed a meat-eater grain? Soybeans have been a protein staple in China for 5000 years. Protein is essential. It makes no difference where it comes from.

Other grains supply energy-giving carbohydrates. The important thing is that the dog food contains all the nutrients in correct proportions.

Another example is vitamin B. It's necessary for growth, appetite and healthy skin. The vitamin B that's derived from brewer's yeast or whole cereal is just as healthful as that which comes from liver.

By now it should be obvious that concocting a special diet is not doing your dog a favor. Pet food is a big business, and the industry has made great efforts to research their product. They not only know what your dog needs, but they make it available for less than you can assemble it yourself.

The industry also produces a great variety of foods. There are dry, semi-moist and two kinds of canned foods: cereal-based and all-meat. What kind is best for your dog?

A recent survey revealed that 46 percent of America's dogs are fed dry food, 21 percent get semi-moist, and 59 percent eat canned food. Some people used more than one type, so the total exceeds 100 percent. I don't know how gun dogs fit into these figures, but I do know the majority of people in that survey chose palatability over cost and convenience.

Perhaps if I fed one dog, I'd cater to his tastes, too. But cost is an important factor to anyone who keeps several hunting dogs. Just to compare, I asked my sister-in-law what she feeds her 15-pound Dachshund. When we added up the milk bone, top quality canned food and milk the dog consumes each year, it totalled nearly $225. That's almost twice what it costs to feed dry food to one of my dogs, and mine weigh more than three times as much. Dog-food makers estimate a 50-pound hunting dog will need about 1½ pounds of dry food each day. Hard-worked dogs may require more. My dogs burn up different amounts of energy according to their temperaments. They also need more food when working than when not and more in cold weather than in hot. But averaging all of my dogs over the entire year, they consume only a little more than the manufacturer's estimate.

Not all canned dog food labels advise how much of the contents to feed. I'd judge about 2½ cans, at the minimum, for a 50-pound dog, maybe more in cheaper brands. According to prices in a nearby supermarket, annual costs would be two to six times as high as dry food. The broad range of price is caused by the type and quantity of meat in the contents.

Semi-moist products in the same supermarket cost two to three times as much as dry dog feed.

Despite the much higher price, a good brand of canned food may contain only 13 percent crude protein compared to 25 percent in dry food. Besides that, the canned food is 74 to 78 percent water compared to 10 percent moisture in dry food. Semi-moist products are only 30 percent moisture and closely compare with dry rations in calories. A pound of semi-moist has 1,318 calories, while a pound of dry has 1,550. Any of the nutritionally complete foods in the correct amounts will maintain the dog's health

"The printing on this box, as far as I can make out, says, "Free, please take one.' "

The point is (pardon the pun) this connoisseur is taking a multiple choice flavor test. Whichever you think he's pointing out, you're wrong. There's a pigeon behind those cans, which conclusively proves that dogs don't know what's best for them.

and well being. Meat is expensive, but there's no question that it tastes better. Dry food is a better dollar value and can't be as palatable, yet dogs eat it readily and eagerly. Perhaps it depends on how you feel about it.

Dry rations have one other advantage. They can be offered in a self-feeder. This is very useful for pregnant or nursing bitches and, later on, their pups. During the last four weeks of gestation, the bitch may need 25 percent more food. When she's nursing the pups, her nutritional needs may triple. You can't know how much she needs at the time she needs it most, but she can. If given a self-feeder at that time, her intake is self-adjusted.

Pups can't keep a lot of food in those little bellies, but their growing bodies have large demands. So pups need to eat frequently—three to five times daily. A self-feeder allows the pups all they can eat when they need it.

Except for these special instances, I don't recommend self-feeders for everyone, however. Dogs generally do fine nutritionally. They overeat at first, but soon taper off, and almost always eat just what it takes to keep them in good shape. There are gluttons that can't use self-feeders, but the main objection I have to using them concerns the masters, not their dogs. It's too easy to fill the feeder and a big bucket of water and forget the dog for days. Dogs do not thrive

with that kind of neglect.

Jack Godsil brought up a point I hadn't thought about. Dogs go off of their feed as a first symptom of illness. If they're on self-feeders, you may not know something is wrong until it reaches an advanced stage. Then it may be too late.

Whether to feed dry rations as is or moisten them seems immaterial to the dogs. I have noticed that an occasional change seems to be appreciated by the dogs. If they're accustomed to it wet, they seem to enjoy chewing on the dry chunks. Those that normally eat it dry seem to find wet rations tastier.

Mine are fed moistened rations most of the year because I mix Caracide with the food to prevent heartworms. I notice the dogs particularly appreciate warm water mixed with their rations during cold weather. Of course, the heartworm preventative can't be given in a self-feeder, but see more on that in the medical section.

What about table scraps? Dogs relish them. Will they upset the balance of nutrients in prepared rations? I mix scraps with the rations to spice the meal. It won't cause deficiency problems if scraps don't average more than 10 or 15 percent of the total food bulk.

Despite the fact that dogs love bones, there are dangers in feeding them. Chicken bones shatter. Other bones get stuck between the teeth across the roof of the mouth. Bones also tend to become compacted in the intestines, making it difficult, and in some cases impossible, to defecate. If you must give a dog bones, make sure the amount is small compared to the total meal.

How often should you feed your dog? Most dogs are ready to eat any time. Yet they don't seem to experience real hunger pangs as we do. Wolves may gorge themselves on a big kill and have to sleep it off, but as soon as they're up and moving, they're again interested in food. Spoiled pets may go for days trying to hold out for favorite foods, and it doesn't harm them. Dr. Leon F. Whitney says well-fed dogs don't become really hungry for 36 hours. The important thing is not how often the dog is fed, but how much. Once a day seems convenient for most people. Feed whatever it takes to keep your dog in shape—not too fat, nor too skinny—using the manufacturer's recommendation as a guide or starting point, not an absolute rule.

Don't worry about variety. While we would soon tire of eating the same thing day after day, it doesn't affect dogs' appetites at all. They look forward to their meal with the same eagerness day after day. In fact, a change of diet or brand sometimes creates loose bowels. Try a few brands at first. See which makes firm stools for your dog, then stick with it. Adding table scraps occasionally will be enough of a change to provide a treat, if you want the dog to have it.

Hard-working dogs sometimes may not consume quite enough dry rations to maintain good weight. If you're hunting your dog hard and he's growing thin, add up to 25 percent fat (especially in colder climates) or mix in any amount of nutritionally complete canned food. A temporary diet of half hamburger-half rice cooked together will also put weight on a sick or hard-worked dog. It's not a superior diet, but dogs love it, so they'll eat as much as they're given.

There's one other consideration in feeding dogs. Feed them plenty of sunshine. This is especially important to pups. Old dogs are rarely inside all of the time, but pups often start life in basements and outbuildings. Vitamin D is essential to unlock calcium and phosphorus in the body. Teeth and bones cannot form properly without them. If sunshine cannot be provided, ask the vet how much halibut liver oil, or whatever he recommends, should be added to the diets of the nursing dam and her pups.

Care and Grooming

Have you ever considered scraping the tartar from the teeth of a seven-week-old pup? Ridiculous? Yes! But that's the age to lay groundwork for that and all later care and grooming. Begin by handling the pup—all over and a great deal. Lift his lips. Run your fingers over his teeth. Raise his ears, and gently rub the underear and opening with cotton or a finger. Open his

Self-feeders are especially good for pregnant or nursing bitches and growing pups.

This Lixit automatic waterer provides water at all times. Dogs catch on in minutes how licking gets them a drink.

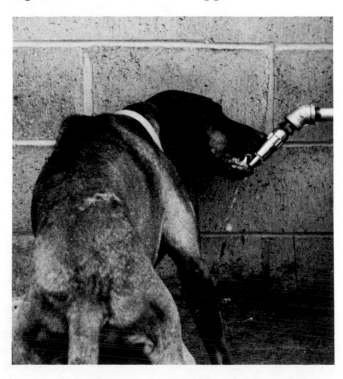

Nelson Nungesser, of Highland, Illinois, demonstrates cleaning tartar from teeth with a new dime.

mouth and hold his jaws apart for a few moments as if to give a pill. Pick up his paws one at a time. Hold his tail. Stroke it. Squeeze the anal glands. Do it gently. Nothing will come out. It's just training. Talk soothingly all the while you're handling the pup.

By handling, I *do not* mean rolling the pup on his back and teasing him into biting and struggling. Even while you're handling him gently, he'll probably squirm and wiggle, Keep it up anyway. If you don't, you'll have a real fight on your hands when handling is necessary to his care and the full-grown pup has become touchy, ticklish and skittish. Make it a form of attention. The pup will not only learn to accept it, he'll begin to enjoy and look forward to it.

If the pup lives in the house, probably the first outrage to his person that he'll experience is a bath. Pups don't care where they walk. Despite how careful you are when taking them outside to answer nature's call, pups will make mistakes. They'll run through it.

And they'll smell like it. Perhaps bathing once a week will be enough. Let your nose be your guide.

If the pup is small, he can be gently placed bodily into a tub of lukewarm water. Talk soothingly the first few times. Even when an action seems threatening to a dog, speech can reassure him.

If a dog is bathed in the bathtub, push a wad of steel wool in the drain to catch the hair.

Don't try to introduce an older dog to bath water by depositing him unceremoniously into a tub. You'll both be wet before bathing starts. Lead him to it. Talk to him. Lift his front feet into the tub. Tell him how nice it is. Begin soaking his front end. Go slow and easy. If he remains calm, it won't be difficult to lift his rear end into the water.

A little thought and planning will almost always improve the relationship by avoiding violent reactions. If it doesn't work, make a believer of him. He can't be allowed to bluff you out of taking a bath or

Author begins bath by putting the dog's front legs in first. There is less struggle with a gradual entry.

After the dog is wet down and accustomed to the water, it's easier to lead him all the way into the tub.

anything else.

A great many kennel dogs aren't bathed from one year to the next and don't suffer from it. In fact, bathing is something we do to make the dog acceptable in our company. Except in rare cases, it's not for the dog's benefit. In fact, bathing too frequently makes the hair dry and susceptible to dirt. A good oily coat stays rather clean if the dog is in clean surroundings, and especially if he gets new bedding frequently.

When bathing is being done for the dog's benefit, it's to remove something that may be toxic or to kill a parasite. When bathing dogs for any reason, I like to use a shampoo containing hexetidine. It not only cleans and deodorizes the dog, but also destroys bacteria and fungi associated with skin problems.

The old flea soap was and is good for its purpose, too. With all the other products available, however, there are easier and more effective flea controls than bathing. Powders have always been effective, but I personally prefer the newer sprays when numbers of fleas need to be destroyed in a hurry. Hands sometimes smell for days after rubbing powder into the dog's coat. If dusted around the inside corners of his house, the dog may experience the discomfort of getting powder into his nostrils for a time. Sprays penetrate the dog's coat as well as every corner of his house without the attendant discomforts.

The best flea control of all is the flea collar. I used to fight fleas every year. About the time I'd lick the problem, my dogs would bring a new strain of flea from someone else's dog. Now I give each dog a new flea collar every summer. They last about three months. If there are fleas in your pen, the collar not only kills the adults, but later on it also gets the young that hatch from eggs in the kennel. And it's fatal for the flea that hops a ride on your dog when away from home.

There's one caution about flea collars. Take it off of

After a bath allow the dog to shake himself thoroughly, then dry him with absorbent cloth. Keep him away from loose dirt until completely dry or he'll roll in it and wind up dirtier than before his bath.

A flea collar is the most effective flea control ever invented. Remove it whenever the dog might become wet, however. Water hastens the release of insecticide which can cause a rash on some dogs.

a dog if you expect it to get wet. Or if wetting happens unexpectedly, remove the collar. Water quickens the release of insecticide in flea collars, and too much around the neck at once can cause skin irritations. It happened to one of my dogs the first year I used flea collars. I removed the collar and the infection healed completely in a couple of weeks. This can happen to certain dogs without getting wet. Watch for it.

I have an idea that collars are also preventing some of the skin disorders that can be caused by mites. Sarcoptic mange is a common one. Dr. Whitney cured a dog of mange by installing a Vapone Bar, or no-pest strip, in its quarters. It's my understanding the insecticide is the same in both flea collars and no-pest strips.

Demodectic mange mites get into the hair follicles. If your dog develops bald spots, get it to the vet. I've cured sarcoptic mange with one bath in livestock dip, but demodectic mange mites are difficult to reach and kill. Humans can become infested with them, so it doesn't pay to fool with home remedies.

If your dog has been exposed to mange mites by being near an infested dog, dust him thoroughly with flea powder. If you're quick enough, chances are good of destroying the parasites.

Most hunting dogs that are kenneled outside need little coat grooming unless they're entered in shows. They look rough when shedding the winter coat, so

you may want to hurry the process with a brush or comb, but otherwise they keep themselves presentable enough to suit most men. I've seen Setters come in from a hunt with their undersides caked with mud and their coats tangled with burrs, and the next morning they'd be spick and span. They should have help in this, however. A steel comb and a knife to break up burrs will speed the job considerably.

I asked dog-show judge Herb Hardt what he considers important to coat grooming for hunting dogs that live in the house. "Get a comb," Herb said. "Loose hair hangs in the coat. Brushing over the top doesn't catch it all. A comb rakes it out."

Dogs that are kept inside shed a little the year round instead of seasonally. There's always some hair to get on the furniture and aggravate the wife. It's especially noticeable with long-haired breeds. Nearly all of this problem can be eliminated by daily combing.

Dogs that loaf in the pen all summer grow soft and should be conditioned before hunting season by road work or running in the field. Roading is running in front of or beside a car, bicycle or horse. Taking a dog for a walk will be exercise for you but nothing at all for him.

The summertime loafer will probably grow nails like an ancient Chinese empress. Nail clippers are reasonably priced and easy to use. Frequent clippings

The only really necessary grooming tool for a hunter is a steel comb. It speeds removal of burrs, beggar lice, etc., after a day in the field. If the dog is kept in the house, a daily combing avoids sanitary problems by raking loose hair on the coat's surface. Lynn Nungesser, of Highland, Illinois, demonstrates on Star, a descendant of Irish field champions.

Some dog lovers like to go over the coat with a hound glove after a good brushing. Actually better for breeds with short coats, the small, closely set wire or fiber bristles in the glove-type brush puts nearly every hair in place.

will cause the quick to recede, making a shorter nail that is less likely to break off during a hunt. Getting the dog accustomed to handling as I recommended at the beginning of this section will make nail clipping an easy job. Otherwise it may be a two-man tussle.

The same thing applies to giving medicine or cleaning tartar from teeth. The edge of a new dime cleans scale, but don't try to remove stain with it. And if the dime doesn't do the job, let a vet handle it. A harder instrument in the hands of an amateur could damage the dog's teeth.

Anal glands are just inside the anus. There's one on each side. Sometimes they clog and cause the dog to scoot around on his rear trying to empty them. With the forefinger on one side of the anus and the thumb on the other, squeeze. But don't have your eye in line

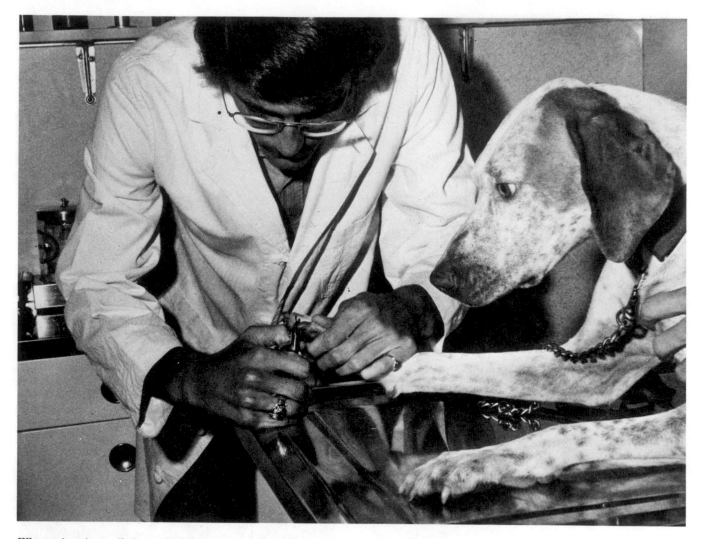

When trimming nails be careful not to cut into the quick. Frequent trimming makes the quick recede which eventually shortens the nails if they're too long on your dog. Long toenails will cause painful toes after the dog's first hunt of the season or pre-season conditioning.

of fire. And do it outside. The odor is foul. And don't squeeze hard enough to break the sac. If in doubt, let a vet do it.

Ears should be cleaned regularly. A cotton swab dipped in alcohol loosens and wipes away the waxy discharge. The amateur shouldn't swab deeply, however. A better method may be to just pour some mercurochrome down each ear and let the dog shake out the excess. If done every couple of weeks during warm weather, ears will remain clean and, according to a friend, free of canker mites.

Eyes should be inspected after each hunt. Dogs breasting cover invariably end the day with the eyes full of small seeds. Work them out with a twist of cotton. An eyewash will also help flush out seeds and dirt. But don't neglect it. The eyes could be badly inflamed by the next morning.

I've saved a pet peeve for last. Give your dog a proper collar. A choke chain is not a collar. It's a training device. Yet great numbers of dogs are afield with the hangman's noose around their necks, tempting fate every time they're out of their master's sight or reach. And every now and then I hear of a dog dying because of it.

I wrote about this in *Field & Stream* and two readers sent me a method of locking the chain in a non-slip position. I can't see the point. The manner of locking the chain makes a loose collar that slips over the dog's head. It's of no value as a restraint in tying a dog, say, in the farmer's yard. It's of use only when your hand is on the chain. In the field it's worthless. Why not simply remove it?

When hunting, a dog should have a collar with a name tag in case of misfortune. I can understand why

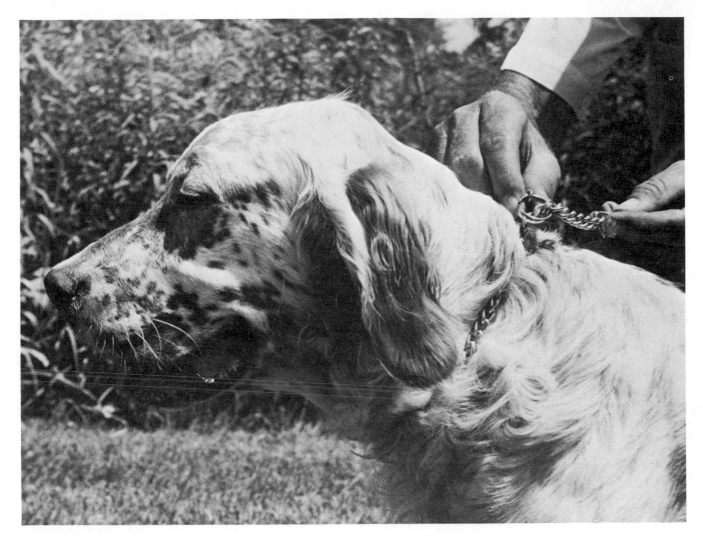

If you must use a choke chain for a collar, run a large-size split key ring through the links to hold the collar open and prevent the dog from being strangled if the chain catches in a fence when he is out of your sight.

A blaze orange sleeve over the dog's collar makes him easier to see and safer while hunting.

hunters like metal collars, especially for Retrievers. Metal doesn't stay soaking wet all night after the hunt. But a good chain collar with a name tag is available at a reasonable price from the Slip Check Company, Centralia, Missouri 65240. There is absolutely no need to insist on using a choke chain for a collar.

Dark dogs that blend well with the background should wear a blaze-orange collar while hunting. Deer hunters have proven blaze orange to be the easiest of all colors to see in the outdoors. This can be a second collar to be removed after the hunt, or it can be the name-tag collar. Blaze-orange sleeves are also available to slip over another collar.

After all of the time and money invested in buying a dog, feeding and housing him, providing his shots, and training for months, it just doesn't make sense to stop short of safety by refusing to spend a few more dollars for a proper collar.

Medical Care

Today's most insidious of all threats to dogs is the heartworm. By the time the average hunter can recognize something is wrong, it's usually too late to save his dog. The animal begins coughing. Gums turn yellow. Urine is the color of coffee. And the vet is helpless. The heart is already hampered by too many adult worms. The shock of killing them would probably kill the dog.

Yet there is a way to diagnose heartworms in time to save the dog. There's even a way to prevent heartworms. In fact, if we carry out the heartworm prevention, we'll knock out two other prominent parasites in the bargain. What are we waiting for then? Probably public awareness—and willingness to perform a simple daily task.

Despite persistent rumors to the contrary, there is not a one-time or once-a-year shot to immunize dogs against heartworms. Let's look at the life cycle of the heartworm to understand why.

First, there are no eggs that might be destroyed in the pen to stop the reproduction cycle. Adult heartworms live and breed in the bloodstream, mostly in the heart and arteries to the lungs. The young, called microfilariae, are born alive at the rate of 20,000 per adult female every day.

Microfilariae are prelarval embryos that are too small to be seen without a microscope. They circulate throughout the bloodstream, but cause no trouble to the host animal while in that stage. In fact, if the dog was never exposed to a mosquito, these microfilariae would circulate harmlessly until they or the dog died of old age.

But the mosquito has to stick his nose into things and ingest a microfilaria in the process. If the microfilaria doesn't kill its new host, it remains in the mosquitoe's excretory organs until it changes into a shorter, fatter larva. This takes place within two weeks after which the larva migrates to the mosquito's snout.

The mosquito becomes a deadly syringe. If his next victim is a dog, the larva is injected into muscle where it molts to a more mature stage. It then bores into a vein and migrates to the heart. In about nine months the young heartworm will become sexually mature.

Not everyone realizes the widespread seriousness of the situation because at one time heartworms were restricted to the South. The greatest infestation is still in the South. Nearly 80 percent of the dogs around Brownsville, Texas, are thought to have heartworms. The situation is even more serious in Florida. But a greater interest in dog trials and shows, coupled with affluence and good transportation, has

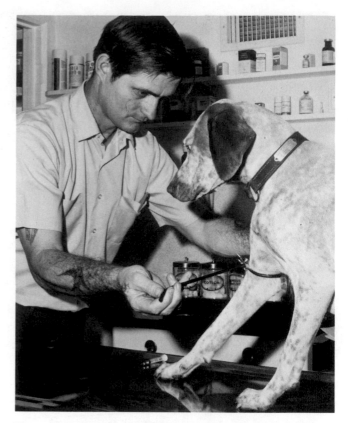

There is no "shot" to immunize against heartworms. Dogs must be checked by a veterinarian to determine if they have the parasite.

spread heartworm all over the country. All it takes is one infested dog and a bunch of mosquitoes. A couple of weeks later, dogs of the area are exposed. In a recent examination of foxhounds in three Maryland hunt clubs, 45 out of 102 had heartworms. There's an infestation around Minneapolis. Routine checks by the St. Louis Humane Society revealed that 15 percent of the dogs brought to them had heartworms.

Dr. Dennis Groom, my veterinarian friend and advisor in these matters, says the profession is more cautious of heartworms today than it used to be. Therefore, more cases are discovered and treated. Many vets now recommend routine blood tests whenever a dog comes in for any reason. Presence of microfilariae in the blood indicates adult worms are present, of course.

Whether heartworms are a newly exploding menace, or it just seems so because of increased awareness, is beside the point. The menace exists. One vet kept records for a time and found he was able to treat only 15 out of 80 dogs that had heartworms. The remaining 65 were beyond help.

To kill adult heartworms, an arsenical medication is injected into the veins at 12-hour intervals. Dead worms break up and lodge in the lungs where the pieces are covered with scar tissue. Too many worms killed at once could kill the dog. The arsenic can also

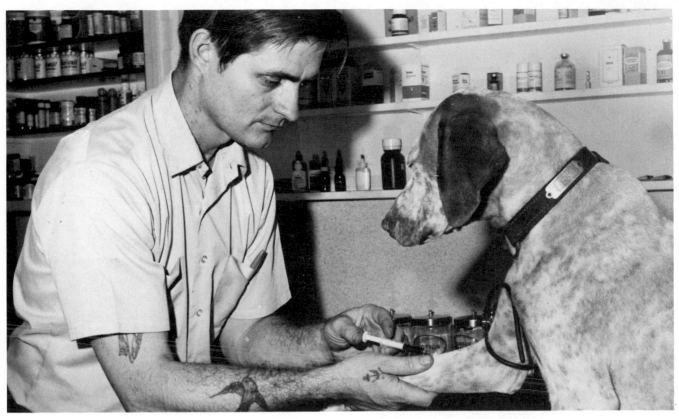

Dr. Dennis Groom draws a blood sample . . .

. . . to be checked under the microscope for microfilariae
(the prelarval embryos of heartworms).

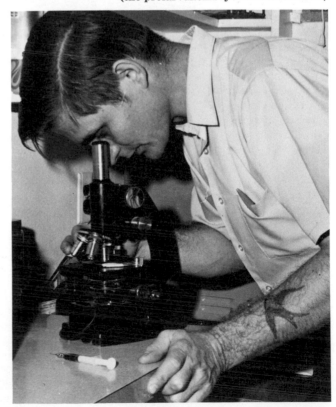

harm or even kill the dog. It's unlikely that a treated dog ever recovers the full health he enjoyed before the heartworms.

Arsenic doesn't kill the microfilariae circulating in the bloodstream. After recovery from treatment, the vet will destroy the pre-embryo young with another drug, probably dithiazanine iodide.

After spending $45 to $90 for treatment and watching the misery of the dog—not to mention the likelihood of permanent damage—we don't want it to happen again. And if we have a promising young dog, we don't want him to ever have heartworms.

Fortunately, a preventive medicine is available: Styrid Caracide. It can only be given after a vet finds the dog to be negative for heartworms, however. *If you acquire Caracide from a friend and give it to a dog that has heartworms, it will kill the dog.* The worms all die at once and the shock is too great for the dog.

Caracide is easy to administer. One cc per 20 pounds of dog is mixed with the food daily. It takes just a moment every day to avoid a great deal of misery. Puppies can be started on Caracide right after weaning. Dogs over nine months of age should be checked by a vet first.

Veterinarians recommend giving Caracide from a month or two before mosquito season until a month or two after the first killing frost. Since frosts are not

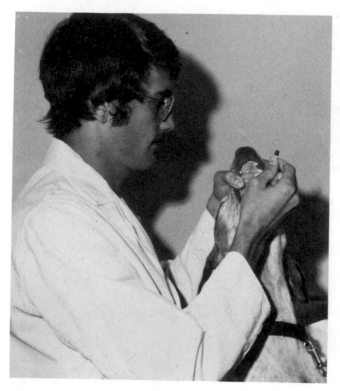

Kevin Rushing, veterinarian assistant, demonstrates the correct way to give a pill.

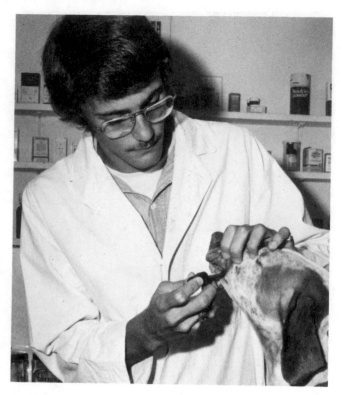

Liquid medicine is more effectively given with an eyedropper than with the old spoon method.

consistent over a wide area, don't be too quick to discontinue treatment. In warm climates the treatment is continued year round.

Some dog owners have feared that feeding a daily dose of an insecticide might itself be damaging. There is no evidence of that, however. Tommy Sorenson gives Styrid Caracide to his field-trial Retrievers the year round. At this writing, he's going into the sixth year of using it. His dogs must be in top shape for competition, and none have suffered any ill effects.

Styrid Caracide also has a welcome side effect. At the level given for heartworms, it controls roundworms and hookworms, too. In one fell swoop, that takes care of a lot of problems. Another drug, Dirocide, is more palatable to dogs, but only controls heartworms and roundworms.

Canine roundworms have been discovered to be rarely, but seriously, dangerous to humans, so we have added incentive to eliminate them.

Infected dogs pass roundworm eggs in every stool. The eggs incubate on the ground in correct humidity and temperature. The larva forms. When the dog or human swallows the egg, the shell is digested and the larvae migrates to the lungs. Normally careful humans are unlikely to ingest roundworm eggs, but it's not impossible—especially for children.

In dogs, we all know the symptoms: pot bellies, thin backs, dull coats and anemia. Roundworms can kill puppies. Humans are not natural hosts for roundworms, so the parasites' life cycles can't be completed. But they may invade lungs or liver and cause pain and discomfort. On very, very rare occasions they have entered the eye or brain.

Don't sit around worrying about it. Take the dog and one of its stools to the vet, and have him checked for all worms, including heartworms. Then get the dog on Caracide, and forget it.

Tapeworms and whipworms seem to trouble dogs less frequently than the other parasites, perhaps, but don't forget the possibility. If the dog is on Caracide and is still showing signs of having worms (stiffness, disinterest or anemia as indicated by white gums) get him to a vet.

Distemper is something we shouldn't even have to discuss. Inoculations have been available for so long that the disease should be stamped out. My friend Dr. Groom gets so riled up over distemper that I know the threat is far from licked. Unwanted, abandoned dogs probably don't get shots. They continue to keep the disease alive. Humane shelters are often infected with distemper. And if the owner of a pup is neglectful, chances are it will be exposed.

Distemper causes cold-like symptoms: coughing, runny nose, watery eyes and fever. Half of the dogs

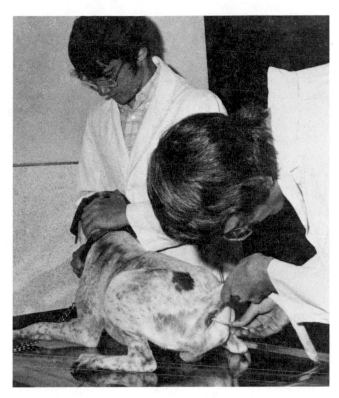

Dog's temperature should be 101° or 101.5°. Take it with an anal thermometer. Temperature is a good indicator if illness is suspected.

Broken bones are always a job for the vet. Never try to set a break yourself. This Wirehair puppy got around quite well with the cast on his leg.

infected don't survive. Those that live frequently suffer permanent damage.

Pups should receive temporary shots at seven weeks and permanent inoculations at twelve weeks. The vet will advise you when to return for booster shots.

The vet won't simply give a distemper shot, however. He'll give a multiple inoculation that also prevents hepatitis and leptospirosis. Hepatitis causes permanent kidney and liver damage in most dogs that survive it. Leptospirosis kills half of the dogs infected with it and endangers humans as well.

Rabies shots are required by law and for good reason. Oppian, the Greek who wrote about the dogs in Brittany about 150 A.D., thought their teeth contained a poison. No doubt the poison was rabies.

Rabies virus is so tiny that it can pass through porcelain. There is no cure for man or dog once infected by rabies.

Dogs infected with furious rabies refuse food, hide from light, and bite anything and everything. Dumb rabies causes the dog to drool and have throat spasms if offered water. Don't go near nor touch either animal. The germs can enter the slightest scratch. Inoculations must begin immediately if a person is bitten by a dog with furious rabies or has a scratch and handles one with dumb rabies. Wild animals may also have rabies. Avoid any animals that do not show

normal fear of humans. Get the pup his rabies shots at twelve weeks, and ask the vet when he should return for the next one. Some types of shots are good for a year, others three.

Dogs may go off their feed for a day and have nothing whatever wrong. Then again, it may be the first symptom of an illness. Temperature will usually reveal whether a dog is sick or not. Normal dog temperature is 101°-101.5°. Use an anal thermometer to find out whether the dog should see a vet.

Most dog books show how to give liquid medicine by pouring a spoonful in a pouch formed by pulling the lip away from the jaw. Dr. Groom says that's doing it the hard way. Use an eye dropper and squirt the medicine between the dog's teeth which are certain to be clenched at this time.

To give pills, open the dog's mouth by pressing his lips against the teeth of the lower jaw with your forefinger and thumb. Tilt the dog's head up, and drop the pill as far back in the throat as possible. Close the dog's mouth immediately, hold it shut, and stroke the underside of his neck until he swallows.

If the dog puts up more struggle than you want to cope with, stick the pill in a wad of meat or dog food that he likes well enough to gulp right down.

A really serious medical problem with today's dogs is hip dysplasia. This is simply abnormal development of the hip socket which cripples the dog as it grows older.

No breeds are immune. According to records kept by Dr. John Bardens, of Lowell, Indiana, as high as 78 percent of all Labrador Retrievers may have it. It may be 86 percent among Goldens.

The disease is hereditary and can only be eliminated by never breeding dogs that suffer from hip dysplasia. Before breeding, have your vet take an X-ray of the bitch's hips. He can send it to the Orthopedic Foundation for Animals, 817 Virginia Avenue, Columbia, Missouri 65201. At a very small cost, Foundation radiologists certify the absence or presence of hip dysplasia. Insist on the same certification of a stud dog. If you're buying a pup, ask for proof that both dam and sire are free from hip dysplasia.

First Aid

When it comes to first aid, too many of us are extremists. Some of us excuse ourselves from knowing about first aid on the grounds that "we take all of our problems to the professional veterinarian who knows what he's doing." The rest of us tend to regard our meager knowledge of first aid as the last word in medical science, and our dogs have to be very nearly

dead before a vet sees them. Actually, first aid is the thumb in the dike that wards off disaster until the engineers can arrive and perform permanent repairs. It makes sense to be prepared and to do what we can. It does not make sense to stop short and fail to let the vet complete repairs.

I've had dogs shot, caught in steel traps, hung in fences, torn open by barbed wire, quilled by porcupines, sprayed by skunks, bitten by animals, chewed by other dogs, and what have you. The one thing I've learned about all dogs that need first aid is that they only know they're being threatened, not how or why or that you're there to help. If they feel sufficiently desperate, they'll protect themselves the only way they know how—with their teeth.

I've had situations I regarded as too dangerous to take time for caution. And I've been bitten. Whenever possible your first action should be to restrain the dog. If you have a first-aid kit—and you should—unroll two or three feet of gauze bandage to muzzle the dog. Approach the dog slowly, and reassure him with soothing talk. Form a loop in the center of the gauze with an overhand knot. Slip it over the dog's muzzle and pull it tight. Bring the ends down and make a knot under the chin. Now draw the loose ends behind the dog's neck and tie securely.

If there is no gauze or other bandage available, look

The first thing to do when a dog needs first aid is muzzle him. He only knows he hurts and will very likely try to bite. Begin by tying an overhand knot over the muzzle.

Bring the ends of the cloth or gauze under the muzzle and tie a second overhand knot. Then draw the ends behind the head.

around for a rope or reasonably strong cord, necktie or woman's cloth belt. In the field where nothing else is available, it may be necessary to use part of your shirt. A handkerchief around the muzzle is better than nothing, but the dog may scratch it off.

When help is around, the shirt can be saved. Draw a belt into a noose, slip it over the dog's muzzle and pull it tight. There's no way to tie it, however, so the helper will have to keep enough tension on it to restrain the dog.

Some dogs snap so viciously that it's next to impossible to muzzle them, yet they must be moved rapidly. Maybe the dog was hit by a car on a busy street or highway. Slip the belt noose over the dog's head, pull it closed as gently as possible, then use the loose end to drag the dog onto a coat or shirt. After that, the coat can be the drag.

A coat can also be used as a stretcher for two men to carry an injured dog out of the field. If there's no help, drape the dog over your shoulders, and carry him out. A stretcher method is much preferred, however, because extra moving, twisting and bending may cause further injury. A broken rib may pierce the lungs. A shattered leg bone may cut an artery. Pressure on damaged internal organs may complicate the injury.

If internal injury and bleeding are suspected, look at the dog's gums. If they remain red and healthy, the dog isn't bleeding. If they turn white, he is. In that case it may be wise to wrap the dog rather tightly to hold organs in place. Tuck the coat snugly around the dog if nothing else is available. Use a folded sheet or blanket or very wide cloth bandages if they can be gotten in a reasonable length of time.

A badly injured or extremely frightened dog may go into shock. If so, treat him for that before anything else. Carry him inside for warmth if it can be done quickly and safely. Otherwise cover him with a coat. Keep his head lower than his body. Calm down yourself, and avoid further excitement to the dog.

The dog in shock may appear to be oblivious to pain. Muscles are relaxed. Gums may be white. His body is probably cold. The nervous system is in a state of depression, so don't administer alcohol. That's a depressant. Give a stimulant such as warm coffee only if there is no bleeding and only if the dog is capable of swallowing. The liquid could choke the dog. The important treatment is keeping the dog warm.

If there is external bleeding, it can best be stopped by applying pressure with a thumb or both thumbs on the wound. Use just enough pressure to stop the bleeding. Continue patiently until the blood has time to clot.

A pressure bandage may also be used to stop bleeding. Apply a wad of cloth to the wound and wrap

Tie the loose ends behind the head.

If no coat or stretcher material is available and you're a considerable distance from the car, the dog can be carried out across the shoulders.

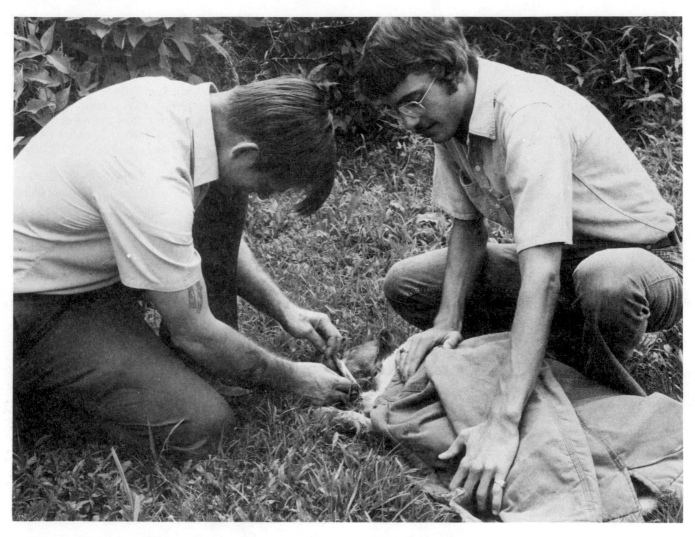

Always treat for shock first. Simply cover the dog to keep him warm. Dr. Dennis Groom is looking at the color of the dog's lips. If they're white, it could mean internal bleeding.

tightly. Unless wrapped very tightly, however, the bandage is useless.

If the wound is too expansive to stop bleeding by these methods, a tourniquet may be necessary. I hesitate to advise this, however, because so many people know how to apply a tourniquet, but don't remember to loosen it every 10 or 15 minutes. This allows some blood circulation. Without it, the limb can be destroyed. If it's essential, use a stick to twist a cloth around the limb above the wound. When bleeding stops, it's tight enough. Just don't forget to loosen it every 10 or 15 minutes on the way to the vet.

Dogs frequently suffer deeply cut pads. These wounds bleed profusely because of the many blood vessels in the dogs' feet. Make sure nothing foreign remains in the cut, and stop the bleeding by the methods already discussed. But let a vet suture the wound to hasten healing.

Hunting dogs have their problems with barbed wire,

the most frequent of which is the triangular tear. The hide is caught and torn back, sometimes for several inches. If there is no further injury, the dog may administer better first aid then you can. Let him lick it. Clean the tear with peroxide if the dog can't reach it. A tear is not something that endangers the dog's life, so it doesn't require emergency treatment. When it happens late and a vet can't be reached, there's no danger in waiting until the next day to have the wound cleaned and sutured.

Don't hesitate to give the dog an aspirin every four hours for pain. Whether it's a tear, serious wound, infection or illness, the dog's misery should be relieved. I find that many dog owners never think of aspirin in first-aid treatment. Perhaps because the dog can't complain and carry on about the severity of his pain as do humans, we're not motivated to relieve it. Unfortunately for them, dogs are most quiet when most miserable. But we're intelligent enough to know

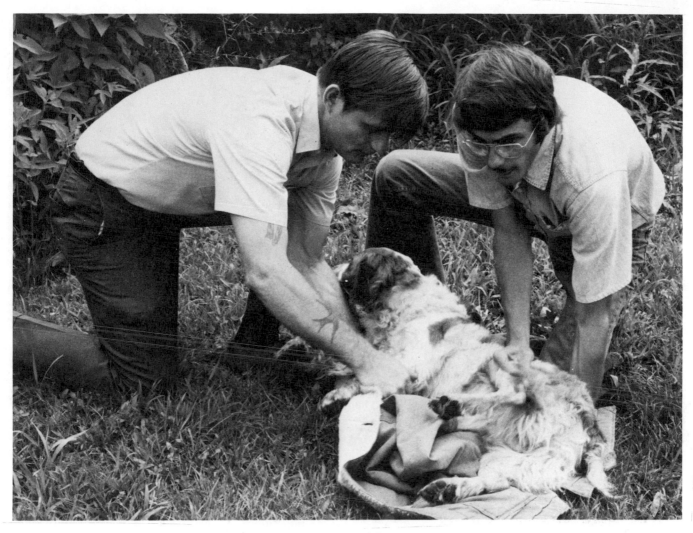

A coat can be used to carry a dog if a better stretcher isn't available.

Wrap the dog tightly, especially if internal injury is feared, and pick him up carefully.

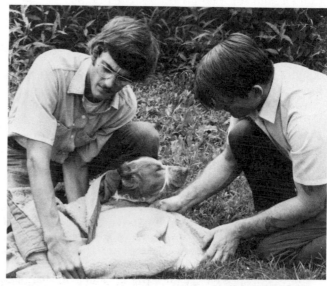

when it has to be hurting the dog. And it only takes a moment to give an aspirin.

Punctures of any sort, including nonfatal bullet wounds, carry the danger of lockjaw. Tetanus germs do not grow in an open wound that's exposed to oxygen, but will if the puncture heals at the surface, sealing in the deadly bacteria. Punctures must be opened and cleaned. The vet will also give an antitoxin injection.

Broken bones carry the added danger of a sharp edge cutting an artery. Make a temporary splint if necessary to keep the bones in place, but *do not set the bones yourself.* Carry the dog on some sort of stretcher to avoid further injury.

Dislocation of a joint requires quick veterinary care. Swelling that occurs during a delay can make it impossible to reset the joint. Apply a cold compress to reduce swelling and pain, and get to the vet fast.

First aid in dog fights is getting them apart. Treat-

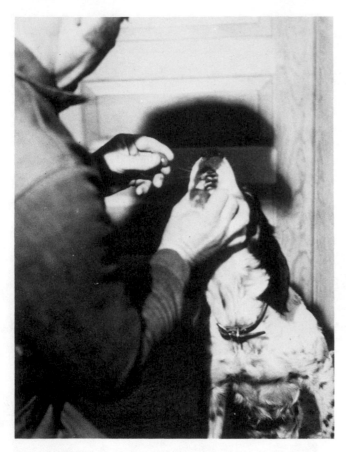

Dogs suffer from pain just like humans, but are quiet about it. Don't hesitate to relieve that pain with an aspirin or other pain reliever that your veterinarian might prescribe.

Kevin Rushing demonstrates how to restrain a dog while administering pressure to a wound to stop the bleeding.

ing cuts and bruises comes later. If a bucket of water is handy, drenching the combatants may stop the fight. Sparring dogs can be parted by grabbing the aggressive dog's tail and slinging him out of the way. But don't reach for a collar unless the dog has locked his jaws on the enemy and won't let go. When teeth are flying, the dog very likely won't realize he's biting you. He's lashing out at whatever he feels is threatening him.

Once a large dog has a jaw hold, it's difficult to get him loose. There's no time to search for a pry-bar, and it could cause more damage. Slide your hand under the dog's collar from behind. Get a good grip. That takes the slack out of the collar and makes it impossible for the dog to turn against your clenched hand. A friend has stopped fights by blowing into the dog's ear after he has a grip on the collar, but I wouldn't get my face that close to the action.

Kicking, hitting and yelling have no effect on fighting dogs. They seem oblivious to pain. I had one fight in which it just wasn't physically possible for me to separate the two by twisting an ear or pulling and shaking. When I got desperate enough to take the chance, I even tried pulling the jaws apart with both

hands. Finally, I choked the aggressor by twisting his collar with all of my strength. When he ran out of air, he let go. By luck he wore a Slip Check chain collar that could be twisted. Perhaps a belt pulled tightly around the neck would work as well or better. I didn't think of it until later, and I hope I never have a chance to try it.

Fights occur mostly when a little common sense would avoid them. It seldom happens in the field. It's usually before or after a hunt, around the kennels or anywhere jealousy motivates the dogs.

The dog I feel most sorry for is the one suffering heatstroke. Dogs have enough sense to make themselves comfortable. Heatstroke can only happen when the dog is forced to overexercise in hot weather, is tied out in the hot sun for too long or, worst of all, is left in an automobile in the full sun with the windows closed. The temperature can reach 200 degrees inside such a car. And a prolonged 115 degrees can damage a dog's brain.

Heatstroke symptoms are heavy breathing, glassy-eyed exhaustion, vomiting, purple tongue and inability to stand. Carry the dog into the shade and soak his body with cold water. Take his temperature with a

Dogs that are fed bones often get one wedged between the teeth across the roof of the mouth. Gary Arbergast demonstrates how to hold a dog's mouth open in case such a bone must be removed.

This pheasant dropped beside the porcupine. Fast action prevented the dog from making the retrieve and getting a face full of quills. Carry pliers in porcupine country. The quills must come out quickly.

rectal thermometer. If it doesn't drop quickly, immerse the dog in a tub of cold water. Dry the dog when his temperature is back to a normal 101 degrees.

Dogs can also suffer heatstroke from lack of water. Actually too much sun and heat causes heatstroke, but water can prevent it. Retrievers especially need lots of water during the summer. They often put their feet in the water bucket because it's very cooling. Chances are, they'll overturn the bucket and be without water until you return. An acquaintance lost a valuable Labrador just this way. Hardware stores carry non-swiveling, double-ended bolt snaps that are excellent for fastening the bucket to a fence. Some Retrievers may require two buckets of water during the heat of the day.

Nearly all dogs can swim, so we seldom worry about their drowning. But it can happen, especially to sporting dogs that are afield during trapping season. A muskrat trap near shore where the dog wades in to cool off or drink is attached to a drowning wire. As the dog struggles to free himself, the trap works into deeper water.

To give artificial respiration lay the dog on its side. Press and release the rib cage in rhythmic two- to four-second intervals. If the heart is beating, the dog can usually be saved.

If there are porcupines in the vicinity, carry a pair of pliers. If you have no pliers, you'll have to pull quills with your fingers. Do it on the spot. They have to come out. These quills are barbed and work deeper with every movement the dog. The easiest time to remove them is just after they're stuck. Do it, otherwise they'll work through the dog's body dangerously.

That pair of pliers should also be along if the dog accompanies the family on fishing trips. Whether by trying to eat a hook covered with smelly catfish bait, or just being in the way, dogs often need to have fish hooks removed. Clip the eye of the hook off with the wire cutter part of the pliers and shove the barb through.

Stings of bees, hornets and wasps can be fatal, depending on the number of stings and the size of the dog. Wrap ice in a towel and hold it on the stings to slow swelling and spread of the poison while rushing the dog to a vet.

Tomato juice is said to reduce skunk odor. So is lemon juice. I've never had either when I needed them most. A friend and I did make one badly skunked dog somewhat suitable for human company by swinging him by the legs through the dense smoke of a smouldering leaf fire. A kennel dog that isn't suffering is not apt to receive the various bathings I've seen recommended. The dog is brought home in the trailer or the trunk of a car and left for nature to take its course. No one wants to show up for work smelling like a skunk and that's about all that will be accomplished by bathing the dog. If it happened to a house pet of mine, he'd get a cozy bed in the garage for a while.

If the dog's eyes were badly sprayed, use an eyewash and ointment.

We've finally learned what comes naturally for burns and scalds. Pour cold water over your own or the dog's. That removes the painful heat and actually prevents the blisters we used to think it would cause. Cover the damaged area with a clean cloth and see the vet.

Screw worms and maggots will feed on live flesh of the dog. They may feed on a wound, or biting flies may start the wound that maggots will later attack. Apply antiseptics, but see the vet if infestation is serious.

Dogs are more susceptible to electric shock than humans. Treating the dog first depends on your remaining healthy, however. If he is still touching the wire, unplug it before touching him. Or pull the fuse to that circuit. If that's not possible, move him with a belt, dry stick or something that will not conduct electricity. The dog may not be breathing. Give artificial respiration, and keep the dog warm.

Dogs suffocated from gas or smoke can also sometimes be revived by artificial respiration.

Bites from venomous snakes require immediate action. Induce bleeding by cutting over the fang marks. Get to the vet by the shortest, fastest route for an antivenin injection.

Poisoning is another emergency that demands instant action. Symptoms are convulsions, trembling and coma. Mix hydrogen peroxide with water in equal quantities. Measure one tablespoon for every ten pounds of dog, and pour that amount down his throat. Hopefully, he'll vomit.

While this is going on, have someone else phone the veterinarian. If you know what the dog consumed, the vet may be able to prescribe something immediately.

When the symptoms are stiff neck and limbs, the poison is strychnine. In this case, the dog must avoid vomiting and should be given nembutal or phenobarbital at the rate of one grain for each seven pounds of dog.

Put together a first-aid kit that can be kept around the house and carried along in the car. It should include such things as gauze, cloth bandages, adhesive tape, hydrogen peroxide, one of the better antiseptics, sharp knife or razor blade, cotton, aspirin, Vaseline and whatever else your vet may recommend.

A dog that gives faithful service while young deserves considerate treatment when he's old.

Retrievers are frequently wet while working and are susceptible to rheumatism and arthritis.

Eller's dog also suffered from what appeared to be long-term hip dysplasia. Although his joints couldn't be repaired, after Neo-Arth treatment he no longer shows evidence of pain from either hip dysplasia or arthritis.

Just as important, perhaps more so, is to make room in the shell pocket for just a few essential emergency items. Having a small bottle of antiseptic, a little roll of adhesive tape and some gauze or cloth bandages at the site of an accident can make a life or death difference.

The Old Dog

The most exciting promise for old dogs hasn't been approved by the Food and Drug Administration at this writing. I hope it is approved soon because its capability for relieving misery is nothing short of incredible. The product is Neo-Arth. It was discovered by Generics Corporation of America. It relieves the pain of osteo-arthritis in dogs and one day may do the same for humans.

Aspirin, cortisone and butazolidin also relieve the pain of arthritis. Why another pain reliever? Because these products give very temporary relief. And heart or kidney patients might not find them safe. Neo-Arth is non-narcotic and to date has caused no side effects. But that's not the incredible part. Neo-Arth when given daily for two weeks permanently ends the pain of osteo-arthritis in the vast majority of dogs!

How can pain relief be permanent? I don't know. As this is written, Generics doesn't either. And that's why the delay in getting the new drug approved for veterinary use. The F.D.A. hesitates to allow a drug on the market until it is proven to be safe and effective, either by a "manner of action" study or through a great many successful tests on individual dogs.

My friend Dr. Dennis Groom was a cooperating clinician for a time, and I was privileged to see the drug work. One dog was kept at my home. He could barely crawl out of his house to eat and relieve himself. In the two-week period of treatment, I watched him go from almost a vegetable to a dog with a lively interest in his surroundings. He got his pill in a wad of canned dog food and considered it a treat. By the end of the second week, he was trying to run to greet me. The poor dog was 15 and suffered from other ailments, so he didn't live much longer after that. But the pain of arthritis never returned.

Another dog owned by Bud and Janet Hollingberger was younger by four years and had no other ailments. But arthritis forced it to walk up steps sideways to avoid pain as much as possible. At the end of two weeks on Neo-Arth, "Wag" showed no significant change. But a week after treatment ended, the dog returned to behaving just as she had before becoming crippled with arthritis.

A Labrador Retriever belonging to Don Eller was found lying outside his dog house in severe weather because arthritis made the pain too great to crawl over the retaining board to get inside. After two weeks on Neo-Arth, Eller's dog began showing an interest in

Pointing breeds are also wet during much of their work.

life. Swelling reduced around the afflicted joints.

When I saw the Lab, he was happily retrieving a dummy and begging for it to be thrown again and again. Hollingberger's Wag was fairly flying up the basement stairs. Yet it was obvious that none of these dogs had repaired joints. There's no way to rebuild worn out sockets or to smooth off abnormal bone growth. They simply felt no pain.

I'm quite sure that early diagnosis and treatment would get added hunting years from dogs afflicted with arthritis. Many years ago doctors prescribed bed rest for arthritis, and people ended up as cripples. Today, exercise is advocated to keep joints from getting worse. It's possible for dogs to get that exercise, and most will, when the pain is relieved by Neo-Arth. I think the drug can be curative in that respect while yet unable to rebuild joints.

When I learned about Neo-Arth, Generics had already tested the drug on 101 arthritic dogs. Anywhere from good improvement to excellent recovery was reported for 80 percent of the dogs. When the treated dogs numbered 203, the positive response changed just slightly to 77 percent.

Michigan State University has since begun a manner-of-action study in an effort to learn how Neo-Arth works. Generics hopes they will discover something in the synovial fluid of the joint that becomes elevated or

Old dogs slow down, but sometimes the wisdom of old age helps them find birds the young canines race right past.

suppressed when diseased with arthritis but which is returned to normal by Neo-Arth.

Not all dogs have responded alike. Some dogs seem recovered after a week's capsules. Most require two weeks. But some don't show relief of symptoms until a week or more after treatment has ended. A very few improved for a time, then returned to a crippled state. These few dogs have shown relief only while continually taking Neo-Arth. Perhaps age, type or area of affliction or other health complications are causing different reactions to the drug. It's new, and much yet remains to be learned.

What is known, however, and what I've seen for myself, have convinced me that this combination of metallic oxides is capable of relieving the misery of the majority of the estimated 3.75 million dogs that are afflicted in the United States today.

I also took note when Dr. Groom pointed out that the X-ray of Don Eller's Lab showed probable long-term hip dysplasia. It's another form of joint disease. The Lab was not showing signs of pain from any joint disorder. I have no business jumping to a conclusion from the behavior of one dog, so I'll only hope that the pain of this dread disease might also be minimized by Neo-Arth.

Since Neo-Arth is so new, there's no way to predict when it may be approved for veterinary use. If I had a dog showing signs of arthritis, however, I'd certainly ask my vet if it has become available.

Arthritis, of course, isn't the only complication suffered by our aging dogs. Parts wear out, and there are no replacements. Organs don't function as they did, and each new disorder is one more thing the old dog must learn to live with. Sometimes we have more trouble learning to live with these disorders than the dog does.

When an old dog that has been housebroken for years begins to slip; don't regard it as defiance of the rules. He may not even know it is happening. The sphincter muscle has probably weakened. He dribbles.

Bladder control diminishes in old dogs. They drink more, exercise less, and urinate oftener. It will go unnoticed in kennel dogs, but house dogs should be given paper at night for emergencies and taken out often during the day.

Insufficient exercise may cause constipation. Mineral oil may help, but see the veterinarian if constipation continues.

As the metabolism of an aging dog slows, he needs less calories per day and often has a strong tendency toward obesity. Don't continue to feed a certain amount just because that's what you're both used to. Watch his weight and cut down as necessary. Make gradual changes or he'll think you're trying to starve him. He may beg for more, but obesity is not in his interest or yours. A fat dog is quickly exhausted in the field. A fat old dog is finished before he starts. But old dogs in good condition are often assets in the field.

They won't run as wide and fast, but the wisdom of age helps them find valuable shortcuts. The old-timers often locate game the fast young fireballs run right past.

Old dogs may have a problem with protein digestion. In that case, the veterinarian will advise a prescription diet.

Special diets are also available for dogs with kidney or liver irritations. These dogs begin drinking more water than usual, so salty and spiced food that encourage this should be avoided. Nephritis is a common kidney ailment among old dogs. Other symptoms besides increased thirst and urination are vomiting, trouble in walking and bad breath. If you suspect this, press on the dog's back over the kidneys. If the dog reacts with pain, he should see the vet promptly. Collect some of the dog's urine before going as the veterinarian may want to make an albumin test.

Deafness and blindness are common in various degrees among very old dogs. However, both can sometimes be postponed or minimized by good care. Keep the ears clean and free of wax. If the dog begins scratching his ear, find out why. Keep the eyes free of dirt, weed seeds, etc. Use an eyewash occasionally, especially if the eyes are watering. If you notice a glassy look beginning to glaze over the eyes, see the veterinarian. Cataracts or growths under the eyelids may be forming.

Keep in mind that diminished sight and hearing leaves the dog more vulnerable to danger, such as from automobiles. His senses won't alert him to your approach as quickly as normal, either. You or someone may be upon him before he realizes it. It may seem threatening to him, and he may snap. Find a way to alert him to your coming.

Since poor digestion and bad breath are common among old dogs, avoid foods such as liver and vegetables that form gas. Dogs also react differently to various manufactured dog foods. Try a change.

Tartar on the teeth also contributes to bad breath. Have a vet scale it if you can't. Dogs seldom have cavities, but it can happen. An abscess may result.

A product with two percent activated charcoal, available from pet shops, will help sweeten the breath.

Skin problems are more common with increasing age. Brush and comb the dog as much as possible to promote healthy skin and hair. Bathe only as absolutely necessary and then be sure to avoid chills. Be keenly alert for parasites. The old dog is more susceptible to them as well as their effects.

Watch the toenails of inactive dogs. They aren't being worn off as they had in the past, and long nails will soon cause sore toes. Clip the nails regularly.

Tumors and cysts are common in old dogs and may be malignant. The best insurance is to let the veterinarian advise whether surgery is recommended. If caught early, malignancy can be controlled.

Routine semiannual veterinary checkups may reveal problems that can be stopped or minimized before they get a good hold on the dog.

And don't forget that the old ones need the reassurance of love every bit as much as the very young. Don't neglect to give it while you can.

Traveling

Hunting dogs travel, so they should become accustomed to it early. Read the puppy play section for the proper introduction to riding in a vehicle. It will save a lot of grief later.

Most bird hunters have one or two dogs they transport to the field in an automobile. For this situation, it's hard to beat wire cages. Even well-trained, well-behaved dogs are better off in cages than on the floor of a car. There's no danger of forgetting their manners and sticking a nose in your face, or

trying to jump in your lap, in a moment of impulsive affection. Accidents happen in split seconds. An obedient dog just out of the field may sit on the floor and still put his muddy paws on the seat. And the dog may have to be confined for some time while you talk to a landowner friend before or after the hunt. Especially before a hunt, the excited dog may tear up the upholstery in his eagerness to get into the field. And finally, if the dog wasn't travel-trained early and suffers from motion sickness, the cage can be covered with a canvas or blanket. The dog will be more comfortable if he can't see objects whizzing by.

Whatever way the dog travels, don't let it be in the trunk of your car. Valuable dogs are constantly being suffocated by exhaust fumes in automobile trunks. People have propped the trunk lid open and tied it in place to provide ventilation only to discover this just sucked more fumes into the compartment. If the dog is worth feeding, he's worth the price of a crate.

A crate came in handy for an entirely different

Temperature inside a closed car in the hot sun can reach 200 degrees. Prolonged 115-degree heat will damage a dog's brain. Kennel-Aire crates allow the dog to be comfortable and the car windows can be left open.

reason during a Montana bird-hunting trip. We had pulled the truck camper inside a machine shed. There wasn't room for the dogs in the camper, so I bedded one on hay bales and the other in a crate. When we turned out the light, the Retriever in the cage decided to cry about his loneliness in a strange place. I went out and threw the tarpaulin over the cage, and that was the end of it.

That's a good trick to remember if you patronize motels or hotels during your travels. Dogs left alone whine, cry, bark and sometimes tear up the room in their anxiety to get back to your side. A cage will prevent damage. And you can quiet your dog and bring peace to the neighboring rooms by covering the cage. In this kind of closed-in darkness, dogs quiet down and spend most of their time sleeping.

Of course, there are other ways of transporting dogs. Quali-Craft of St. Louis makes a carrier that mounts on a standard trailer hitch. The unit can double as a dog house and comes in one- or two-dog models.

Quality trailers and truck units are available to those who carry several dogs.

Sportsmen who fly to distant hunting grounds can take their dogs as air baggage. A sturdy, leakproof cage that can be locked must be supplied or rented. Rules and regulations of the various airlines differ and change, so telephone ahead of time for specific instructions and requirements. It wouldn't be much of a hunt without the dog, so keep an eye on him during transfers. Baggage has been lost.

Whenever crossing state lines, it's wise to have a health certificate from your veterinarian and proof of rabies inoculation. Various states have different time limits, and some are quite strict. Give the vet your destination. He can advise you on requirements. Having the right credentials can save a lot of grief in case the dog is bitten or bites someone.

And suppose the dog gets lost. Can you give its weight, height and markings accurately? Try it, and check yourself. It might be a good idea to carry a color

A new, revolutionary way of carrying a dog, the Canine Carrier attaches to any standard frame-mounted trailer hitch. Collapsing legs fold down so the unit becomes a dog house.

Holiday Inns provide outside kennels for dogs that aren't housebroken.

photograph with vital statistics on the back.

When hunting trips are planned in advance with friends in other states, I think it makes sense to have address tags made up in the friend's name. Second collars with name tags may be preferred. If the dog is lost, it might be returned to the local party before you must return home. There's little chance of getting the dog back in time if the finder has to reach you through your own address.

Canada's rules parallel those of the States. The dog must have a health certificate and have had a rabies vaccination within the past year. A border official initials the certificate that the dog owner must carry at all times while visiting Canada.

Mexico asks for a certificate of rabies inoculation and a health certificate which has been certified by a Mexican consulate. When the dog enters Mexico, it will be inspected and a local certificate issued. The dog owner should also ask the consulate how to obtain an import license which is required before arrival in Mexico.

Sportsmen wanting their dogs along on overseas hunts may find that impossible in some countries. Iceland, Scotland and England, for example, require a six months' quarantine before the dog may enter. Check with a consulate of the country you intend to visit or write to the American Society for the Prevention of Cruelty to Animals, 441 East 92 Street, New York, N.Y. 10028 for the pamphlet *Traveling Abroad With Your Pet*. It contains the latest rules and regulations for taking your dog into more than 60 countries.

Every bit as important as good planning and making proper arrangements, I think, is the dog owner's behavior while traveling and during the visit. Many people expect problems the moment they see a dog. Prove their fears well founded, and you help ruin it for all dog people that follow.

My wife and her sister spent several sleepless nights in a Miami hotel because someone was thoughtful enough to take the dog along, but thoughtless enough to leave the dog in the room while out on the town until the wee hours. The annoyance could have been eliminated with a cage and cover. I'm sure the hotel manager considered prohibiting dogs in the rooms after that incident.

I've heard people complain about having to pay for the things their dogs chewed up in motel rooms. The usual claim is that they were overcharged for the item. If true, I'd say it's a well-deserved penalty. Again, these incidents can be avoided with a cage. If the cage would be in the way at times during the travels, buy the type that folds into a flat package.

Oddly enough, dog people who worry about others thoughtlessly destroying everyone's right to travel with dogs seem more vocal about the problem than motel managers. Or maybe I talked to the wrong people.

The Holiday Inn at Marion, Illinois, had been headquarters for the English Springer Spaniel National Championship for two years when I talked to manager Dick Bittle.

"I'll assure you," Bittle told me, "we have less trouble with dogs than with people."

When making arrangements for the championship, Dick thought that many dogs might create a noise problem. He was amazed when it didn't. Most of the dogs were caged in station wagons and they made no noise.

Field-trial Springer Spaniels are well-trained, well-mannered dogs. So are the owners and handlers. I asked about other field trialers because the Crab Orchard Wildlife Area is also a popular trial grounds for the pointing breeds. Bittle couldn't think of anything more serious than a little hair on the furniture.

Thinking that motels in the country might be more accustomed to dogs and therefore more tolerant, I contacted one in St. Louis. The hostess assured me that field and show dogs cause no trouble. These people come prepared with crates, and the dogs are trained and accustomed to traveling. Even pets cause little trouble.

I hadn't meant to single out Holiday Inns. It just happened because they headquartered the Springer event. But I do appreciate their attitude. Dogs are welcomed as a corporate policy. Except in states where it's prohibited, people are encouraged to keep their pets with them in the rooms. And I do believe the lack of friction from dog problems isn't an accident. Nor is it entirely because people's dogs are so well trained. I think it's planning and forethought. Holiday Inns provide safe outside kennels for dogs that aren't prepared to stay inside.

Many other motels allow dogs. But not all do. As a public service Gaines Dog Research offers a 54-page brochure called *Touring With Towser* that lists thousands of motels and hotels in the United States and Canada that allow pets. Send 50 cents for postage and handling to Gaines TWT, P.O. Box 1007, Kankakee, Illinois 60901.

Dog trailers provide comfortable traveling and double as kennels during extended hunting trips.

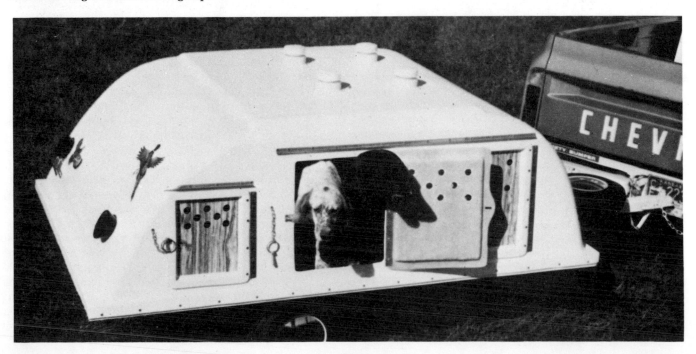

9/Breeding Dogs

Breeding dogs is a simple procedure. Twice a year the bitch comes in season for 21 days. Her vulva swells. Her appetite increases. A bloody discharge appears, and in a few days she'll accept a stud. About 63 days later, there are pups. In fact, it's so simple dogs can do it. But breeding good dogs—that's another matter. That is a highly complicated practice (ambition might be more accurate) guided by art, science and a bright star.

If the bright star has shown on your destiny, you've been blessed with an outstanding animal that is worthy of reproducing. If the star has left you in the dark, don't proceed without it. Borrow someone else's. Never breed a mediocre dog just because it's available. The best of dogs throw too many mediocre pups. Pick an excellent stud that has proven himself in other matings. If your bitch has faults you don't want in a litter of pups, don't breed her. She supplies half of the genes. Get a better bitch, or forget breeding.

I'm reminded of a quip attributed to Georger Bernard Shaw, the playwright. A movie queen supposedly suggested, "You and I should have a baby, Mr. Shaw. With your brains and my looks, we could have the perfect child."

"Yes," Shaw allegedly replied, "but what if it had my looks and your brains!"

Shaw would have made a great dog breeder. The average fellow thinks like the movie queen. He mates a running bitch that won't point to a pointing dog that won't run and fully expects to get pups that both run and point.

Let's forget optimism. We can do more toward improving the odds by taking an objective look at the science of mating.

Every cell in a dog contains 39 pairs of chromosomes. Each chromosome consists of a beadlike string of genes. The dog's color, size, type of hair, general appearance—all of its physical traits—are programmed in the genes before the animal is born. The inherited mental capability is also programmed in the genes. Good training can develop it to the fullest, and bad training can destroy it, but this capability can never be exceeded or changed.

Genes which program characteristics are arranged in a definite order on each chromosome. Genes that determine color, for example, are situated in the same place on the chromosomes of every dog.

The reproductive cells divide and become 39 single chromosomes. In the mating process, these half-cells unite to form 39 new pairs that become tomorrow's pups.

Obviously, the genes are also present in pairs—one each on corresponding chromosomes. If they weren't, a pup could receive no genes whatever for color or ears or what have you. So, when the half-cells join, each parent is contributing genes for every last feature in

Inbreeding has risks, but should be attempted to hold the traits of a great individual and, if possible, build an inbred family on those traits. And always be on the lookout for the outstanding bitch—she's scarce while great studs are always available.

the new pup. Some genes may determine a single characteristic. But more often these genes and arrangements of genes interact to influence several characteristics.

To get an idea of how genes program an individual, let's examine color. It's more obvious and understandable than most other characteristics.

Mongrels are mixtures that carry a great variety of possible genetic color combinations. The chances of reproducing one of the parents when mating two mongrels are as slim as filling the same bingo card in the same way two times in a row. Purebred dogs are different. They've been selected for certain characteristics including color for a long time, and the many choices are simply not available. Certain colors are available in certain breeds, and that's it.

Let's look at the color genetics of a Curly-Coated Retriever. Two colors are available: black and a brown which is called liver. The liver dog is that color because its genes programmed the hair pigment in less dense clusters than in a black dog. A black gene is given the symbol B. A liver gene is b. Remember that genes come in pairs—one on each corresponding chromosome. A dog that is pure for black would have BB genes. Pure for liver is bb.

When pure black and pure liver dogs are mated, the cells divide. Black contributes B; liver, b. The resulting pups have B on one chromosome, and b on the

corresponding chromosome, making their color programming genes Bb.

Another factor enters at this point. Some genes are dominant, others recessive. Black is dominant to liver, so B overpowers b, and the Bb pups are black.

We could breed pure liver to pure black endlessly and never get a liver pup. But suppose a friend also bred liver and black, and we mated a Bb pup of ours to a Bb pup of his. B's of each could join to create a pup pure for black, or BB. The b's of each could also join to make bb, or pure for liver. The B of ours might join the b of his to make Bb, or black carrying liver recessive. And the b of ours could join the B of his to make the same thing. You can see there are four possible combinations. Three will make black pups; one comes out liver.

If BB dogs are mated, all pups are black. When bb dogs are joined, all are liver. There are no other possible combinations.

Understanding the above is essential to scientific dog breeding. And what we will discuss from this point forward builds upon that minimum knowledge. We've deliberately put color genetics in its most simple terms to establish this basis from which to work. All genetic relationships are not that simple. Just adding a third color, such as yellow in Labs, greatly complicates it. It's obvious that ability, which combines many physical and mental characteristics, would be

Breeding dogs is so simple dogs can do it. Breeding *good* dogs takes real planning.

Be sure the dog you breed has the conformation of a working dog. Shoulder slope, angulation, well-bent stifles, slightly bent pasterns and well-sprung chest cavity are all important to the dog's ability to run and hunt.

impossible to describe in simple terms. Yet the genetic relationships are much alike. If the simple basic relationsips are understood, that understanding can be applied to complicated genetic combinations which defy mathematical analysis.

One of those very complicated combinations of genes gives us a dog that points. In his breeding experiments, Dr. Leon F. Whitney found pointing to be dominant over non-pointing, but that's only the beginning. How well the dog functions at pointing also depends upon head carriage, nose, bird interest and many other inheritable traits.

It's almost overwhelming to recognize that the genes of every one of today's specialized breeds were all present in the original dogs or wolves or combinations of wild canines. In other words, those original canines were on a mongrel level in carrying a grand assortment of genes. How in the world, you might reasonably ask, did man ever reduce the numbers of possible combinations of genes in dogs to make them breed true for one important characteristic like pointing?

It had to begin with a lucky accident. Some ancient dog's bingo card filled up just right to make him especially interested in and especially good at per-

forming some task that men of the time considered worthwhile. The rest was achieved by inbreeding.

If inbreeding dogs conjures up thoughts of incest and immorality, you are allowing emotion to close your mind. If it's impossible to open your mind and dispassionately, rationally study the science of genetics, you're wasting your time reading this section.

Inbreeding is so badly misunderstood because its disadvantages have gotten far more attention than its advantages. Brilliant breeders like Laverack, Llewellin, McCarthy, Marjoribanks—and in our time, Le-Grande—established great strains, and even breeds, with the help of inbreeding. But their achievements are continually negated in the minds of dog men by those with inadequate knowledge and poor stock whose efforts produce the spooky, deformed idiots so many have come to expect from inbreeding.

Of course, there are many degrees of inbreeding. And, here again, the names we give these degrees—incest, family breeding, etc.—are clouded by emotion. So let's forget preconceived notions and accompanying words and get right to the facts.

Inbreeding is the doubling of genes, no more, no less. If we choose to get b on corresponding chromosome pairs in the Curly-Coats mentioned earlier, we might

The blond coat in Wirehairs should never be bred.

Outbreeding is usually the expert's method of trying for the superior individual that occasionally crops up when many good dogs of different families are bred.

call it selecting for liver, but it's also inbreeding for that particular characteristic. If we want a pointing dog, we don't outcross on a Retriever. We breed two dogs that point because the genes for that quality will likely double and assure us that the pups will also point. That's inbreeding although most people don't realize it.

Ancient people often inbred dogs without realizing it, too. Someone's dog performed a valuable task, so the man tried to get an offspring like him. Maybe friends also wanted that kind of dog and bred their bitches to him. Maybe none of the pups had the sire's good qualities. But a lot of his offspring were running around with his genes, perhaps recessive and masked as with the liver color in Bb Curly-Coats. If brother and sister were accidentally or deliberately mated, the genes would again double and a new generation would possess their grandfather's good ability. The same might have happened with sire/daughter or sire/granddaughter or half-brother/half-sister matings. Or the genes may have passed along for several generations until they became paired when the right two individuals mated

Inbreeding also took place in earlier times because poor transportation isolated various districts. Dogs

couldn't be found that weren't related. Certain outstanding dogs were bred more often than others and this increased family relationships. Because the genes were similar and joined often, all the dogs of the area conformed very roughly to a type. They were distinctive enough to become known as a breed. The Brittany Spaniel is a good example of that.

After Mendel discovered the basis of genetics, men learned how to speed up the process of developing a breed. Instead of gradual inbreeding under the influence of selecting for ability among a limited number of available dogs, men deliberately bred related dogs because they carried like genes. A favorite method of the English was breeding an outstanding dog to his granddaughter. Histories of the breeds in the front of this book are full of cases where men created or standardized breeds by inbreeding. Histories are full of a great many more outstanding dogs whose genes were lost to us forever because they were never inbred.

Why do most prefer outbreeding to inbreeding? There are two reasons. The first is fear of defects from inbreeding. If there are poor qualities or abnormalities in a strain of dogs, inbreeding will double those genes as well as those of desired characteristics. If a dog is a little shy, for example, spookiness could be a real

Springer Spaniels, although all registered by the A.K.C., come in two distinct types: show and field. Don't breed the two together just because they happen to be available.

Irish Setters were brought back from near extinction as field dogs by both inbreeding and crossbreeding.

If you're not satisfied with a dog's pace and range, don't breed it. Mate dogs only when *both* have the qualities you want.

problem in his inbred offspring.

The second reason for outbreeding is the search for a better dog. Inbreeding should begin with a truly outstanding dog whose characteristics ought to be preserved in future generations. The great individual's good qualities can be held by inbreeding, but not very likely surpassed. Outbreeding creates that one-in-a-thousand dog that is much superior to the average of his breed. If a man isn't quite satisfied with his stock, he should certainly outbreed. If he's lucky enough to get that superior dog, he can then inbreed to hold its qualities.

We said earlier that breeding good dogs is a matter of science, art and a bright star. It takes the bright star to own a dog worthy of inbreeding. We've already looked at some of the science of breeding, and although a whole book could be written on that subject alone, I hope I've provided a basic understanding. The art of breeding is knowing which dogs might join in a procreation better than either of themselves. It's knowing dogs so well that a sire with a slight excess might be chosen to balance a bitch with a slight deficiency.

If art and luck have blessed you with an outstanding bank of genes, by all means inbreed in an effort to keep what you've earned. But choose a related mate that's very much like your dog in the qualities you want to hold. Being related doesn't guarantee they carry the same genes. And if you select dogs that exhibit like characteristics, they carry even more like

Breed dogs that point early. If your bitch took three years to point, you'll probably feed her pups for three years to find out if they're worth keeping.

Only 20 percent of the Wirehaired Pointing Griffons and German Wirehaired Pointers have coats good enough to be used for breeding, according to Don Smith, Connecticut Wirehair authority.

genes—especially the ones you want.

The first inbred mating should always be considered a test, however. If it uncovers undesirable qualities that have been hidden as recessives and most of the pups are worthless, have the courage to cull them. Don't repeat the mating. If only a pup or two are defective, however, and all the rest show the sought-after characteristics, don't hesitate to keep and breed from the good offspring. Inbreeding then becomes a way to flush out and destroy slight defects in a strain of dogs.

Sometimes an outstanding dog has sufficient faults to make a close inbreeding program inadvisable. If we already know of serious faults, it's not wise to attempt sire/daughter or brother/sister matings. If we're sincerely ready to expect and cull the bad ones, we might try a sire/granddaughter mating. Half-brother/half-sister offspring from a great dog might also be test mated.

If these tests are unsuccessful, it may be necessary to wait until the outstanding dog with faults has had great or even great-great grandpups. Select a dog and a bitch that both show Mr. Great in the fourth or fifth generation of the pedigree. If both are chosen carefully for showing good qualities, genes from the outstanding ancestor may have some doubling influence while not unmasking serious problems.

Throughout this discussion, I've referred to sire/daughter, sire/granddaughter, etc., without a mention of possible dam/son or dam/grandson matings. I wasn't motivated by male chauvinism. I did it partly for brevity, but mainly because male dogs can produce a great many offspring by various matings. With many daughters and granddaughters (and sons for brother/sister breeding) there is considerable choice in finding related dogs very much like the Great One. Females produce comparatively few litters. If the right son or grandson is available, however, don't hesitate to test mate it back to a superior female.

I've placed more than average emphasis on inbreeding. I did that in an effort to dispel prejudices. Inbreeding is a valuable tool that has its dangers and must be used intelligently by those who don't fool themselves about the results. But it's no cure-all. It's simply one more way to achieve desired results in this art-science-luck game called dog breeding.

Directory

Pro handler, Elmore Chick, of Lemont, Illinois, exercises his dogs.

AMATEUR FIELD TRIAL CLUBS OF AMERICA (AFTCA), Miss Leslie Anderson, Secretary, Hernando, Missouri 38632. Comprised of over 300 member clubs, this organization sponsors regional and national competition for the pointing breeds.

AMERICAN BRITTANY CLUB, Mrs. Nicky Bissell, Secretary, Rt. 3, Box 14 Sherwood, Oregon 97140. AKC parent club for the Brittany Spaniel. Publishes *The American Brittany* monthly, same address as above.

AMERICAN CHESAPEAKE CLUB, Jim Nicholes, Secretary, 1218 Purdue Dr., Davis, California 95616. AKC parent club for the Chesapeake Bay Retriever. Publishes club bulletin quarterly; Mr. Bill Boyson, editor.

AMERICAN FIELD, THE, Bill Brown, Editor, 222 W. Adams St., Chicago, Illinois 60606. Weekly publications primarily about pointing breeds. Contains listing of Field Dog Stud Book.

AMERICAN KENNEL CLUB, 51 Madison Ave., New York, N.Y. 10010. Largest registry of dog breeds. Licenses competition. Publishes *Pure Bred Dogs, American Kennel Gazette* and will send upon request "Orange Book" of field trial rules.

GERMAN SHORTHAIRED POINTER CLUB OF AMERICA, Mrs. Geraldine Green, Secretary, 125 Arlene Dr., Walnut Creek, California 94595, AKC parent club of the German Shorthair.

GERMAN WIREHAIRED POINTER CLUB OF AMERICA, Mrs. Sandy Bertrand, Secretary, 2201 Essex Rd., Minnetonka, Minnesota 55343. AKC parent club of the German Wirehair (Drahthaar). (Also see Verein Deutsche Drahthaar.)

GERMAN SHORTHAIRED POINTER NEWS, Mrs. Shirley Carlson, Editor, Box 850, St. Paris, Ohio 43072, monthly.

GOLDEN RETRIEVER CLUB OF AMERICA, THE, Mrs. Robert A. Bower, Secretary, Route 1, Constantine, Michigan 49042. AKC parent club for the Golden Retriever. Publishes *Golden Retriever News* Mrs. Judy Tredwell, editor, bimonthly.

GORDON SETTER CLUB OF AMERICA, Mrs. William S. Miller, Jr., Secretary, 6100 Eastwood Terrace, Norfolk, Virginia 23508. AKC parent club for the Gordon Setter. Publishes *Gordon Setter News* monthly, Mrs. Bobbie Jones, editor.

IRISH WATER SPANIEL CLUB OF AMERICA, Mrs. John L. Hopkins, Secretary, Center Rd. RFD, Bradford, New Hampshire 03221.

MORRIS ANIMAL FOUNDATION, 531 Guaranty Bank Bldg., Denver, Colorado 80202. Sponsors and coordinates research in animal health.

NATIONAL GERMAN SHORTHAIRED POINTER ASSOCIATION, (American Field affiliate) John Rabidou, Secretary, Rt. No. 2, Box 169, Cambridge, Wisconsin 53523.

NATIONAL RED SETTER FIELD TRIAL CLUB, Robert B. Kerans, Secretary, R.R. No. 1, Newton, Illinois 62448. Publishes *The Flushing Whip,* monthly, same address as above.

NORTH AMERICAN VERSATILE HUNTING DOG ASSOCIATION, (NAVHDA) Dr. E. D. Bailey, Secretary, R.R. No. 1 Puslinch, Ontario, Canada. Organization is sponsoring trials which emphasize the versatility of some hunting breeds. Dogs tested on land and water, open to any dog registered in national stud book.

ORTHOPEDIC FOUNDATION FOR ANIMALS (OFA), University of Missouri, Columbia, School of Veterinary Medicine, 817 Virginia Ave., Columbia, Missouri 65201. Founded to help eliminate hip dysplasia in dogs through effective x-ray programs.

PET FOOD INSTITUTE, 111 E. Wacker Dr., Chicago, Illinois 60601 will provide clubs with material to help celebrate National Dog Week, which is observed in September.

RETRIEVER FIELD TRIAL NEWS, Mrs. Toni Reynolds, Editor, 1836 E. St. Francis Ave., Milwaukee, Wisconsin 53207. Primarily reports field trial results of Retrievers; 10 issues annually.

THE SPRINGER BARK, Mrs. Evelyn Bui, Editor, P.O. Box 2115, San Leandro, California 94577, quarterly. Covers field and show activity for Springer Spaniels.

VEREIN DEUTSCHE DRAHTHAAR GRUPPE NORD-AMERIKA, Mrs. Dagmar Howell, Director of Breeding, Star Route, Marlow, Oklahoma 73055. North American group of Drahthaar (German Wirehaired Pointer) fanciers and breeders affiliated with the German mother organization (Verein Deutsche Drahthaar) and continuing the German breeding and training practices in America.

VIZSLA CLUB OF AMERICA, THE, Mrs. Barbara Berlenbach, Secretary, 15 Middle Court, Mill Valley, California 94941. AKC parent club of the Vizsla breed. Publishes *Vizsla News* monthly.

WEIMARANER CLUB OF AMERICA, Mrs. Janette Jana, Secretary, P.O. Box 6086, Heatherdown Station, Toledo, Ohio 43614. AKC parent club of the Weimaraner. Publishes *Weimaraner News* monthly, same address as above.

WIREHAIRED POINTING GRIFFON CLUB OF AMERICA, Mrs. Edward D. Bailey, Secretary, R.R. No. 1, Puslinch, Ontario, Canada, publishes *Gun Dog Supreme* bi-monthly, same address as above.

Picture Credits

For the many excellent photographs kindly contributed to this work, I extend my special thanks to:

Joan and Edward Bailey
Dr. Robert B. Ballinger
Verne Brand
Francis Clasen
N. Dale Detweiler
Dexter Hoyle Eaton
Pete Frierson
Wayne Fruchey
Charles and Dorothy Goodnow
Hill Greer, Jr.
Dave Grubb
Gladys Harriman
David J. Hasinger
Dr. Walker Heap
Marion Hopkins
T. C. Marshall
Mrs. H. C. McGrew
Beth McKinney
Douglas C. North
Drs. Dorthea and Mick Robinson
H. P. Sheely
Lewis and Sharon Simon
Delmar Smith
Roy Speece
Joe, Sharon and Jeff Tryba
W. F. Whittal
Sigbot Winterhelt
Custoglass
Dogs Unlimited
Kennel-Aire Mfg. Company
McKee Industries
Quali-Craft Industries, Inc.
Sensitronix

and game departments of the states of:

Arizona   *Maine*
Colorado   *Nebraska*
Georgia   *New Mexico*
Idaho   *North Dakota*
Illinois

If anyone has been overlooked, please accept my apologies. It was not intentional.

—Larry Mueller